# Praise for *In My Jewish State*

*"One of the most insightful observers of contemporary Israeli culture, Elana Sztokman gives us a passionate critique of its political conflicts. With a sharp eye on the ways religion and gender are manipulated, she opens new ways of thinking about Judaism and Zionism that offer possibilities of a peaceful future."*
Prof. Susannah Heschel, Eli M. Black Distinguished Professor, Dartmouth College

*"A challenging and important read for those brave enough to question their beliefs to make the world a better place."*
Julie Gray, author, *The True Adventures of Gidon Lev*, and *Let's Make Things Better*

*"This is a must read for any American Jewish person who cares about Israel-Palestine and the people in it. It's a mirror we all need to look into."*
Becca Strober, political strategist, educator, former senior director with Breaking the Silence, and Instagram influencer @becca explains the occupation

*"A searingly brave look at Israel today and at what the area between the river and the sea can be, if only we can imagine a future defined by equality for everyone. Sztokman is the best kind of patriot: one who is not willing to give up on freedom, justice and compassion."*
Mira Sucharov, Professor of Political Science at Carleton University, and author of *Borders and Belonging: A Memoir*

*"Elana Sztokman's journey – and her memoir capturing it – shows how the Israeli-Palestinian conflict is perpetuated in part by the over-simplifying narratives people often hold. As an Israeli (and American) Jew, she shares her own process of gradually questioning and deconstructing the Jewish narrative, and then reconstructing a narrative which gives space for the legitimate needs and identities of both Jews and Palestinians while staying rooted in deep commitment to Israel and the Jewish people.*
Rebecca Bardach, writer and activist

*Elana's book highlights the transformative power of education rooted in inclusivity and care, embracing complexity, fostering human connection, and strengthening democratic values to challenge patriarchy, militarism, and violence. From an ultraorthodox girl in Brooklyn to an awakened adult in Israel, her journey reflects the profound impact of education. Captivated by her charismatic 9th-grade teacher, Tomer, she later recognized his latent agenda reinforcing patriarchal, messianic Jewish nationalism. Encounters with Palestinians in Israel profoundly reshaped her views, sparking disillusionment and growth. Her story underscores the vital role of education in nurturing meaningful human relationships across all contexts and platforms. political strategist and educator, former senior director with Breaking the Silence*
Dr. Tammy Shel (Aboody), philosopher of education, and expert in pedagogy of caring.

# IN MY JEWISH STATE

## How I was trained in pro-Israel advocacy, and how I learned to talk back to my culture, find my own humanity, and fight for peace

### Elana Sztokman

Lioness

**Publisher:** Lioness Books
**Editor:** Maayan Sharon
**Cover Designer:** Rebeca @Rebecacovers
**Author photo:** Jacob Sztokman

IN LIBRARY IN-DATA-PUBLICATION
In My Jewish State/ Elana Sztokman
 p. cm.

ISBN 978-1-957712-19-2 ebook
ISBN 978-1-957712-17-8 paperback

 1.  Memoir  2. Israel/Palestine  3. Anthropology

*This book is dedicated to*
*the people who have tragically lost their lives*
*in this war,*
*to the hostages, the displaced, the wounded,*
*and the traumatized.*
*And to the people who love them, mourn them,*
*and fight for them.*
*My work is for you. Always.*
*With prayers for peace.*

# Also by Elana Sztokman

# Contents

*"I am not free while any woman is unfree,
even when her shackles are very different from my own."*
Audre Lorde


*"The world is upside down,
it's going to take a lot of hands to turn it right side up....
It is our duty to stand up for humanity.
Step in and correct things that are wrong."*
Nobel Peace Prize Laureate Leymah Gbowee

# Prologue

This was not an easy book to write.

For one thing, it is personal. I don't like writing about myself. My books until now have been, for the most part, about social trends and cultures. I'm a sociologist/anthropologist, not a memoirist. I like to present ideas based on research, on data meticulously collected and organized. It's what I'm trained in, and what I am good at. I prefer to share insights and ideas based on structured observation, not based on my own limited experiences. And yet, here I am doing exactly that, grounding my anthropological observations in my own personal history. It's risky, and uncomfortable.

What's more, I am looking back at my life and my culture, and facing aspects of myself that make me uneasy, angry, at times even ashamed. To do the research that makes up the core of this book, I had to admit to my own mistakes, failings, and at times stupidity. That's not much fun. But as they say, sometimes the only way around is through. So here I am. Doing the hard work — publicly.

The topic of this book is also extremely charged. The war in Israel/Palestine — a topic that literally alters global events, gets celebrities canceled and university presidents fired, affects world markets, redraws world alliances, and has been a pivotal issue that determines who gets elected to Congress and even as President of the United States. My writing career was going well! Why would I want to sabotage it by venturing into this particular fire pit?

Perhaps most scary for me is that I am about to release into the world some unpopular opinions. Well, I should qualify that. They are unpopular in the community to which I belong. That is, I am about to suggest to my people — the Jewish people, who are currently experiencing levels of antisemitic violence not seen since World War II — that we look at some of those difficult events through a different lens. That we look at our own actions before labeling everything as antisemitism. I'm not sure that's a good idea right now. Some might experience it as me kicking-'em-while-they're-down, or victim blaming.

And yet, here I am, doing it anyway.

I'm putting this book out into the world because I believe it is important, and urgent. I have to do it, no matter how difficult or risky it is. Lives are at stake.

My observations of language, power, and hierarchy are not some abstract thesis, like an exploration of ancient Roman tongue-washing habits. The topic of my research here, around which I wrap my life story, is one that is impacting the daily lives of millions of people, often in unconscionable ways. I see my research not as a theoretical, detached analysis; rather, I am looking at social processes that urgently demand our attention and rethinking.

Simply put, innocent lives are being lost on a daily basis, and the cultures of discourse that I am trained in observing and analyzing are actively contributing to that. I believe that if we don't change our language, we will continue to participate in that ongoing travesty.

So how did I get here? Born in Brooklyn, New York, I was brought up on Orthodox Judaism and religious Zionism and was an advocate for those ideologies during my formative adulthood, even as I fought to make them better. For many years I was a Jewish educator and an Orthodox feminist activist, working to improve our culture — change from within, as it is often called. I hung on to the belief that Judaism and Israel are inherently good, or even amazing. My job was to fix what was wrong with it, like the patriarchy and other power structures.

Indeed, this mission was the focus of both my personal and professional life for many years. I earned a Bachelor of Arts degree in education and political science from Barnard College, then moved to Israel at the age of twenty-three with a husband, a child, a long skirt, and a hat. I went on to earn a master's degree in Jewish education from the Hebrew University in Jerusalem, aspiring to teach about the beauty of Judaism and Israel. Eventually, the patriarchy became too much for me; I took off the skirt and the hat, and became an active religious feminist. My doctorate in education and sociology/anthropology with a specialty in gender studies, which I completed also at Hebrew University in 2006 after my youngest child was born, combined these passions. I dedicated my career and my life to smashing gender norms and cultures. I wrote books, conducted research, built communities, spoke at conferences, worked in many organizations, and advocated for change within my culture in all things gender-related.

For most of that time, I did not look too hard at what Israel was doing with the Palestinians. I was hyper-focused on my own struggles and on raising my children. Perhaps I could only break down small bits of my culture at a time without breaking down myself. I was living in the pro-Israel bubble — believing that Judaism and Israel were basically good and simply needed some tweaking. I was a good soldier of the rhetoric. I shared pro-Israel axioms and wrote about antisemitism and the pain and traumas of being a pro-Israel Jew in the world.[1] I also experienced many of the struggles of living as an Israeli Jew: terror attacks, wars, excessive reserve duty of my family members, tragic killings of people we loved and of relatives of people we love, and the endless stress of

---

[1] See for example, Elana Sztokman, "Why It's Hard To Be a Zionist and a Feminist," *Forward*, November 17, 2009 https://forward.com/life/119097/why-its-hard-to-be-a-zionist-and-a-feminist/.

effectively living in a war zone. For a brief period, I even lived over the Green Line. I've done all that.

I stayed in that pro-Israel bubble for quite some time. Until I didn't.

A series of turning points in my life gradually burst open that bubble I was living inside. There was the writing job I was fired from for refusing to manipulate the truth. An encounter with a Palestinian peace activist, hearing about her son's experiences with Israeli soldiers. A visit to East Jerusalem where homes were being demolished. Speaking with Palestinians about their lives — checkpoints, discrimination, and many challenges that I as a privileged Jewish Israeli never experienced. Driving a group of children from Hebron to the beach — illegally — because even though they lived only an hour away, they had never seen the sea. And more. One by one, I watched the walls I had put up around me start to crumble.

I realized that much of what I was brought up on was actually a lie. I was a pawn in a steadfast system of crafting history for a particular purpose. And I did not like that. I needed to step out of that bubble and start thinking for myself.

My process can be encapsulated in one exchange, in which a friend wrote to me, "You've been brainwashed to think Israel kills babies." I replied, "You've been brainwashed to think they *don't*."

Over the past fifteen years or so, I have been peeling back the layers and facing my life, my surroundings, and my culture in ways that I was not indoctrinated to consider. And what I found has made me sad, ashamed, and outraged. I have been shattered at the discovery that the pro-Israel community I have been part of my entire life uses emotional manipulation, dehumanization of the Other, and outright lies to justify some of the worst actions in the world. And then we complain that the world hates us. It's twisted. And I have been an active part of it.

Since the events of October 7, 2023, this has all gotten worse — much worse. The extent of bloodshed carried out by the State of Israel under the false pretense of protecting Israelis is unprecedented, and quite sickening.[2] As of this writing, an estimated 45,000 Gazans have been killed by the Israel Defense Forces (IDF) if not more,[3] with at least two thirds of them completely innocent, according to Israel's own admission.[4] The count is likely higher due to the many people who were buried without being registered, or whose bodies are still left in the rubble.[5] Some 1.9 million out of 2.2 million Gazans are homeless, as entire swaths of Gaza have been destroyed. An estimated 69% of homes in northern Gaza have been decimated, and there is so much rubble in Gaza that it

---

[2] Yaniv Kubovich, "'No Civilians. Everyone's a Terrorist': IDF Soldiers Expose Arbitrary Killings and Rampant Lawlessness in Gaza's Netzarim Corridor," *Haaretz*, Dec 18, 2024, https://www.haaretz.com/israel-news/2024-12-18/ty-article-magazine/.premium/idf-soldiers-expose-arbitrary-killings-and-rampant-lawlessness-in-gazas-netzarim-corridor/00000193-da7f-de86-a9f3-fefff2e50000

[3] Rob Picheta, "More than 40,000 Palestinians have been killed in 10 months of war in Gaza, health ministry says," *CNN*, August 16, 2024, https://edition.cnn.com/2024/08/15/middleeast/gaza-death-toll-40000-israel-war-intl/index.html; Smriti Mallapaty, "Gaza: Why is it so hard to establish the death toll?," *Nature*, September 24, 2024, https://www.nature.com/articles/d41586-024-02508-0; Rasha Khatib, Martin McKee, and Salim Yusuf. "Counting the dead in Gaza: difficult but essential." *The Lancet* 404, no. 10449 (2024): 237-238, https://www.thelancet.com/journals/lancet/article/PIIS0140-6736(24)01169-3/fulltext.

[4] Mitchell McCluskey and Richard Allen Greene, "Israel military says 2 civilians killed for every Hamas militant is a 'tremendously positive' ratio given combat challenges," *CNN*, December 6, 2023, https://edition.cnn.com/2023/12/05/middleeast/israel-hamas-military-civilian-ratio-killed-intl-hnk/index.html.

[5] Raja Abdulrahim et al., "Gaza in Ruins After a Year of War," *The New York Times*, October 7, 2024, https://www.nytimes.com/interactive/2024/10/07/world/middleeast/israel-gaza-destruction-hamas-war.html.

would fill up Central Park some twenty meters high and would take eight years to clear.[6] Palestinians are struggling with starvation, injuries, disease, lack of clean water, destruction of infrastructure, horrific loss of family and friends, a looming climate catastrophe, and an uncertain future.[7] Polio is back after having been eradicated twenty-five years ago, as are some strange bacterial infections and the threat of other diseases such as cholera.[8] There have also been deeply disturbing reports of the IDF using Palestinians as human shields,[9] and some grotesque testimonies from IDF soldiers struggling with PTSD after the things they saw and

---

[6] Abdulrahim et al.

[7] Josie Glausiusz, "The Israel-Hamas conflict one year on: researcher resilience in the face of war," *Nature*, October 7, 2024, https://www.nature.com/articles/d41586-024-03263-y; Patrick Wintour, "US demands proof that Israel does not have starvation policy in northern Gaza," *The Guardian*, October 16, 2024, https://www.theguardian.com/world/2024/oct/16/urgent-un-security-council-meeting-called-amid-pressure-on-israel-to-allow-aid-into-gaza; Ephrat Livni, "Conditions in Gaza Worsen Amid Israeli Strikes," *The New York Times*, October 9, 2024, https://www.nytimes.com/2024/10/09/world/middleeast/gaza-israel-military-strike.html; Matthew Mpoke Bigg, "Gazans Are So Malnourished That They Could Face Famine, Report Warns," *The New York Times*, October 17, 2024, https://www.nytimes.com/2024/10/17/world/middleeast/gaza-malnourished-famine-warnings.html; Nathalie Rozanes, "The Gaza war is an environmental catastrophe," *+972 Magazine*, September 5, 2024, https://www.972mag.com/gaza-war-environmental-catastrophe/.

[8] Mohammed Aghaalkurdi, "Polio Threatens Gaza Today. Tomorrow, It Could Be Cholera." *The New York Times*, October 14, 2024, https://www.nytimes.com/2024/10/14/opinion/gaza-polio-infectious-disease.html.

[9] Natan Odenheimer, Bilal Shbair, and Patrick Kingsley, "How Israel's Army Uses Palestinians as Human Shields in Gaza," *The New York Times*, October 14, 2024, https://www.nytimes.com/2024/10/14/world/middleeast/israel-gaza-military-human-shields.html.

did.[10] Aid workers are saying that the trauma in Gaza is worse than anything they have ever seen — more prolonged, more intense, with no respite or way out.[11] Meanwhile, members of the Israeli government are openly calling for a complete wipeout of Gaza and the creation of new Jewish settlements throughout the strip.[12]

At the same time, the rights of three million Palestinians in the West Bank are routinely trampled on. Palestinians can barely move, they are subjected to random arrests and rampant home demolitions,[13] and the number of Palestinians

---

[10] Nadeen Ebrahim and Mike Schwartz, "'He got out of Gaza, but Gaza did not get out of him': Israeli soldiers returning from war struggle with trauma and suicide," *CNN*, October 21, 2024, https://edition.cnn.com/2024/10/21/middleeast/gaza-war-israeli-soldiers-ptsd-suicide-intl/index.html.

[11] Arwa Damon, "Opinion: How the suffering in Gaza is different from other conflicts," *CNN*, May 7, 2024, https://edition.cnn.com/2024/05/05/opinions/israel-gaza-psychological-trauma-damon/index.html; Ahmad Ibsais, "I've never felt more disillusioned as a Palestinian," *The Guardian*, May 17, 2024, https://www.theguardian.com/commentisfree/article/2024/may/17/palestinians-gaza-news-coverage.

[12] Dana Karni, "Israeli minister says it may be 'moral' to starve 2 million Gazans, but 'no one in the world would let us'," *CNN*, August 6, 2024, https://edition.cnn.com/2024/08/06/middleeast/israeli-minister-smotrich-starve-gazans-intl/index.html?utm_source=substack&utm_medium=email; Ruth Margalit, "Itamar Ben-Gvir, Israel's Minister of Chaos," *The New Yorker*, February 20, 2023, https://www.newyorker.com/magazine/2023/02/27/itamar-ben-gvir-israels-minister-of-chaos?utm_source=substack&utm_medium=email; Channel 4 News, "The hardline Israeli settlers planning their future homes in Gaza," October 22, 2024, YouTube video, 7:49, https://www.youtube.com/watch?v=riLA5r8D4ac.

[13] See, for example, this report by Ir Amim: https://www.instagram.com/p/DBWoKb6uz5l/?utm_source=ig_web_button_share_sheet&igsh=ZDNlZDc0MzIxNw==.

killed by settlers and the IDF is on the rise.[14] Bedouin villages are being demolished to make way for Jewish settlements.[15]

And let's not forget that even within Israel, the same government that ignores human rights abuses and international law in Gaza and the West Bank is also actively threatening citizens' rights — firing or even arresting people for dancing on TikTok, protesting in the streets, daring to express sympathy for children in Gaza, or wearing a "FCKBNGVR" T-shirt at a soccer match.[16] As the famous

---

[14] Ephrat Livni, "Surge in Violence by West Bank Settlers Draws Ire of Israel's Allies," *The New York Times*, July 16, 2024, https://www.nytimes.com/2024/07/16/world/middleeast/settler-violence-west-bank.html.

[15] Lorenzo Tondo, "'We will not go away': Israeli demolitions leave Bedouin homeless," *The Guardian*, June 6, 2024, https://www.theguardian.com/world/article/2024/jun/06/israeli-demolitions-bedouins-homeless-negev.

[16] "Ben-Gvir orders Arab educator be arrested for dancing on Oct. 7 on TikTok," *The Jerusalem Post*, October 9, 2024, https://www.jpost.com/israel-news/article-823840; "Ben Gvir tells police to start arresting anti-government protesters who block roads," *The Times of Israel*, January 10, 2023, https://www.timesofisrael.com/ben-gvir-tells-police-to-arrest-anti-government-protesters-who-block-roads/; "Gallant calls for probe into Ben-Gvir amid suspicions he prevented police response to riots at IDF bases," *i24NEWS*, July 30, 2024, https://www.i24news.tv/en/news/israel-at-war/artc-gallant-calls-for-investigation-into-ben-gvir-for-inciting-rioters-in-idf-bases; Iddo Schejter and Gavriel Fiske, "Police use considerable force near PM's home to disperse protesters urging hostage deal," *The Times of Israel*, September 3, 2024, https://www.timesofisrael.com/police-use-considerable-force-near-pms-home-to-disperse-protesters-urging-hostage-deal/; Maayan Lubell, "Tel Aviv police chief quits, citing government meddling against protesters," *Reuters*, July 6, 2023, https://www.reuters.com/world/middle-east/tel-aviv-police-chief-quits-citing-government-meddling-against-protesters-2023-07-05/; "Police briefly detain teen wearing anti-Ben Gvir T-shirt at Jerusalem basketball game," *The Times of Israel*, October 14, 2024, https://www.timesofisrael.com/police-briefly-detain-teen-wearing-anti-ben-gvir-t-shirt-at-jerusalem-basketball-game/; "Beersheba girl suspended from school after voicing concern for Gazan kids," *The*

poem goes, first they came for the stateless Palestinians, then they came for citizens who think Palestinians are human beings, and then they came for anyone whose T-shirt they didn't like.

While all those killings and arrests and home demolitions are happening, and while the world is trying to stop it and at times accuses Israel of committing genocide and ethnic cleansing, Jewish communities are crying out that such accusations are antisemitism. As in, *How dare you say such a thing about us!* Like, *We're the Good Guys.* Case closed. Nothing more to discuss here.

I have been observing and writing about this for a while. I spent seven years working on a book about sexual and emotional-sexual abuse in the Jewish community that was published in 2022.[17] During that process, I became familiar with tactics of emotional manipulation — such as lying, deflecting, and gaslighting — that are used in grooming practices of abusers. I observed a horrifying overlap between the rhetorical tactics used by sexual predators against their victims and those used by Israel's advocates against Palestinians.

But over the past year, since October 7, this has all gotten worse. Even as I am living out the war in my own living room, I have been able to pull back the curtain to see the propaganda that is being shoved in my face. These tactics of emotional and rhetorical manipulation have now been adopted by Jews of

---

*Times of Israel*, September 23, 2024, https://www.timesofisrael.com/beersheba-girl-suspended-from-school-after-voicing-concern-for-gazan-kids/; Emma Graham-Harrison and Quique Kierszenbaum, "'It is a time of witch hunts in Israel': teacher held in solitary confinement for posting concern about Gaza deaths," *The Guardian*, January 13, 2024, https://www.theguardian.com/world/2024/jan/13/it-is-a-time-of-witch-hunts-in-israel-teacher-held-in-solitary-confinement-for-posting-concern-about-gaza-deaths.

[17] Elana Sztokman, *When Rabbis Abuse: Power, Gender, and Status in the Dynamics of Sexual Abuse in Jewish Culture* (Lioness Books, 2022).

the world as they face their own demons, and thus the fight against antisemitism has morphed into a massive campaign to support massive, unjustifiable bloodshed.

I realize that antisemitism in the world right now is a very painful subject. Jews are being attacked in many corners of life that used to feel safe. In campuses, workplaces, the subway, and synagogues — incidents of Jew baiting, graffiti, verbal assault, and exclusion of Jews have become commonplace. This is hard. For many Jews, it is terrifying. I get that.

The problem is that not everything that is being labeled as "antisemitism" is actually antisemitism. Some of what is called "antisemitism" is in fact an expression of protest against Israel's actions in Gaza — very legitimate and necessary criticism of the Israeli government. And the more we sweep this criticism under the rug or lump it together with actual antisemitism, the more we justify and enable Israel to continue to carry out those terrible actions.

By resorting to the knee-jerk claims of "antisemitism", we fail to engage in authentic conversations, we ignore those who are trying to engage with us about our shared reality, and we avoid taking responsibility for our own actions. All of that is extremely toxic. If this were happening in individual interpersonal relationships, where one person kept saying to the other, "You are hurting me!" and the response was, "How dare you suggest that! You are just a bigoted hater!", we would clearly see how toxic this dynamic is. It is emotionally manipulative abuse and gaslighting. What I am suggesting is that we as a people have been engaged in that kind of toxic behavior on a collective, communal, cultural scale. And I would like us all to stop doing that.

I know this is hard. Jews and Israelis have suffered throughout history. Israel is indeed under attack and people are in great pain. And antisemitism is a very real thing in the world. In addition, the rhetorical tactics are at times nuanced and complicated, and they rest on some of the oldest Jewish tropes and traumas that send Jews back to images of the gas chambers. We all carry some severe collective traumas and our triggers are justified. Moreover, the desire to protect one's people often comes from a genuinely good place of honor.

Nevertheless, we must learn to distinguish between actual antisemitism and legitimate feedback about the pain we have been causing to others. To do that, we must stop with the rhetoric for a second and take a closer look at what is really happening, what we are actually doing. We must learn to put aside our own communal propaganda and be truthful with ourselves about our own actions, and the actions being conducted in our name. We must stop with the knee-jerk reactions to events and try to better understand the rhetorical war in which we are being used as pawns. Because at this point, *not* speaking out is no longer an option. Not if I want to keep my humanity.

And so, here it is. I am talking back to my culture and hoping you will do the same. Because to achieve peace, we must first create peace within ourselves.

This book has three parts. Part One is my own personal journey with Zionism and Israel, so that you, my reader, understand where I'm coming from, how I have evolved, and how I know what I know.

Part Two is a compilation of social media exchanges and content written while wearing my anthropological hat. I offer a narrative analysis of the language used in pro-Israel advocacy[18] circles since October 7, and explore the social media amplification of some of the most problematic and violent ideas that have driven Zionism for the past century.

---

[18] I use the term "pro-Israel" in the way that it is most frequently used in the media, in politics, and in the Jewish world — which is to say what I set out to explore in this book, that "pro-Israel" generally means defending Israel's actions no matter what. But I think this is a misnomer and misguided. Nevertheless, it has taken me an entire book to explain that position. And so, for ease of identification of the issues I'm addressing, that is the phrase I'm using all along.

Part Three is a return to the here and now, in which I share what I have been doing since October 7 to activate peace in myself and in the world around me. I share insights from my work with my Palestinian colleague Eva Dalak to activate peace. I present ideas from my work with Forum 1325, a collective of women experts on conflict resolution who offer an array of solutions for ending this conflict and creating a normal, functioning state and society.

Finally, I revisit my own understandings of "A Jewish State" — my Jewish state within, and the Jewish state without. I explore what a Jewish state that is also a humane state may look like — inside of me and in the world around me. I make peace with the clear and unequivocal realization that what exists currently is not sustainable. A Jewish state that relies on violence is unethical and cruel. We need different thinking — not only for the sake of the Palestinians, but also for the sake of our own souls, our own humanity.

## About This Book

I have spent the war watching my social media feeds fill up with 50-year-old tropes that promote misguided and even horrific ideas about the conflict. At times I write back to the original posters as well as in my own blogs and essays. But it's not enough. There is an urgent need for more in-depth, substantive, and thorough push-back and deconstruction of the rhetorical onslaught.

I realized that I cannot fight the rhetorical battle alone in my little Facebook page. There is a need for a more culture-wide movement to talk back to all this. We need to fight the toxic language with truth, morality, and shared humanity.

To tackle this issue more systematically and hopefully effectively, I began collecting pro-Israel posts, graphics, and memes about the conflict. I want to address the problems in this language war more systematically.

In this book, I've selected some of the most egregious memes from my collections and organized them according to

IN MY JEWISH STATE | 25

themes and talking points. I am looking at these ideas straight on, holding up a mirror to them, and explaining why they are so horrible and wrong. All these arguments are ultimately used to justify mass killings, oppression, and displacement of Palestinians. And it's time to put a stop to all that.

## Caveats

A few points about my own process that are worth noting:

### I'm writing what I know.

This is a book about my own life, speaking to my own people, from the place I come from. I am not doing an analysis of texts coming out of Palestinian culture. I'm writing about my own culture. Our core responsibility as human beings is to fix ourselves rather than blame others. That's what I'm doing here. Nothing else.

### I'm not engaging in "whataboutism".

One of the most common responses I get when I talk about this issue is, "But what about *them*?!" Whichever tactics I argue that Israelis engage in, I'm told that Palestinians do it more, or worse. "Lying? Gaslighting? Distorting history? Tribalism? Racism? Dehumanizing the Other? What about the Palestinians? They are worse!"

This response is an example of deflection, an avoidance tactic, commonly known as "whataboutism". It is a way to evade personal responsibility and accountability. It is toxic and wrong and I'm not doing it. My job is to change my own bad behavior in the world first, not blame others for it. We need to look in the mirror with honesty about ourselves.

Israel's advocates have been engaging in whataboutism for a very long time — blaming the world, blaming Palestinians, labeling everything as antisemitism — instead of doing the work of candid introspection. It has not served us but instead has brought us to this place of seemingly endless cycles of escalating violence. I'm proposing that we try something different, something humane and truthful.

### Even truth can be manipulative.

You might also notice that some memes that I use as examples of toxic behavior contain kernels of truth. I am not claiming, for example, that antisemitism doesn't exist. Rather, I'm saying that the use of antisemitism as a justification for Israel's actions is twisted and manipulative. In other words, while antisemitism is an actual thing, it can also be a smokescreen blocking other discussions.

### I'm protecting posters.

You will notice that I do not include the actual graphics here. My aim to linguistically and logically analyze texts and images that are being widely used to defend Israel without legal or personal entanglements. I'm addressing ideas, not individuals. Although this is hard for me as a researcher who tries to be meticulous about sources and citations, social media has changed the world, and I am adjusting accordingly. My solution for these conundrums is to simply share the core content of social media posts and rely on readers to check their origins using the many online tools available. It is the best solution, all things considered.

### I'm sure there's more.

Once you start unpacking manipulative language, you will likely find more themes that I missed. I consider that a victory. This book is meant to be just the beginning of a process of cleaning up our act. I would be thrilled for readers to take the process further and continue to talk back to the rhetoric.

# Part I: My Israel Story

# What I Was Doing on October 7

At 6:30am on the morning of October 7, 2023, I was lying in bed in the sleepy town of Modi'in, Israel, where I have lived for nearly twenty years, thinking to myself, "Wow, my upstairs neighbor is doing quite a workout this morning."

It felt like massive weights kept dropping on the floor above me — weights so heavy it seemed like they caused the walls and windows to shake every few moments. It made no sense, but to be fair, I wasn't fully conscious yet.

My phone, charging next to my bed, kept beeping. I ignored it. But the beeps became more frequent, in rapid succession.

*Boom. Windows shake. Ping. Ping. Ping. Boom. Windows shake. Ping. Ping. Ping. Boom. Windows shake. Ping. Ping. Ping.*

I opened my eyes, sat up, and grabbed my phone. I was getting WhatsApp notifications from my daughter who lives in the city of Ashkelon.

*Ima, we're being attacked.*

*We're on our way to you.*

*We'll be there in an hour.*

I responded:

*What?!!??!!*

*Okay, of course. Come over.*

I didn't immediately panic. Then I looked at the news.

*Non-stop rocket barrages. Hits. Explosions. Infiltrations. Bands of terrorists roaming the streets. Men with guns hopping out of trucks in front of people's homes.*

Wait, what? What is happening?

I jumped out of bed and got to work. Within an hour, we set up the guest room for my daughter, her husband, and their three-month-old baby, prepared some food fo them, and checked our supplies. And all the while I barely managed to contain my shock while checking my phone for updates.

They arrived an hour later, a bit shaky but mostly calm. They had passed by some terrifying things on the road — a bloody, bullet-ridden car, a few fires, fallen rockets. In retrospect, they had undoubtedly evaded terrorists in very close vicinity.

*Miracles.*

As soon as they arrived, my son-in-law turned around to leave. He said he was going back to Ashkelon.

*What?! Why?! You can't go back there!*

He had to.

*I have to get my brother.*

Oh my God.

My son-in-law's 17-year-old brother was stranded. He had stayed with friends in Ashkelon for the holiday, who also bolted from the city and left him alone. He showed up at my daughter and her husband's house at 8am, not knowing that they were already in the relative safety of middle-of-the-country Modi'in. My son-in-law ran out, back to Ashkelon, some twenty kilometers from Gaza, to what had instantly become a war front.

I tried reaching my older daughter, who was eight months pregnant and living in Be'er-Sheva — a large city in the Negev, about forty-five kilometers from Gaza toward the south where there was currently heavy rocket fire, unsurprisingly, considering that Be'er-Sheva had been a favorite Hamas target for the past twenty years. (In fact, she gave birth to her twins two years earlier in the middle of rocket fire. I wrote about that adventure in *Lilith* magazine).[19]

---

[19] Elana Sztokman, "Rockets, Bombs and Babies: Wartime in the Maternity Ward," *Lilith*, June 9, 2021,

Among the many new experiences that day was the fact that I was *calling* her on Shabbat, something observant Jews don't normally do. But that day was anything but normal. It took a while, but I eventually reached her. She, her husband, and their twin toddlers had spent all morning in their bomb shelter.

*There is a siren every ten minutes. No point in leaving the safe room.*

At least they *had* a safe room in their apartment — unlike many other people in Israel, like my daughter in Ashkelon.

I desperately wanted them to come to Modi'in, too, where there were far fewer sirens than in Be'er-Sheva and where I could help keep them safe. On the other hand, I was also very nervous about them driving on the roads. Gangs of terrorists were now roaming everywhere, apparently shooting at cars on intercity roads. I was glued to the news, and it was becoming clear that no place was truly safe. By the afternoon, they realized they had to leave. Staying under a barrage of rockets was unsustainable.

My other son-in-law was now stuck in Ashkelon, as many roads had been closed. I checked Waze to see which roads might still be open. One route, Road Six, seemed safe. *Drive fast. No stopping for anything. Nothing. Hamas terrorists were masquerading as people needing help. Just go. Just drive. Safely but fast. Whatever you do, don't stop.* Conversations that sounded like they were taken straight from an apocalypse movie. Surreal.

It took my older daughter and her family hours to get to Modi'in, as everyone in Be'er-Sheva seemed to be leaving at the same time. Those were the longest hours of my life. Eventually they arrived. I breathed for the first time all day.

Thank God. *Miracles.*

By late afternoon, my son, who lives in the north, was called to army duty. He stopped by our house on his way

---

https://lilith.org/2021/06/rockets-bombs-and-babies-wartime-in-the-maternity-ward/.

south to pick up gear, food, and hugs, leaving his eight-month-pregnant wife at her parents' house in Haifa. By the end of the day, my older daughter's husband left to report for reserve duty — as did all three of his brothers — leaving behind my pregnant daughter and their two children. By Sunday morning, my other son-in-law would report for duty as well, leaving behind my daughter and her baby.

*Tak-tak-tak. Reporting for duty.*

My husband, who had not yet seen the news directly, was still trying to keep Shabbat. I had long ago given up on that and could not stop looking at my phone. The news kept pouring in. He kept asking me how bad things were. I was his channel to the outside world.

*Bad. Really bad. Worse. Even worse than you can imagine. Worse than they are even reporting.*

I was trying to keep up with the developments, absorbing the shock minute by minute via Israeli news channels, Facebook, WhatsApp. My husband was getting it from me in waves. It was a lot of information. Unbelievable information.

*Are you sure?*

*Pretty sure.*

*Hostages?!*

*I'm afraid so.*

*That can't be right.*

*I know how you feel.*

Social media was far ahead of the traditional news outlets. I was chatting with a friend of mine who lives in Kibbutz Nirim, a community on the Gaza border, one of the spots that was immediately infiltrated. She is in her 80s and lives alone. We studied together in a year-long course in Spiritual Counseling. We had spent a lot of time that year hearing about the traumas of living for years under rocket fire. When I reached her, she was in her safe room. Alone. For hours. We chatted for a while and then she said she had to go because her battery was running out.

It was terrifying. But she made it out alive in the end.

*Miracles.*

Well, miracles for her. We would later learn that of the 416 people who lived in Nirim before the massacre, nine were killed that day, dozens were injured, and five were taken hostage. The rest have not gone back home since.

Reports started coming in about what happened to the soldiers. Rumors about the female soldiers in *tatzpitanut* — *tatzpi* in army lingo, the "lookouts", the ones in charge of the screens of the cameras on the fence. It's a job reserved for female soldiers. Online chatter about a slaughter on their base in Re'im on the Gaza fence. Unofficial and unconfirmed. People sharing stories on Facebook, and then others arguing that it's just rumors and they should stop sharing fake news.

My youngest daughter eventually checked in to see how we all are, to share how she is. She was in *tatzpi* doing her mandatory service. At twenty years old, she had been in the army for nearly two years. She was not in Re'im but on a different base. By chance. Luck of the draw where one gets placed. I kept replaying in my mind a conversation we had a year earlier when she was waiting to hear where she would be headed. Re'im or Maccabim? She actually wanted the Gaza rim base. Less boring, she said. They sent her to Maccabim, closer to home. Luck of the draw.

*Miracles.*

Well, miracles among horrors.

*Miracles among horrors.*

What is the word for miracles among horrors? I don't have one.

That was my October 7, a day that in many ways stands on its own in the annals of human horror. But this is only part of the story of the violence in my region. October 7 is not a beginning or an end, but a chapter smack in the middle of a deeply tragic saga — tragic for Israelis, for Palestinians, and for the history of this bloody region.

It has now become a central part of my own story with my people and with humanity, one which I am more than ready to continue differently.

What I had not anticipated was that the entire Jewish world was also experiencing an October 7 that would linger in their consciousness as a time of slipping into collective existential danger. For Jews of the world, that day was about to be cast as 1933 Germany. It seems strange to me, considering that I was actually here, viscerally living out the *actual* day with its *actual* horrors and *real* threats and losses. But for people thousands of miles away, that day became a symbol of something that I do not fully connect to, a narrative of something that feels completely disconnected from the actual story. I get why people on the Gaza border experienced that day as a kind of Holocaust trauma, the people hiding in closets as if they were Anne Frank, people who were hunted down by monsters with guns, watching everything around them explode. I can understand their Nazi associations. But I was surprised (or perhaps not surprised, as the year evolved) that people living in the safety of America, many of whom had never actually experienced a threat to their life, described that day in more apocalyptic Jewish-survival terms than I did, conflating it with ancient events that had nothing to do with this story.

But that was just the beginning of the twists and turns that day had ushered in.

# The New World

On Monday morning, October 9, I woke up once again to incessant pinging from my phone. I quickly sat up in bed, again. This time it was a manic thread coming out of Brooklyn. Overnight, I had apparently been added to a new WhatsApp group of high school alumni. The WhatsApp group of my 1987 graduating class from my yeshiva day school in Brooklyn was blowing up, and someone thought it would be a good idea for me to join the fray.

For some perspective: I had been hanging onto WhatsApp like a lifeboat since that awful October 7. On that unfathomable day, I was glued to my phone checking in on family and friends most directly affected by the events — some living in the line of rocket fire, some hiding in safe rooms in the kibbutzim under attack, some in the army, some whose children or relatives were missing. In the weeks that followed, WhatsApp groups would become a vital source of minute-by-minute information about the needs of displaced communities and soldiers, locations of sirens and rockets, funerals, bios of hostages, and important political developments. Almost immediately, all the groups of the pro-democracy protest movements created the previous year pivoted to mobilizations and volunteering, from collections for families from the Gaza rim whose homes and lives have been shattered and who are now scattered all around the country in temporary dwellings, to supporting families of hostages, volunteering on farms to pick produce so that people's businesses are not destroyed and the country doesn't face a massive food security crisis.

I was following all those events and participating in that new mobilization in a variety of ways, while at the same time caring for my two displaced daughters — whose respective husbands would end up spending months in reserve duty, and their children. I was on 24/7 grandmother duty — a blessing and a privilege, if an exhausting one. I was and still am grateful not only that thank God my family is okay, but also for my strength and my home and my ability to protect them and care for them, and for the partnership of my spouse without whom the job would have been much harder. Still, it was quite the juggle.

Two minutes in bed to see what my former classmates were talking about seemed like a good idea at the time. A wartime version of "me time".

Then I read the thread.

Someone posted a video from Channel 14, an Israeli version of Fox News with a religious Zionist slant (the one where, for example, a panelist had recently opined that Yigal Amir, the assassin of Prime Minister Yitzhak Rabin, is a hero and should be pardoned and released from jail; to be fair, the anchor was sacked, but not before being applauded in the studio).[20] The clip offered a view on the current war which argued that the Hamas attack is proof that all Palestinians everywhere want to wipe Israel off the map. Also, people should stop talking about the West Bank like it's a problem because there is no difference between Hebron and Tel Aviv — it's all the same, and "they" are coming for all of us.

I sat up in bed.

I kept scrolling. The next message was from a high school teacher who taught us forty years ago whom I'll call Tomer, who was backing up those ideas about how "they" hate all of "us" and the end goal is to kill us all and wipe Israel off the map. I hadn't realized our former teachers were still alive, let alone still schooling us middle agers via this alumni group.

---

[20] Michael Horovitz, "Panelist on right-wing TV calls to free Rabin assassin, to audience applause; is booted," *The Times of Israel*, July 31, 2023, https://www.timesofisrael.com/tv-panelist-sacked-after-calling-to-free-assassin-yigal-amir-to-audience-applause/.

But Tomer has a special role in this story. I'll get back to him later.

I desperately wanted to reply to that thread. I wanted to write that we have to stop using words like "they" to refer to all Palestinians when we mean Hamas terrorists. I wanted to say that people criticizing the IDF's plan to wipe out entire neighborhoods in Gaza are not necessarily "antisemitic" but perhaps just against killing innocent civilians. There was so much I wanted to say, but I knew it would not go down well.

I could feel my whole body tensing up, my blood pressure rising, heat filling up my chest.

I decided to reach out to the group moderator, a woman I'll call Frieda who I thought was a friend, with whom I had spent many years together in class, who had visited me years ago when she was in Jerusalem. I thought I could talk to her.

"You realize the people in Gaza are human beings," I wrote. "Why are you sharing these radical religious ideas that justify mass murder?"

I may as well have been reaching out from another planet.

"Do you have any idea what happened on October 7?", she replied.

*She wanted to know if I had any idea...* I felt the room beginning to spin.

I started to describe my life to her. I told her about my children, my grandchildren, the army duty, the displacement, my worries, the panic. I was trying to prove my credentials. It was crazy. "And with all that, I'm saying that it's not okay to promote the wanton destruction of all of Gaza."

"We're worried about you", she wrote back. "Clearly, you're not well. You need help. Why don't you go back to being a grandmother and leave the thinking to the rest of us."

In one fell swoop I was rendered mentally incompetent for daring to suggest that Palestinians are human beings. My own vulnerability was used against me, with a toxic combination of ageism and sexism, lobbed at me by a woman from my own cohort. Just like that. All because I challenged the idea that all Palestinians deserve to die.

I switched off my phone, blocked my former classmate and the alumni group, and ran to find a bucket.

*Ugh. It's happening again.*

# Israel and Me

I was twelve years old the first time I visited Israel. The summer of 1982, when Ariel Sharon led the Israeli Defense Forces (IDF) into what would become the first Lebanon War, was also the summer of my cousin Duvi's bar mitzvah. My extended family descended upon Jerusalem, and I was excited. Like so many Orthodox Jews, we were entranced by the dominance of our religion in the place. We loved the way the chicken in the supermarket was kosher, the way the country came to a halt on Friday afternoon, the way everyone — from postal workers to bus drivers — wished one another Shabbat Shalom. After years and generations of feeling like an unwanted guest in our home country, forced to tolerate an entirely Christmas-focused December, to explain to countless professors and employers why we couldn't show up for most of September, and to endure occasional representations of Jews as big-nosed money-hungry powerbrokers, it was nice to suddenly feel at home. Part of the majority culture. Not having to say "No" to all the amazing-looking restaurants we pass by or excuse ourselves for our skullcaps and long skirts. *To be understood.* That's quite a relief. And fun, too. It was like the streets were suddenly ours.

I wouldn't say that I personally experienced much antisemitism in my life. I didn't feel unsafe as a Jew walking the streets of Manhattan. (Although I felt very unsafe as a girl. Much less interesting to my community, then and now. But I digress). My father, in contrast, described being beaten up as a kid along with his brothers, the fear of wearing his skullcap in public as an adult, and recollections of university quotas for

Jews or clubs where "no dogs or Jews" were allowed. My experience of Jewishness in America was not quite as sinister. It was more like a bit *uncomfortable*. It was more about living your entire life in a place where you are not fully present or grounded; you live there, but you always feel a bit on the outskirts, perhaps waiting for the moment when you will be discovered as an imposter or be forced to leave the way your ancestors were. Whether that threat is real or imagined is irrelevant. When you carry around centuries of violent discrimination in stories that are relentlessly inculcated into your consciousness in a million big and small ways, there are existential fears that weigh on you even if they don't match your own life experiences.

Israel felt like a salve for all that — even to my teenage self. To come to a place and feel like you don't have to hide your identity, where your strange cultural quirks — like eating kosher supermarket chicken — are fully out in the open, not only tolerated but embraced and supported and dominant, well, that's healing. It's like taking a deep breath for the first time in, I don't know, eons.

I fell in love with Israel that summer. Even then, at the tender age of twelve, I knew I wanted to live here. It felt meaningful in ways that living in America did not.

Still, I know now that despite countless emotion-laden visits to historical Jewish sites — the Western Wall, Masada, The Diaspora Museum — we only got part of the story about what Israel is. We did not engage with Palestinians, leftists, or Reform Jews. Actually, that's not *entirely* true. We took photos with the Arab charging money for rides on his camel. We ordered schnitzels and Fanta from Arab waiters. And once when we walked through the Muslim quarter of the Old City of Jerusalem, an Arab shopkeeper stopped my father and offered him 200 camels for me. The two men had a great chuckle, and my father loved telling the story at Shabbat dinner tables about how he could have sold me for the right price. I laughed along. I suppose I was happy that those men thought I was cute. What else could a girl want, right?

The trip that gave me such deep pride and significance was also badly skewed. But what do we do when the experience or the narrative we so desperately want to embrace is something of a lie?

Well, we know what people generally do. They tend to stick to what's comfortable and ignore the rest. If we ever had doubts about the human psyche's ability to ignore facts and reality because people are attached to something being shown to them, we only need to look at America since 2016. Our minds are apparently ready to hang on to some awful ideas by ignoring the worst, as long as those ideas feed some kind of deep need.[21]

Am I shocked by this cognitive dissonance? I don't know. I lived it for a long time.

---

[21] Carol Tavris and Elliot Aronson, *Mistakes Were Made (but Not by Me): Why We Justify Foolish Beliefs, Bad Decisions, and Hurtful Acts* (Mariner Books, 2015); Bruce Peterson, "The scary power of cognitive dissonance," *Star Tribune*, October 21, 2024, https://www.startribune.com/the-scary-power-of-cognitive-dissonance/601165383; Charlie Warzel, "I'm Running Out of Ways to Explain How Bad This Is," *The Atlantic*, October 10, 2024, https://www.theatlantic.com/technology/archive/2024/10/hurricane-milton-conspiracies-misinformation/680221/.

# That Zionism Class

My education about Israel in text form began in ninth grade at my yeshiva day school in New York, where we had a mandatory semester-long course called Zionism.

The teacher — that Tomer who had dominated my grade's alumni WhatsApp group with right-wing religious media following October 7 — was unlike any other teacher at the school. Back in the 1980s, he was young not only in appearance but also in his overall attitude. He could easily pass for one of the students, with his horn-rimmed tortoiseshell glasses, argyle socks, Levi's jeans, and boyish tussled hair. He would eat pizza in class while teaching, and even more enticingly, he did not bother much with things like attendance, homework, or even learning our names. He would just sit there in that tiny room, unbothered by rules or routines or the rest of the school. None of that applied to him. An adolescent's dream! What's more, his father was the school's principal, so he could pretty much get away with whatever he wanted without consequence. He told jokes and had an air of twenty-something coolness, the kind that teenagers tend to envy. These were very attractive qualities in a teacher.

Tomer's teaching method was a cross between training at a sales seminar and a TED talk. We were enchanted by his mighty world, where he would shoot off talking points in a clear and purposefully directed script. Every word was planned, recited, and repeated like Absolute Truth. Had we not been Orthodox Jews, we might have called them catechisms, only more thrilling and less fire and brimstone. He would pace up and down the narrow aisles of the classroom, animatedly planting his ideas in our impressionable brains in such a way that we would totally get and remember them. We would not consider for even the slightest of nanoseconds that he might be wrong. *Impossible!* The class was not about discussion or dialogue or sharing feelings or different perspectives. There was exactly one idea, which was his, and which was so undeniably and inarguably correct that our sole mission in life was to ingest it, make it our own, and regurgitate it frequently for the rest of our lives. His job was to turn us into Fierce Defenders of Israel, and he did it with aplomb. I loved it!

You may not fully appreciate what a big deal it is for me to say that I *loved* a class. I was quite an unproductive student throughout high school. I never took notes, I spent inordinate amounts of time napping in the student lounge, I wandered the halls aimlessly, I looked for any excuse to get out of class by getting involved in anything and everything that was going on elsewhere, often by playing the glockenspiel in the school orchestra, which allowed me to attend rehearsals for every assembly, school play, and holiday event. When I was really lucky, I got to play the piano in the orchestra which gave me permission to work on entire plays or accompany day-long outings to an old age home. Anything but attending class. I was not one to notice when anything of interest was happening in the classroom. I got through four years of high school by cramming the night before each final exam, having photocopied and memorized someone else's entire notebook. I could not recite most of what I ingested in those four years if I tried.

Except for Tomer's Zionism class. That class I could recite almost verbatim. It felt clear, directed, decisive, comprehensible, and, perhaps most importantly, convincing. I might even say I was inspired. He totally won me over.

The first lesson was, "*What is Zionism? Zionism is Jewish nationalism*", followed by an outline of words in nuclear code precision about why this is true.

The next lesson was, "*What is Judaism? Judaism is not a religion. It is a nation*", again followed by a clear, concise, and conclusive outline of irrefutable talking points.

Just like that, Tomer would spend each class with exactly one point to make, and he was clear and organized in proving his thesis. We would lap it up, absorbed and engaged. For me, it felt like I understood for the first time who I was and what I was doing in school. It was invigorating.

It also didn't matter that many of the students had never been to Israel. Or, like me, had the sum total of Israel experienced in one summer family bar mitzvah tour. We were all becoming experts on Israel, often sight unseen.

# Becoming a Soldier in the Language Wars

It's hardly surprising that Tomer had me hooked from day one. I was an easy target. I wanted to know it all, I needed to absorb everything he was saying. I was eager to master every nuance, every detail, every persuasive argument. I was all in.

Still, despite having been to Israel and being extremely motivated, many topics in that class were new to me. For example, when Tomer refuted the United Nations' assertion that "Zionism is racism" I was very confused. I could not comprehend how anyone could say such a thing. Didn't the UN realize that Jews have been facing antisemitism since forever? How could they not realize that Israel is simply Jewish nationalism? It made no sense to me. I suppose that was the point; Tomer gave us talking points to repudiate ideas I did not know existed. As with so much of my Orthodox education, I was given answers before I knew the questions.

Another example was a lesson about Deir Yassin, and about how Arabs are lying when they describe the Deir Yassin massacre. None of us had ever heard of Deir Yassin nor could we point to it on a map. We had never heard a Palestinian version of events — in fact, we had never read anything written by Palestinians, unless it was in order to disprove it. But by the end of that lesson, we could assert with complete authority that anything Palestinians claimed about Deir Yassin was a lie. We knew with absolute certainty that any story claiming that Jews killed Palestinians in Deir Yassin was entirely untrue. We were affirmed and validated in our own communal, national righteousness. No matter what anyone else said.

It was only decades later, after the events of October 7, when I began working with my Palestinian partner Eva Dalak on our podcast Women Ending War, that I learned how the Deir Yassin catastrophe affected Palestinians. Eva's family was almost entirely expelled from Jaffa in the first week of May 1948, just a few weeks after the Deir Yassin massacre. In that rampage, Zionist paramilitaries led mostly by Lehi and Irgun attacked the village of Deir Yassin near Jerusalem using firearms and hand grenades, as they emptied the village of its residents, going door to door, killing at least 107 Palestinian villagers, including women and children. The massacre was carried out despite the village having agreed to a non-aggression pact.[22] This event is very much part of Eva's family lore and one of the main reasons they abandoned their generational homes and fled in fear to places like Gaza and Nablus. Needless to say, we never heard this side of the story in Tomer's class. Instead, he delivered a series of rebuttals about how the Palestinians lie, while we nodded and accepted these ideas without question.

In fact, we never used the term "Palestinian", only "Arab" or "The Arabs", as if "they" were all one homogeneous unit. We were taught that there is no such thing as a Palestinian people, that it's a complete fabrication. We also learned that Jordan should be part of Israel, or at the very least the place where Palestinian refugees belong — that any death or displacement of Palestinians was their own fault, and that "The Arabs" should stop complaining about Israel because they have twenty-three Arab nations to choose from and can go anywhere while we Jews have only one tiny little nation so

---

[22] Ofer Aderet, "Testimonies from the Censored Deir Yassin Massacre: 'They Piled Bodies and Burned Them'," *Haaretz*, July 16, 2017, https://www.haaretz.com/israel-news/2017-07-16/ty-article-magazine/testimonies-from-the-censored-massacre-at-deir-yassin/0000017f-e364-d38f-a57f-e77689930000.

leave us alone. We rejected and debunked Palestinian claims to "self-determination", pulling the concept to pieces entirely, without any empathy or even irony about what self-determination means for Jews.

We learned that it is wrong for "The Arabs" to have control over the Al Aqsa Mosque on Temple Mount, because the location is the holiest place in Judaism but only the third holiest location in Islam, so we Jews should really have dibs on it.

We learned that when people say that Israel should stop building settlements that's a smokescreen, because all "The Arabs" want is for Israel to disappear completely — including Tel Aviv and Haifa — so we might as well keep building settlements because whether Jews live in Hebron or in Tel Aviv, it's all the same. "They" all want "us" dead just like Hitler did and like the Spanish Inquisition did and like the Crusaders and Haman and Pharoah did. "They" are all one and the same, all interchangeable and driven by an irrational and inexplicable antisemitic appetite for Jewish blood. And we are not going to give in, so we must just keep doing our thing.

We learned that if someone does not support Israel, or expresses even a hint of sympathy for Palestinians, they clearly hate all Jews and prefer for us all to disappear.

On top of all this, we justified our exclusive entitlement to the land based on the biblical promise from God to Abraham some 3,000 years ago. We used that to prove that our claims were more legitimate than anyone else's claims. After all, we were on the land centuries before Muhammed was even born, and therefore we are its rightful owners. We never questioned the legitimacy or logic of any of these ideas.

Tomer was great. So charismatic. He loaded us with "the facts" and it all seemed so true and logical, it made us feel righteous and God-appointed and morally upright and on a mission. His class filled us with a very specific form of Jewish pride and armed us with everything we needed to defend Israel against rhetorical attacks.

It worked.

I lapped it all up. Tomer was, after all, so articulate and so charming that it was impossible to disagree. And why would I want to? It felt good to gain clarity about who I was and where I belonged. Everything he said made so much sense, and I had no idea that there may be other perspectives. I was perhaps too young or too ignorant or too naïve or too adolescently insecure to consider other sides. I had never met a Palestinian or read a book by a Palestinian writer, and it never even occurred to me that I should.

I was completely enamored with the idea of Israel as a Jewish homeland. It felt so real and authentic. It was so much better than the Judaism of New York's Avenue J, high heels, lipstick, and endless gossip and judgment of women's bodies. It was thrillingly exciting to consider myself as part of one of the most important events in the 3,000-year-old Jewish history — the revival of my people, a reversal of Jewish fortunes, the great Zionist experiment. I was carving my place in my own history, taking my peoplehood seriously, and giving my life meaning and purpose. It's what everyone wants, isn't it?

# My Orthodoxy

All that took place against the backdrop of my Orthodox Jewish upbringing.

A key component of Orthodox day school education, that I only fully understood twenty years later, after I completed my doctorate in education and sociology/anthropology, is this: Critical thinking isn't really a thing in Orthodox schooling. By design, Orthodox educators are not interested in teaching their students to question what they learn. On the contrary, Orthodox educators at times very honestly admit that their purpose is to inculcate complete commitment and loyalty to the lifestyle, to the system. In fact, the entire *raison d'être* of Orthodoxy is the exact opposite of critical thinking.

Lest you think this is some extreme, ultra-Orthodox version of the religion I'm referring to, it is not. I'm talking about modern Orthodoxy, or religious Zionism, where boys and girls sometimes learn together, where many girls wear jeans, where schoolchildren are expected to go to college and get jobs, and where the community ethos is integration into Western society, at least to a certain degree.

Or so they say. In my career as an educator, I gradually discovered otherwise. I started out my post-college working life teaching high school social studies; I earned an M.A. in Jewish Education from the Hebrew University, taught in a variety of settings — from seventh grade through high school, to gap-year programs and colleges, received my doctorate in education and sociology/anthropology with a focus on gender studies, and spent about six years teaching education in universities and colleges in Israel while researching and writing about Orthodox Jewish educational culture. As I went through this career path and explored sociological aspects of education, I uncovered some uncomfortable truths about my own education and the culture I come from. It was not pretty.

I have an astounding memory of a moment of discovery about indoctrination. When my dear friend and colleague the late Dr. Chaya Gorsetman and I were working on our book about gender in Jewish education, *Educating in the Divine Image*, and were conducting interviews with Jewish educators, Chaya had a conversation with a school principal whom she had up until that point deeply admired, as his school is considered to be one of the best and most progressive schools in the Orthodox world in the United States. He said to her point blank: "We are not interested in teaching critical thinking. We are here to give them all the information they need. They can start thinking critically later in life, after they've left our schools and spent a year in Israel. Then they can go to college and start processing on their own."

Chaya was shocked by that conversation, as was I, and we discussed it at length. We considered all the ways in which we had both felt indoctrinated, how it took us years if not decades to disentangle from that indoctrination, how we both dreamed of being a particular kind of educators while embracing our religious culture, and how we had both faced immense roadblocks to those dreams. It was as if the Orthodox school system was never really interested in our offerings — open-mindedness, heart-led experiences, encouraging children to be free-thinking and free-feeling individuals. Suddenly it all made sense. By the end of our conversation, we were no longer shocked. We finally gained true clarity about our own life experiences and the culture we were so desperately trying to change.

I say this to try and explain why, sitting in Tomer's class hearing all those ideas about Israel and Jewish history, I was so uncritical, so intellectually limp in response. I was in a cultural system called "education" that was designed to sculpt eager followers. In that sense, I was a great student. Despite all my cutting classes and overall bad habits, I sponged up the main point: *Be a good Jew.*

I did that, the best way I knew how, for a very long time. Always trying hard to be a good Jew. You might even say I dedicated my life to that ideal. Maybe I still am.

I suppose I shouldn't be so forgiving to myself. I should take more responsibility for my own stupidity. But in my defense, I would just like to say, it is very hard to talk back to one's entire culture, all by yourself, especially when you're still just a kid. And especially when that culture gives you many things your heart craves most: belonging, connections, meaning, purpose, depth, community, friends. Love, in a way. It's what teenagers want most in the world, and probably adults, too. It's hard to reject a system that gives you all that.

If you do talk back to your culture, your entire world may eventually collapse. I should know.

# Jewish Pride

There is one more aspect of the formation of my religious Zionist identity that I feel the need to explain. The lessons of that Zionism class took place in the context of certain political and cultural trends in my community. Those were the years of Natan Sharansky's epic imprisonment and the plight of Soviet Jews, of the Nazi parade in Skokie, Illinois, of Lenny Solomon and Jewish pride and NCSY, of religious outreach, of Rabbi Avi Weiss handcuffing himself to a fence outside the White House. It was an intense, public, feisty reckoning with antisemitism by the Jewish community, fears for our collective safety — real or imagined — and a deep attachment to Jewish historical trauma. World events were seen through a specifically Jewish lens. "Is it good for the Jews?" was the regular response to everything, from presidential elections to commercial trends. Jewish-specific responses couched as resistance to what the world was trying to do to us — that felt like power. This practice, coupled with biblical messaging and charismatic teachers, made you feel like you were flying on the wings of God himself.

There's more. On that scene of Jewish-specific engagement with the world was the visible, audible presence of the JDL — the Jewish Defense League, the militant arm of the late Meir Kahana's racist, violent, Jew-centric nationalist movement. They showed up everywhere. To Soviet Jewry rallies. To the Salute to Israel Parade. To the White House. Wherever Jews gathered to do an angry, public Jewy thing, the Kahanists were there. (Or even not so angry. Maybe it was their job to *make* it angry). They were always there, the agitators, with their raised fists, ready to pounce. Always there, but sort of on the side.

We knew they were a bit, shall we say, extreme. They were aggressive. Untamed. Unpredictable. Troublemakers. We kind of knew to stay away from them. More or less.

But maybe not really. They were also *ours*.

They were part of the community, even if they were a fringe. We were connected even as we tried to pretend that we weren't. They were like the crazy uncle you still invite to Thanksgiving. You pretend he's all talk but mostly harmless. Or at least you hope so. I was only a kid, but it felt like the adults around me had a kind of love-hate relationship with the JDL Kahanists, with people who claimed to represent all of us but had means and tactics we weren't sure were kosher.

Lest you think that the Kahanist JDL culture is a thing of the past, Israel's Minister of Police, Itamar Ben-Gvir, is a protégé of Meir Kahana. He celebrates Kahana's life and death, and he has built his political party on Kahanism — the same party that received fifteen Knesset seats, 12.5% of the votes, and is aggressively pushing to raze Gaza entirely and replace Palestinians with a new Jewish settlement.[23] All those crazy uncles of the JDL morphed into the Israeli police system and leaders of the Israeli coalition.

Where this gets truly murky for me is that it was often hard to distinguish between the message of the JDL and Tomer's message. Jewish nationalism. Jewish pride. Jewish chosenness. Jewish victimhood. The inevitability of antisemitism. The Holocaust. Israel. Zionism. Self-defense.

---

[23] Jeremy Sharon, "Ben Gvir calls to 'encourage emigration,' resettle Gaza at ultra-nationalist rally," *The Times of Israel*, May 14, 2024, https://www.timesofisrael.com/ben-gvir-calls-to-encourage-emigration-resettle-gaza-at-ultra-nationalist-rally/; Eleanor H. Reich, "Israel's far-right kingmaker joins memorial for racist rabbi," *AP News*, November 10, 2022, https://apnews.com/article/middle-east-religion-jerusalem-israel-d1500820cd52562638506cc59843b789.

Jewish power. *Kill the enemy of the Jews.* It was all wrapped up together in religious-scaffolded ideas about Jewish history. About our identity and life mission.

We need the land of Israel because they tried to kill us in the Holocaust and they always try to kill us, and anyway God promised it to us. The world owes it to us. We are the "good guys", against all evil.

*This is why you, Elana, are here right now, why you were put on this earth. To protect your people.*

All this was presented as an all-encompassing truth about everything, about who we are. And I desperately wanted that. I wanted meaning, purpose, connection, truth, and some kind of context to my life.

I completed my Zionism training — the ninth-grade mandatory class and another twelfth grade Zionist elective class — ready for battle. I was eager, excited, and armed. I graduated high school fully ready to engage in the rhetorical battle of our lives, to protect our people and our nation and our right to exist. To live out the dreams of our ancestors and thereby avenge two thousand years of Jewish suffering that culminated in the Holocaust. Our weapons were words. We were raring to go. At least I was.

In college I was heavily involved in Hillel International, I chaired Columbia Students for Israel, I attended AIPAC events, and I rallied and protested on campus against Palestinian student groups. I never veered from my dream. I knew for certain even then that I was going to build my life in Israel. And that's what I did.

By the time I was twenty-three years old, I was married with a child and was enthusiastically moving my new family to Israel.

# The Latest War

October 7, the worst day in modern Jewish history, was like a confirmation of everything Tomer taught us about Zionism. Details emerged in agonizing swaths. From the Israeli perspective, the day looked like this: Over 1,200 Israelis dead, a massacre at the Nova music festival, hundreds of soldiers killed, 250 hostages taken to Gaza including dozens of children and babies, sickening mutilations of bodies including those of children and babies, rampant sexual assault, utter devastation of the region, the destruction of kibbutzim, and 70,000 people from the Gaza rim evacuated and whose future remains uncertain.

All that was followed by an ongoing onslaught in the north of Israel that left dozens of Israeli civilians and IDF soldiers dead, thousands of direct hits on Israeli buildings, and 80,000 displaced people from the north who don't know if, when, or how they will ever get to go home.

The war continued to expand onto more fronts. Hundreds of rockets and ballistic missiles aimed at Israel from Iran and Yemen. Israeli life in complete disarray as schools closed, flights got canceled, weddings were postponed, gatherings became restricted — almost like another Covid lockdown, only with missiles headed toward us.

These events affected me directly as well. As I mentioned, my two daughters were immediately displaced from their homes in the south and ended up staying with me in Modi'in for several months; one of them never returned to her previous home. My son and two sons-in-law were all called up to reserve duty for months, sometimes for several "tours", leaving their children, pregnant wives, and then babies and nursing mothers alone and afraid indefinitely. One was in the army for eleven months straight. They have all suffered personal losses — friends, classmates, and friends of friends who were at the Nova festival or who were injured, killed, taken hostage, or displaced. My youngest daughter, who we didn't see for a month but who was released from compulsory service in February 2024, was dealing with the deaths of friends and fellow soldiers, as well as countless injuries, traumas, and close calls among people she knew. My husband and I were dealing not only with supporting our children, but also with our own losses — funerals of neighbors' children, colleagues taken hostage, a friend whose son was killed at home on the morning of the attack, scores of people displaced and disrupted, and countless fears and trepidations.

Thankfully, my family is mostly okay. *Counting my blessings. Miracles.*

With all this happening, I also had another serious concern, one that most people in Israel weren't thinking about at all during those days. One that is almost never mentioned in the Israeli media, as if it's part of a different reality that has nothing to do with us.

The people of Gaza. The Palestinians in Gaza.

Immediately after October 7, Israel went on the attack in Gaza. Not a small attack. Not a calculated and precise strike or some intelligent strategy that aims only at the actual people holding guns or operating rocket launchers. That's not what Israel did. Israel went for massive, excessive assault, destroying entire buildings, entire neighborhoods. Leaving vast craters where communities once lived.

Of course that's what Israel did. That's what Israel always seems to do. For twenty years, Israel has responded to Hamas rockets with colossal attacks in Gaza, in which many innocent people are killed, and which do nothing to make Israel safer.

As I write this, with over 45,000 known dead in Gaza, 90,000 injured, wanton destruction of homes, and a massive humanitarian crisis that has overwhelmed even the sturdiest of relief agencies, there is still no end in sight and long-term solutions are becoming more elusive by the day. The loss of human life extends to the West Bank as well, where hundreds of Palestinians have been killed by the IDF as a result of loosened or nonexistent rules around shooting, on top of years of callous disregard for basic rights of the entire Palestinian population. All this has been exacerbated by the radical religious right whose government actively encourages settler violence, and whose ministers often participate in the attacks and pillaging of Palestinian villages themselves. Most of this is far from the media, certainly of little interest to most Israelis, and continues unabated. The entire story of what we have been doing to Palestinians is horrific, and frankly, for most Israelis — unimaginable.

And *we* did this. By "we" I mean we the Zionists, the Israelis, the Jews. This is our Jewish pride in action. *My* Jewish pride. The one that has guided me my entire life. This is where it has led.

Again, it did not start on October 7, nor end on October 7. We are smack in the middle of a very long story with new chapters being written in blood every day.

I am horrified by this. And ashamed. And angry. And terrified about what lies ahead. And wondering what being Israeli or even being Jewish really means.

# Revisiting My Israel

I realize that it took me a while to get to this place and to understand my own role in world events and systematic oppression of an entire people. There were many twists and turns along the way. For much of my young adulthood, I was fully invested in the Zionist enterprise, dedicating my personal, professional, and communal life to supporting my people. I was also intensely invested in fixing the patriarchal aspects of my culture, believing fully that my culture is inherently worthy and fixable. During those years, there was no room in my head for questioning the entire foundation, for looking too closely at how the outside world perceives us. I wasn't there yet. It took me a long time, maybe too long. For that I am remorseful, but I'm also working on what my friend Eva Dalak calls "compassionate self-forgiveness". Working on it.

As I've learned, it's not easy to unpack your own personal history so critically. How do you face the discovery that things you were taught as righteous and "good education" were actually forms of indoctrination and manipulation for the sake of power, tools to justify systematic oppression, dehumanization, and even killing an entire population? This has not been an easy journey. But here I am.

One major turning point for me came in 2009, when I landed a position as a writer for an Israeli so-called "media monitoring" organization. I say "so-called" because the term "media monitoring" makes it sound objective and unbiased, though it is anything but. My job was to write organizational copy that counters what was labeled anti-Israel bias in articles, op-eds, and television items. In practice, whenever I came across anything even slightly sympathetic to Palestinians, my task was to find a way to debunk it by claiming that the "Palestinian narrative" is false. If a Palestinian spoke, my job was to argue that they were lying. I took the job, but at a certain point it started to feel very wrong. I thought we were working too hard to delegitimize Palestinian lives and identities. Did our Zionist mission require such an active presence on the debating team to survive? Couldn't we tell our story in a more upright way, with more integrity? Wasn't our own story better than this?

"What's wrong with the Palestinians having a narrative?", I asked the director at a staff meeting. "They are entitled to have their own experiences."

Everyone around the conference table stared at me in astonishment.

The next day I was fired.

Stewing in the shock of my experience, I found myself torn between different pulls on my soul. Sure, I wanted to protect and defend Israel. That has been my whole life. But something about that process of "media monitoring" felt so wrong to me. I was particularly bothered by the idea that by insisting on telling our own story, we were shutting off the possibility of listening to the other person's story. I didn't want that to be true. If our only defense is to argue that everyone else is simply lying, we are doing something very wrong.

I also deeply identified with having everyone around you call you a liar. From my years as a feminist in the Orthodox world I knew what it felt like to be talked about, talked over, discussed by men with power, generalized about, and still never being really heard or understood or believed. That position worsened as I became more active with survivors of sexual abuse. From years of intense research on the subject, I was well familiar with the manipulations involved in telling people who are hurting that they are wrong, disillusioned, or just lying. The practice of telling people that we know what their lives are better than they do — that's classic gaslighting and emotional abuse.

I did not yet have all this knowledge and awareness back in 2009. At that point, I just had a visceral experience of not wanting to be the one who reads someone's life story and concludes that they are lying. And I suddenly realized that my entire Zionist narrative was based on that practice.

I needed to step away.

This started my earnest process of looking beyond the manufactured argumentation and listening to people's real stories. I began to wonder what Palestinians — especially Palestinian women — were experiencing. We were taught to believe that "The Arabs" all hate us Jews and make up lies about us. *Sure. Everyone knows that*. But wait. I started to question whether that was actually true. Yes, there was "proof". Fake photographs, videos of children dressed as suicide bombers, celebrations of martyrs whose mothers are proud of how many Jews they killed — all those images and arguments have been shared ubiquitously on social media with classic grandiose generalizations. *Arabs do not value human life. Arabs cannot be trusted. Arabs raise their children to kill.* It was all fixed in my brain.

Sort of.

I started to dig a bit deeper.

*Really?* Do *all* two million Gazans really feel this way? Why do we look at awful things and say things like "They are all..." or use those images to prove our narrative that "all Arabs lie and hate Jews"? Our insistence to prove our rightness obscures the very real questions about whether Israel has really done right by our neighbors.

I began stepping out of the groupthink and looking elsewhere. I decided to sign my daughter up for Kids4Peace, a mixed Jewish-Palestinian youth group in Jerusalem. One aspect of the program that was particularly impactful for me was the parent gatherings that often took place while the kids were doing their thing. It was the closest I had ever come to having a Jewish-Palestinian social circle. I wouldn't say the parents were all suddenly friends — most of us still knew relatively little about each other's real lives, and didn't engage in normal friends' activities like inviting each other to our houses or going to the movies together. But we shared something close to our hearts: our children were becoming friends. This gave us a common language and experience, and an opportunity to see a human face in one another, to see that we were all more or less the same, just regular parents trying to give our children a good life.

One of those gatherings took place around the time of a war in Gaza. (Which one? There was one every two years. Does it even *matter* which one?) We were all affected by the violence, even if it was almost routine. While our kids were in the program, the parents gathered for an impromptu dialogue circle in which we shared what we were going through.

One mother told a story I did not understand at first. The 40-ish-year-old Palestinian mother of three was a resident of East Jerusalem, fluent in Hebrew, Arabic, and English, and worked at a Jewish institute on a program for building peace and a shared society. Sitting next to a Jewish man she called a colleague and a friend, she described a scene that had taken place recently in Hadassah Hospital where she was taking care of her ailing father. While she and her eight-year-old son were in her father's room, there was a sudden commotion as a slew of ambulances began to rush in from a mass casualty event. Turning to the news, she learned that there had just been a terror attack in the city.

Her son, watching the gurneys pass by, asked his mother, "Who did they kill this time?"

She turned to him and said, "No, not *them*. Us. *We* did this."

At first, her son was confused. Then he shrugged nonchalantly and walked away.

She said that story made her feel like a failure as a mother. If she couldn't educate her own child to feel empathy for the

Other, she — who has dedicated her life to peace work — has failed at her most basic job. As she contemplated her son's attitude, she realized he had never met a Jew who was not a soldier. She felt a strong need to fix that.

This story astounded me, and not because of the boy's indifference. Rather, I was shocked that this boy had only encountered violence in the form of Jews attacking Palestinians and not the other way around. It made no sense to me, because it was the exact opposite of how Jews saw the conflict. Yet, his reality was such that he did not even know there was such a thing as a Jew who was not holding a gun. As the mother explained, her son only knew of Jews who were IDF soldiers who arrested his friends and cousins, who patrolled with weapons, and who enforced curfews and roadblocks.

At first, I couldn't believe this was true. Was there really an entire population of Palestinian children whose only contact with Jews was with IDF soldiers perpetrating violence on their streets? This perspective was so completely new to me that it took me some time to digest.

Then the penny dropped. I was completely socialized into one story. And it's not just that it's only half the story. It's not even a *true* half of the story. All those accepted truths we have been telling ourselves about our righteousness and our victimhood and how "they" all want to kill us — that is not exactly what is happening.

Somewhere in the back of my mind a new thought was forming. It is very possible that the exact same ideas I was taught to believe about Palestinians ("they all want to kill us") were what Palestinian children were learning about us. That thought threatened to explode in my brain and wash away my entire concept of who I am and what it means to be Israeli, or even Jewish.

I began looking for new places to interact and engage more authentically with Palestinians. I started entering spaces I had never been to before. I actively sought out locations for dialogue and collaboration. I attended weekends on Nonviolent Communication between Palestinian and Jewish women, *Sulha* events, interfaith conferences and seminars, tours of the West Bank, joint Jewish-Palestinian memorial services, peace trainings, yoga for peacebuilding sessions, and pretty much anything I could find that would open me up to worlds and understandings that had been closed to me.

Instead of seeing Palestinians as people I needed to fear, to correct, to fix, to control, and to challenge, I started listening to them.

I went to meetings, conferences, events, iftars, and tours. I visited Palestinian villages and encountered issues such as water wars and land grabs. I did not want to believe that Jewish settlers engaged in such violence and aggression, but I discovered that some of the worst things that have been said about Jews are true.

On a tour of Jerusalem and its surrounds led by an organization called "Ir Amim" (City of Nations)[24], I sat in the orchard of an elderly Palestinian man in Walaje whose family had been on that land since the nineteenth century, and whom the Israeli government refused to acknowledge or legalize. Instead, the government built The Wall on his land, separated him from his trees, and repeatedly demolished his children's homes. I heard from Palestinians in East Jerusalem who were unable to get permits to build on their own land, because there was no actual mechanism in place for them and by default everything they built was ruled illegal. Teams of lawyers were fighting this madness and had court decisions on their side, but they are still waiting for Jerusalem's municipality to implement the rulings.

On a visit to the village At-Tuwani organized by my friend Sigal Kirsch, I met people who had been attacked by religious Jews who had moved into Palestinian towns to purposely "Judaize" them — using language I was all too familiar with

---

[24] https://www.ir-amim.org.il/en

referring to Jewish ancient history, connections to "the land", or divine chosenness. The village had no electricity or running water. The place was only a few kilometers from my own home, yet it was like a different world.

At a Palestinian-Israeli women's leadership training by the organizations Itach-Ma'aki – Women Lawyers for Social Justice[25] and The Adam Institute for Democracy and Peace,[26] I heard women's life stories and looked at maps to understand how seemingly "bureaucratic" decisions can ruin people's lives. During a Nonviolent Communication (NVC) weekend in what was then EcoMe, an ecological retreat near the Dead Sea, my daughter and I befriended Palestinian women who were struggling with living under occupation. I met a woman trapped in the cruel marriage system in which "mixed" West Bank/Israel couples are often forced to live in separate homes and struggle to meet.[27] I met a woman who couldn't leave the country without losing her rights, another crazy set of rules and regulations that Israel has set up to disconnect Palestinians from their land. I once drove a Palestinian family from Hebron to the Tel Aviv beach — illegally — because the children had never seen the ocean before. On an Encounter Program[28] through Bethlehem and East Jerusalem, I met a woman who was stopped at a checkpoint for hours on her way to a hospital in Jerusalem with her very sick son, the first of many stories I would hear about the checkpoints and how they ruin Palestinian lives. I stood on the top of Mount Scopus and watched the completion of a Jews-only road,[29] as our

---

[25] https://www.itach.org.il/?lang=en.

[26] https://www.adaminstitute.org.il/home/.

[27] Harriet Sherwood, "Court upholds law banning Palestinian spouses from living in Israel," *The Guardian,* January 12, 2012

[28] https://www.encounterprograms.org/.

[29] Nir Hasson, "New Jerusalem 'Apartheid Road' Opens, Separating Palestinians and Jewish Settlers", *Ha'aretz,* Jan 10, 2019, https://www.haaretz.com/israel-news/2019-01-10/ty-article-magazine/.premium/new-apartheid-road-opens-separating-

politicians insisted that there is no such thing as apartheid in Israel. On a Standing Together[30] tour of Jaffa, I saw the relics of the 1948 "Burn the Chametz" operation, as the new Israeli army described the battle for Jaffa at the time. I heard from Abed Sattel, a nurse in Ichilov Medical Center and multi-generational Jaffa resident, about the loss of his family home to the Israeli authorities in the 1950s after Israel passed a law allowing Israelis to grab Palestinian homes. Working with the group Kulna Yaffa (We Are All Jaffa), I heard from Palestinian families facing harrowing injustices of eviction decades later, with no viable recourse to keep the homes they had been living in for generations. Following a Kids4Peace[31] communal iftar, I went on a tour of The Wall and its impact on cutting off Palestinian communities. I also toured the Road One construction in Jerusalem, built specifically to divide Palestinian residential neighborhoods in two while failing to provide them with access to the road. With my Women Building Bridges dialogue group, I sat in the garden of a friend in Beit Hanina where the wall was just meters away, blocking access to the main road in her neighborhood and her friends' homes just a few streets away, creating endless traffic jams and making it impossible for her to move around, all because Israel never bothered to understand the transportation needs of the community, let alone do basic things like installing traffic lights. I heard from Palestinians held indefinitely in Israeli jails in "administrative detention", a tactic that enables the authorities to hold people — even children — without charges and without them knowing what they are being accused of, for up to six months, a period which can then be extended by another six months, and another, and another.

Things like that. The Wall. The separate roads. The water injustices. Home demolitions. Random settler violence.

---

palestinians-and-west-bank-settlers/0000017f-e8cc-df2c-a1ff-fedda5460000 .
[30] https://www.standing-together.org/en .
[31] https://k4p.org/ .

Palestinian villages completely off the grid. These stories saddened me, like the children I drove to the beach, or the women who couldn't live with their husbands. I take for granted that I can go where I want and live how I want, such basic things. And all those people, so close and yet so far, are denied those basic rights. I could not wrap my head around it.

Then I started to get angry. I thought about the man I met whose son, Basel, was beaten up by settlers who ransacked their vulnerable small electricity-less village just because they could. It was the kind of story that, some years earlier, I would have assumed to be a lie, or to be missing "context". But I was no longer looking for explanations and rhetorical stunts to change the narrative. I knew what I saw and heard.

Something was very wrong — very, very wrong. I didn't yet know just how deep the corruption went. Or what I was going to do about it.

# Rewriting My Identity

I had not grasped how much my views had been shifting until the 2014 war, when I found myself engaged in countless social media exchanges, often being cast as the one who "doesn't get it" and needs to receive proper Zionist education.

Of course, nobody announced that a war has broken out. Instead, we all woke up to the news that seventy-six people were killed by the IDF in Gaza. I quickly wrote a Facebook status update:

**76 people have been killed since the Israeli gov't entered Gaza. 76 people. That is a LOT of lives ruined. There has GOT to be another way.**

At the time, I wasn't advocating for a particular political view. I wasn't trying to express an opinion about whether Israel has a right to exist or whether the Palestinians should be able to establish a state in the West Bank and Gaza. I wasn't delegitimizing Israel or waving a Palestinian flag or equating Zionism with racism. I wasn't addressing any broad political questions about the future of the region. I was talking about life and death, about basic rights, right here, right now, about what the IDF is doing today in terms of the real lives of real people living in Gaza who may have nothing to do with rockets or kidnappings or building tunnels but just want to live their lives, just like we do. I did not accept the idea that the killing of those seventy-six people was some kind of self-defense, or that it was somehow necessary for Israel's security. I am even more certain today that such an idea is just a fallacy — after all, the number of rockets launched at Israel only continued to rise, and the mass bombing of Gazans did not leave Israelis better off in any way, not then and not now. Those thoughts about the bigger questions and root causes were not yet fully formed or nuanced. I was still in a stage of listening and learning, of looking honestly at events around me, removing the cloak of propaganda that was always thrown at us with such alacrity that most Israelis would quickly support the government without giving it much thought. I was letting go of all that and reclaiming my brain. I was questioning an approach that views the killing of Gazan civilians as somehow justifiable, as some kind of normal act to "protect" Israel, or as somehow the fault of the Palestinians being killed, even though Israel was pulling those triggers.

I was mostly putting myself in the shoes of the Palestinians in Gaza who were not the ones trying to hurt Israelis. That's what feminism taught me — to look beyond the official story and ask how major political decisions affect people's lives. It's the basic idea that the personal is political. Or maybe it is basic human empathy. I was feeling for Gazans' pain and questioning whether so much killing was the right path. Such a stance should not feel so radical.

The reactions on Facebook were somewhat confounding for me, although they were tame compared to what was to follow. There was a very clear split: some friends thanked me profusely for writing what they were feeling, while others accused me of caring about the wrong issues, of being unsympathetic to the people in the south of Israel suffering from rocket attacks, and of being pro-Palestinian and thus by default a hater of Israel and a Jew-hater. At the time I didn't consider myself particularly pro-anything or anti-anything. I was just putting into words the feelings I had at that moment. I just didn't want us to be killing so many people, so callously.

Social media became the platform where I found myself confronting my internal angst and the place I came from. Those exchanges became mini battlegrounds on a journey from my past to my present, from my identity as an Orthodox religious Zionist Jew to something else. What that "something else" was took a while to take shape, and it was not without many struggles and lost relationships.

I suppose on some level, my transformation may be qualified as having gone from "right" to "left", although I am loath to view it in such linear terms.

Perhaps I'm reluctant to label myself because it feels dishonest, or even shameful. I know that in my own history, I have had many moments of right-wing inspired diatribes. Yes, in my past, I've been that annoying one who goes into discussions of the "Arab-Israeli conflict" accusing critics of Israel of not understanding Israel's position and of promoting antisemitism and probably some other things. In this internet age where nothing disappears, one day someone will come across something I wrote about Israel ten or fifteen years ago and say, perhaps rightly so, that I'm a hypocrite. A fake. Or just incoherent. And they might be right.

Perhaps I don't easily call myself a "leftist" because in the world in which I dwelled for most of my life "leftist" is a slur, kind of like the way rabbis in Israel who want to insult women call us "Reform" or "lesbians". So many status updates I've seen were aimed at "those leftists" as much as at "those Arabs". I really don't want to go anywhere near that whole dialectic, even if perhaps a smarter tack would be to reject the slurs entirely.

I think I find the labels inaccurate. In my ideological meanderings, "leftist" is no more a home for me than "religious Zionist" is. Often, "leftist" gatherings are averse to anything remotely religious. During the anti-government protest movements of 2023, many events took place on Shabbat without even a thought that perhaps religious people were also interested in preserving democracy. Many feminist and pro-democracy groups are overtly anti-religious, like the "red cloak" protests in the spirit of Margaret Atwood's *The Handmaid's Tale* (which I participated in) that view religion as *the* source of patriarchy. As if Israeli secularism is somehow free of rampant sexism. Even though I'm no longer Orthodox and I have attended protests on Shabbat, part of me also bristles on behalf of religious Jews who are cast as cave-dwelling idiots. I'm not there either.

Mostly I think I wouldn't label myself as "leftist" because it feels so inadequate, a product of a cold, linear construction created by the men who have been running the world for so long. Maybe it has something to do with getting older, where things that seemed so simple and straightforward when we were younger take on more nuance and complexity as we experience life. I hear Billy Joel's voice in my head singing, "I believe I've passed the age of consciousness and righteous rage; I found that just surviving was a noble fight." As my own ideas and identity evolve, I increasingly understand that the perspective I identify with the most is not really represented in the way Israeli politics is so often presented. "Right" and "left" seem to be reductivist labels that attempt to conflate our human complexity into a binary position on a particular issue. I am stepping away from boxes, not wanting to place myself in a new one. That entire way of thinking doesn't work for me anymore.

# Losing Friends (Both Facebook Ones and Real Ones)

The 2014 war was a pivotal moment in my journey, when I began to fully grasp the extent to which the rhetorical war is conducted alongside the military one, and how for many Jews it is no less important. Anywhere you go on the internet, there are battles between people who are like soldiers in a PR war — like I once was — ready to pounce on any suggestion of sympathy for the Palestinians, ready to accuse you of being anti-Israel, anti-Jewish. And that feels so wrong.

My views did not fit in with the black-and-white constructs that engulfed me. I found myself deeply concerned about the people at the Gaza rim and in the south of Israel, the soldiers, the displaced, the wounded, and others living with the trauma of war — many of whom are my friends I love deeply — while at the same time I was deeply concerned about the people in Gaza whose homes, families, and lives are so casually destroyed by Israel, including many who are not Hamas supporters and are certainly not terrorists and simply want to live a normal life. This complex stance — to be both anti-rockets and anti-wanton killing of innocent people and destroying homes and entire communities — did not seem to have a place in the existing framework of understanding the conflict. Especially for Israelis, you're either one or the other.

And so, in August 2014, for the first time in my life, after twenty years of living in Israel and a writing career focused mostly on gender and Judaism while staying mostly silent on the Palestinian-Israeli conflict, I decided to write an essay sharing how I feel about this issue. In an essay for *Lilith* titled "My Political Evolution"[32] I wrote about the path I took from the religious Zionist views I adopted as a right-wing-leaning yeshiva graduate from Brooklyn to the views I now held, that the binary no longer worked and I understood that Palestinians are human beings with a history and a culture and some very good reasons to be angry at us. It was my first time trying to make sense of myself and my political identity, trying to find a coherent way to understand who I am in a world where my position defies common assumptions. I was — timidly and hesitantly, I think — trying to justify the idea that I care very deeply about the lives of Israelis, and *also* care very deeply about the lives of Palestinians living under Israeli rule.

My essay focused on the pain of social media exchanges and the breaking of relationships.

> *When I first began saying these things out loud, this monolithic black-white thinking found expression in some deeply painful exchanges. In one on my status updates, when I suggested that we are painting all Palestinians with the same brush, a friend of mine told me I would never say that if I lived in the south. Really, I asked? So everyone living in the south automatically hates all Palestinians? It's a terrible condemnation of humanity, actually. And unfair and untrue. And by the way, I told her, my son, a Givati soldier, was serving down south. Not that I need to use my kids as proof of anything within myself. I hate doing that, and it makes me cringe when others use their children's lives to explain themselves. But let me say something anyway. My son is often out there in those 'open fields' where Iron Dome doesn't bother shooting down rockets and he has had*

---

[32] Elana Sztokman, "My Political Evolution," *Lilith*, August 12, 2014, https://lilith.org/2014/08/my-political-evolution/. https://www.theguardian.com/world/2012/jan/12/israel-palestinian-spouses-ban.

*rockets fall within meters of him. And Givati has been in the news plenty for their bravery as well as their casualties. My experience as a mother of soldiers does not make me revert to seeing all Palestinians as one and the same. On the contrary, now I feel even more strongly that we have to hang on to our humanity, to think about the real lives of Palestinians as human beings, too. But I should not have to say this. I should not have to talk about my son or find other ways to 'prove' that I adequately experience the rockets in order to be able to have an opinion about whether we are overly bombarding the civilians in Gaza. But that is how bifurcated the entire discussion has become.*

*Even worse was what came afterwards in that particular thread.*

*Another woman whom I've known for years, and who also believes that I don't 'get it,' wrote to me to tell me that she has decided to block me on Facebook, but first she needs to educate me, and sent me some links to a film on an Israeli propaganda site that 'You must watch,' as if I need to see this in order to truly understand. And then she wrote, 'Think about your son.' What I responded to her was that she should definitely block me, and that my conversations with my son are none of her business. Her little chat with me was infuriating, using my son as a tool to win me over in the rhetorical war. The revolting implication was that if I dare express sympathy with Palestinians then that means that I haven't thought enough about my son, that I need someone else to educate me, because clearly anyone who is a parent of a soldier must understand that all Palestinians are evil. Even just thinking about this makes me livid.*

*There has been worse, too. I have been unfriending people on both sides of the divide for being completely obnoxious and abusive. One man, a non-Jewish colleague, kept insulting anyone who suggested that Israelis are acting in self-defense. I asked him a few times to try and express his view without being attacking, to stop implying that Israelis are murderous animals, to which he replied that anyone defending Israel deserves to be insulted. I eventually private messaged him that I'm unfriending him not for his political views but for being a jerk.*

*Another man, who lives on a settlement in the West Bank, whom I've known since we were in third grade and whom I kept as a friend even though he regularly leaves anti-feminist, hateful comments on my page, used my status updates to mock me. 'My radical feminist friend' he wrote on his page (meaning me, even though I've never called myself a radical feminist; I think he doesn't know what a radical feminist is but just thinks that my feminist ideas are radical, and hence I'm a radical feminist), 'my radical feminist friend actually posted something today about sexism in Turkey. The world must be coming to an end.' Haha, isn't that funny. Well, I blocked him, too. My outrage at having my entire person be used as someone else's 'material' is assuaged by the knowledge that I'm doing the exact same thing to him right now. Maybe there is some karma at work after all.*

*These conversations can be very destabilizing, as you wonder who your friends are, and to whom you can talk freely.*

*When I think back to those social media exchanges, I am filled with sadness. I think we were all learning about the destructive nature of social media back then. We did not know how to manage our emotions and our language on such a public, quick-paced platform. In many cases, we still don't, although today we understand the risks more clearly. The long list of blocked profiles I have amassed is in some ways a sign of the times, but also a reflection of the particular awfulness of discussions about the Palestinian/Israeli conflict. Even as our understandings about the dangers of social media have evolved, I'm not sure our understandings about the language of the conflict have. Most of the people stuck in those battles do not yet realize that we are living in a rhetorical war, and that often our exchanges are reflections of what our leaders want us to say, more than of what we as human beings might genuinely feel.*

The pains of social media eventually migrated into real life. I'll never forget the day Hadar Goldin and two other soldiers were kidnapped. My son was very close to that event, and one of his commanders was killed. He was supposed to be coming home that day, but then this disaster struck and impacted the entire country.

My essay went on:

> *On one particularly bad day when many people were struggling with the death of soldiers, a friend of mine saw one of my pained updates about how one of the casualties was my son's commander, and she came over so we could cry together. As we sat there with damp tissues piling up between us, she said, 'You've changed.'*
>
> *I thought she was going to say that I've become more left-wing this war. Instead, she said, 'You used to post much more sympathetically for the Palestinians, but you've stopped. You realize you can't, because they want to kill us. What can you do, they won't stop shooting rockets.' I stopped crying and stared at her. I wanted to say, 'No, it's not true.' I wanted to say that I don't believe that two million people of Gaza wanted to be shooting rockets. I wanted to say that most Gazans are also victims here, used by the uncontrollable Hamas military wing as targets, losing their homes and their families, dragged into a war that most of them do not want. I wanted to ask, who is the 'they' who want to kill us? Who is the 'all of them'? And I really wanted to say that the change she thought occurred in me had not in fact happened. But I didn't — because she is my friend and because I was emotionally exhausted, and I just didn't want to get into a debate. So maybe she is right after all; maybe I'm posting less. Maybe all the talking is almost as hard as all the death and destruction.*

The attempt to hold space for suffering on all "sides" is fraught with challenges. In many ways I still dwell in the world I came from even as I try to break open confining boxes.

The friend who sat on my couch crying with me while reprimanding me for having "pro-Palestinian" views also happened to be a fellow yeshiva alumnus. We have known each other since we were teenagers. I am not sure if it is possible to shift these views while also maintaining relationships. We are still friends, but no longer close ones.

> *The rhetorical war accompanying the military war — which has drastically increased interpersonal hostilities and decreased my number of friends — is so very unsettling. I feel like we're doing this all wrong. That nobody is experiencing real events as they are happening but are simply running off into the rhetorical battle. Like we're all on the debate team and determined to win. Nobody is trying to really understand the other's experience but is just determined to prove that they themselves are right about everything. It's as if we have been conditioned in an unyielding binary and overly competitive system for framing this war in a way that leaves little room for complexity or nuance, not to mention empathy, compassion, and real human connection.*

> *I think that there are probably a lot of people like me out there who do not have a home in the current rhetorical construct of the Arab-Israeli conflict. The truth is, despite all these difficult experiences, I have also had many very reinforcing exchanges with people who are also looking for another way, for a way to be both pro-Zionist and pro-Palestinian, or perhaps pro-Jewish and pro-human. My prayer is that when all this is over, that we will all learn how to step out of our respective inherited narratives and start our conversations from the basic premise that we are all human beings.*

Today, I look back at this essay and think it makes perfect sense, and I shouldn't have to try so hard to explain it. I have also come to know many wonderful people over the years who share this perspective. It's about humanity first. It's about the very simple concept that we are all human beings — that we don't want our own babies to die, and we don't want anyone else's babies to die either. It seems so obvious.

And yet, I fear that while for me this concept is clearer than it has ever been, for the Jewish people as a culture and as a community, this very simple and powerful idea is further away from our grasp than ever.

# Returning to My Self

October 8, 2023. In the WhatsApp exchange with my yeshiva alumni group that I was unwittingly added to, where I was cast as old and demented for daring to suggest that Palestinians are human beings who don't all deserve to die, all the twists and turns in my journey with Israel and my Brooklyn Jewishness came full circle.

The experience revealed to me that I had a volcano erupting in my heart and searing my soul. After all, part of me desperately wanted to reconnect with my classmates. These are my roots in some way, even though I'm not entirely sure what that means to me. For the first two decades of my life — significant ones by most accounts — that was all I knew. And it was a place that reflected my family of origin, the values of my ancestors, the ideals and sacrifices that were toiled at for generations by the people who made me and gave me their DNA. There is something primal about wanting to stay connected to that, even if I know deep down that I disconnected long ago. Part of me still wanted to believe that I could belong there.

I also thought, I have been living in Israel for thirty years, I have four children and children-in-law currently serving in the army, I'm living in this war right now. Maybe my perspective has value. After all, I did what we were all taught to do. I dedicated my life to the Jewish people. I moved to Israel. I became a Jewish educator. I'm doing it, the thing so many American Jews claim to only dream of. So isn't anyone interested in hearing from me? Learning the truth about, you know, how it's going for me?

Apparently not. Sometimes, fantasy is more important or more interesting than reality. My community of origin was no longer a place where my current views would be welcomed, or even of interest. That broke my heart. But it also freed me.

I let go of my own need to connect to this ancient part of myself and gave myself permission to be completely honest with myself. I could go back to my anthropologist self, the one trained in observation and analysis. The one slightly on the margins of what is happening, able to see without judgment and describe events as they happen, even in my own culture and community.

Since then, I've noticed something extremely jarring: The entire pro-Israel social media sphere uses the exact same rhetorical argumentation we learned in Flatbush forty years ago. *The exact same lines!* That Palestinians don't exist, that Muslims are all terrorists, that Israel does no wrong, and the world just hates us because of antisemitism. The same statements rehashed, recycled, and regurgitated. We were so well indoctrinated that we keep falling back on the exact same points.

Only now, there are more sophisticated tools at people's disposal. Canva-made memes, AI photographs, TikTok reels, and some frighteningly powerful influencers. In fact, one such influencer I was assigned to interview for a news story told me that the Israeli government has sent her and a group of other bloggers with many followers to no less than three "missions" to Israel for "fact gathering". The Israeli government is literally paying people who have memorized Tomer's talking points so that they can share them far and wide. She now has tens of thousands of Substack followers and is often cited as a hero of Israel.

Pro-Israel PR is working. Jews of the world eagerly share ideas thinking they are "protecting Israel" when they are protecting the Israeli government, justifying horrors. Every attempt at raising awareness about the plight of Palestinians is met with pro-Israel responses screaming "antisemitism".

In fact, the Israeli PR machine is so powerful that it has an indelible impact on American politics, too. When Israel-advocacy groups actively target members of Congress for being "anti-Israel", those representatives stand a good chance of losing their seats.[33] As one friend who is active in that congressional activity proudly told me, "AIPAC works."[34] Some pundits believe that this issue even threatens to upend the entire Democratic Party.[35]

Prime Minister Bibi Netanyahu is seemingly thrilled at how this is going. He himself invokes antisemitism and the Holocaust at every opportunity, his government actively and violently silences opposition, and capacity for nuance seems to have disappeared from our cultural landscape entirely. In fact, there is some evidence that his government actively works on influencing American political campaigns using the tools of American pro-Israel advocacy.[36]

Netanyahu has clearly perfected his ability to train and mobilize the rhetorical army. After all, he's been working on it for nearly half a century. While I was sitting in Tomer's class in the 1980s, Netanyahu was becoming the spokesperson for Israel. He served as Deputy Chief of Mission at the Israeli

[33] Geoffrey Skelley, "Pro-Israel groups spent big to oust two Squad members in primaries. But they didn't splash cash to oppose all high-profile progressives," *ABC News*, September 17, 2024, https://abcnews.go.com/538/pro-israel-groups-spent-big-oust-squad-members/story?id=113675889.

[34] Joan E Greve, Chris McGreal, and Will Craft, "Five things we learned from our reporting on the US's pro-Israel lobby," *The Guardian*, August 16, 2024, https://www.theguardian.com/us-news/article/2024/aug/16/congress-election-pro-israel-lobby-aipac.

[35] Ross Barkan, "How the Israeli-Palestinian Conflict Drove a Wedge Into the Democratic Party," *The New York Times*, February 7, 2024, https://www.nytimes.com/2024/02/07/magazine/israel-october-7-democrats.html.

[36] Sheera Frenkel, "Israel Secretly Targets U.S. Lawmakers With Influence Campaign on Gaza War," *The New York Times*, June 5, 2024, https://www.nytimes.com/2024/06/05/technology/israel-campaign-gaza-social-media.html.

Embassy in Washington, D.C., from 1982 to 1984, including during the 1982 Lebanon War when he became the face of Israel's rhetorical defense while I was going on my first family trip to Israel. Netanyahu was Israel's UN ambassador from 1984 to 1988, and he continued speaking, honing his American accent, his polished language, and his wry smile that made him a darling to the press and a hero to Zionist high school students. While we were preparing for college debates, for AIPAC advocacy, and for a lifelong mission of "defending Israel", Netanyahu was advancing a career that would make him the king of Israel.

In practice, Netanyahu has been running the country for most of the past twenty years. His rhetoric has become Israel's entire policy. My former classmates are still turning to Tomer, who has been Tomerizing Bibi for fifty years, and here we are.

The language war continues. In fact, there would be no military war without a language war to uphold it. How could Israel get away with human rights abuses and violating international law without the rhetoric to support it? I believe it couldn't. The language war keeps Bibi in his seat, and keeps Israel protected and able to do whatever it wants without serious repercussions.

And if we don't start systematically knocking down these talking points, they will continue to enable him to carry out his awful practices. We need to fight back against the rhetorical war. Urgently, and immediately.

# Part II: The Language War

# Overview

The ideas used to justify Israel's violence against Palestinians fall into four key themes:

**(1) Israelis/Jews are good and do no wrong**
**(2) Palestinians are bad and completely at fault**
**(3) Israelis/Jews are the real victims**
**(4) Everything Israel does is justified**

In the following section, I explore each of these four themes in detail.

# (1)  Israelis/Jews Are Good and Do No Wrong

One of the core elements of pro-Israel advocacy is the effort to prove that Jews are inherently good. I consider this a form of the "good-guy defense", a classic tactic of abusers who, when confronted about their abuse, often respond that they cannot possibly have done wrong because they are essentially "good guys".[37] The idea of Jews as the ultimate "good guys" is at the core of much of the rhetorical war. This line of argumentation has many variations and is arguably an underlying theme in all pro-Israel advocacy in some form.

## Jews are good/righteous

One of the memes that has come across my feed is a quote from the late UK Chief Rabbi Lord Jonathan Sacks:

---

[37] I wrote about the "good guy defense" at length in my book, *When Rabbis Abuse* (Lioness Books, 2022). I also refer to this as the "Eric Schneiderman phenomenon", as Schneiderman's public persona was of the great savior of women, literally spending his career prosecuting sexual predators and bringing justice to rape victims, but in private he was a violent misogynist who had a bad habit of nearly choking his girlfriends to death. They were reluctant to come forward because they didn't want to ruin his important work as the "good guy". See Jill Filipovic's excellent article on the subject: Jill Filipovic, "The Problem With 'Feminist' Men," *The New York Times*, May 8, 2018, https://www.nytimes.com/2018/05/08/opinion/schneiderman-abuse-feminist-men.html. I would also add that there is a kind of feminized version of the "good guy defense" that I call the "Who, *moi?*" defense. It's where women are completely impervious to criticism or even the prospect of them saying or doing something wrong or hurtful, and where they respond with a kind of indignance at the idea that they could have possibly done something wrong. It's the same idea but with a gendered twist.

**Israel has taken a barren land and made it bloom again. It's taken an ancient language, the Hebrew of the Bible, and made it speak again. It's taken the West's oldest faith and made it young again. It's taken a tattered, shattered nation and made it live again. Israel is the country whose national anthem, Hatikva, means 'hope'. Israel is the home of hope.**

The essential point of this meme is to frame Israel's existence and actions as part of a pure, angelic, and divinely inspired triumph. In this framing, Israel is exceptionally good.

It is easy to understand the appeal of this quote. The flowing, poetic language uplifts Israel to an angelic status. It tells a story of triumph amid despair, destruction, and barrenness. It depicts Jews as having been on the cusp of death when Israel miraculously revived us.

There is certainly a kernel of truth in this narrative, but it omits a few facts. The land wasn't barren when Jews arrived — Palestinians were living there. Similarly, while Israel is the home of hope for Jews, it is something completely different for other indigenous inhabitants of the land.

There is a deeper issue in this quote that I think defines much of the current tension between Israel's actions and the world of pro-Israel advocacy among Jews around the world. That is, why does a country that exists somewhere other than where the speaker lives need to be wrapped in such saintliness? Why is this preservation of the image of purity and perfection so vital for people around the world? Obviously that need is key to Jewish diaspora identity, the same identity I was socialized into and that drove me to move to Israel all those years ago. But I suspect that this language has taken on an urgency since October 7, and it highlights a split between those living in Israel's reality and those living in Israel as an abstract symbol of identity. Put differently, Israel for people living in it is complex and messy, while Israel as a perpetual safe haven in the distance or in the imagination is flat, unnuanced, idealized, and fictional.

The idea of Israel's pure goodness is framed in many other ways. One meme that appeared on my feed opens with the line "Jews don't kill". This, during the war in which the IDF has killed over 45,000 Gazans, including more than 12,000 children and babies. The meme reads like this:

**Jewish people don't kill while screaming *"Baruch Hashem!"* [Thank God]**
**We don't fly planes into buildings**
**We don't blow ourselves up, conquer lands, spread our faith or language.**
**We grow gardens, toast to life, light candles to remember, and eat.**

This text, which is also aimed at presenting Jews as pure angels, is filled with self-delusion. Jews absolutely *do* kill, often while praising God or justifying their actions as God-driven. Throughout Jewish history, Jewish groups have engaged in killing those branded as enemies — from the first century Sicarii who attacked Romans as well as fellow Jews perceived as "traitors", through early twentieth century Mandate-era terrorist groups like Irgun and Lehi that targeted Arabs, British, and fellow Jews, to more recent groups of Kahanists, Lehava, and more. Jews such as Baruch Goldstein, Yigal Amir, and Yaakov Teitel also killed — both Jews and non-Jews — in the name of religion. During the Duma arson attack by religious terrorist Amiram Ben-Uliel and others that killed an 18-month-old Palestinian baby and his parents, the killers reportedly shouted, "Long live the messiah!"[38] The rallying cry "Death to the Arabs!" can be heard not only in

---

[38] Robert Tait, "Palestinian baby killed in arson attack 'by Israeli settlers'," *The Telegraph*, July 31, 2015, https://www.telegraph.co.uk/news/worldnews/middleeast/israel/11774900/Palestinian-baby-dies-in-fire-started-by-Israeli-settlers.html.

chants by soccer fans and in flag parades,[39] but also in sermons by rabbis who argue that the Torah permits the killing of all Palestinians in Gaza.[40] So much for the premise that Jews don't kill in the name of their religion or God. It is not true historically and certainly not true today.

The current war has exposed chilling accounts of killing in cold blood, such as at the funeral of one soldier whose friends eulogized him by describing how he loved to burn houses and shoot at Palestinians, even unarmed women and children, in order to enact "revenge".[41] Similarly, religious settler groups have been relentlessly attacking Palestinians, especially in the West Bank.[42] Even on the holy day of Yom Kippur, religious Jewish attackers went on violent, armed rampages against Palestinian olive harvesters in the village of

---

[39] Associated Press, "Israeli nationalists march through Palestinian area of Jerusalem, some chanting 'Death to Arabs'," June 5, 2024, YouTube video, 0:35, https://www.youtube.com/watch?v=g8O-6e9M864&ab_channel=AssociatedPress; Sam Sokol and Charlie Summers, "Far-right violence, chants of 'Death to Arabs,' at Jerusalem Day Flag March in Old City," *The Times of Israel*, June 6, 2024, https://www.timesofisrael.com/jerusalem-day-flag-march-marred-by-far-right-violence-under-shadow-of-war/; "Beitar Jerusalem fans sing 'Death to Arabs' on train en route to soccer game," *The Times of Israel*, October 2, 2023, https://www.timesofisrael.com/liveblog_entry/beitar-jerusalem-fans-sing-death-to-arabs-on-train-en-route-to-soccer-game/.

[40] Chen Maanit, "Israeli Police Recommend Closing Case Against Yeshiva Head Who Said All Gazans Should Be Killed," *Haaretz*, June 18, 2024, https://www.haaretz.com/israel-news/2024-06-18/ty-article/.premium/police-recommend-closing-case-against-yeshiva-head-who-said-all-gazans-should-be-killed/00000190-27d9-d95e-a3ff-effdb62c0000.

[41] Einav Shiff, "We have to talk about the disturbing things from Shoval ben Natan's funeral," [Hebrew] *Ynet*, October 28, 2024, https://www.ynet.co.il/news/article/yokra14128906#autoplay.

[42] Kat Lonsdorf, "The war is in Gaza, but Palestinians in the West Bank are targeted with violence too," *NPR*, October 12, 2024, https://www.npr.org/2024/10/12/g-s1-27704/west-bank-palestinians-violence-israel-settlers.

al-Mughayir and the al-Qabun community.[43] The movement to starve or remove all Palestinians from Gaza is being supported by the Likud party, including some of its prominent ministers — a movement that held a large conference/festival on the Gaza border during the Sukkot holiday in 2024.[44]

As for some of the other points in this meme, while it may be true that the IDF does not engage in kamikaze suicide missions, the fact is that the army is able to destroy entire buildings and neighborhood by plane without the pilots having to die, and it does so regularly.

As for the idea that Jews do not "conquer lands", the question would be what, then, is Israel doing in Gaza and the West Bank?

The final point, that Jews simply "grow gardens", "toast to life", and "eat", it may be true that many Jews do many of these things. But that does not mean that Jews do not *also* at times kill in the name of God. One does not negate the other. In fact, one has nothing to do with the other. Many people who kill also grow gardens. And I would venture to say that *all* people who kill also eat.

This meme is wrong and has no logic. It is meant to imply that Jews are good because we are not like the Palestinians, and therefore we deserve support, even when we are in the process of doing some killing. But the idea that "Jews don't kill" in the name of religion is a false generalization and defies both Jewish history and the Jewish present. It's a nonsensical

---

[43] "Israeli settlers threaten and attack Palestinian olive harvesters in the village of al-Mughayir, Ramallah District. Soldiers threaten and drive away the harvesters," *B'Tselem*, October 15, 2024, https://www.btselem.org/video/20241015_israeli_settlers_attack_palestinian_olive_harvesters_and_soldiers_threaten_and_drive_away_the_harvesters_in_the_village_of_al_mughayir_in_ramallah_district#full.

[44] Channel 4 News, "The hardline Israeli settlers planning their future homes in Gaza," October 22, 2024, YouTube video, 7:49, https://www.youtube.com/watch?v=riLA5r8D4ac&t=12s&ab_channel=Channel4News.

idea that Jews are all good while everyone else is bad, and therefore Jews can do no wrong.

> **In a nutshell: Memes that try to present Jews as the most noble and pure in the world, or as people who "don't kill", advance the idea that Jews are the "good ones", and therefore Israel's actions are justified and good, even when Jews and Israelis are actively engaged in killing.**

## The IDF is the most moral army in the world

Israelis are inculcated into the idea that "The IDF is the most moral army in the world" during their military induction and even earlier. According to former Shin Bet head Ami Ayalon, this maxim was created as part of the IDF publicity machine during the 1980s, with intended audiences both in Israel and on the world stage.[45] In effect, this dictum enables soldiers to carry out actions despite their own moral dilemmas about those actions. In a chilling example of this, Shira Eting, a former Israeli air force combat helicopter pilot who is one of the leaders of the Brothers in Arms protest movement, said in a 60 Minutes interview that "If you want pilots to be able to fly, and shoot bombs and missiles into houses knowing they might be killing children, they must have the strongest confidence in the people making those decisions."[46] Eting was explaining why she was determined to overhaul the government, but she ended up admitting that she is asked to carry out bloody missions that involve killing innocent

---

[45] Ami Ayalon and Anthony David, *Friendly Fire: How Israel Became Its Own Worst Enemy and the Hope for Its Future* (Steerforth, 2020).
[46] "On '60 Minutes,' anti-overhaul protest leaders decry threat 'from inside' Israel," *The Times of Israel*, September 18, 2023, https://www.timesofisrael.com/anti-overhaul-protest-leaders-decry-threat-from-inside-israel-on-60-minutes-segment/; 60 Minutes, "60 Minutes travels to Israel to report on historic protests," September 18, 2023, YouTube video, 5:13, https://www.youtube.com/watch?v=kt3aVD8HLXc&ab_channel=60Minutes.

civilians, and that she has her own moral questions about those missions even as she carries them out.

There are copious amounts of online chatter in the pro-Israel world justifying all the IDF's actions. But often these justifications inadvertently end up exposing horrors themselves. In one widely shared post, for example, a tweeter writes:

**Fact: Israel could wipe out Hamas & Gaza from the air without losing a single soldier.**

**Fact: Israel has soldiers on the ground losing lives in order to prevent the civilians in Gaza from consequences caused by Hamas.**

**Fact: Media and terrorist supporters ignore facts 1 & 2 above**

So many issues to unpack in this post. Let's break it down.

First of all, "Hamas and Gaza" are not one and the same. The goal of wiping out all of Gaza would unequivocally constitute an act of ethnic cleansing and a war crime. This post asserts that "wiping out Gaza" is an idealized goal without any hesitation or self-consciousness about the awfulness of it.

Second, Israel does very often engage in massive air strikes that destroy entire buildings and neighborhoods. U.S. intelligence investigations found that half of Israel's aerial bombs in this war were "dumb bombs" — that is, indiscriminate bombings with no precision or strategic value.[47] The IDF has admitted that at least two thirds of those killed were "uninvolved" or innocent civilians. The army considers that ratio to be "tremendously positive".[48] During

---

[47] Natasha Bertrand and Katie Bo Lillis, "Exclusive: Nearly half of the Israeli munitions dropped on Gaza are imprecise 'dumb bombs,' US intelligence assessment finds," *CNN*, December 14, 2023, https://edition.cnn.com/2023/12/13/politics/intelligence-assessment-dumb-bombs-israel-gaza/index.html.

[48] Mitchell McCluskey and Richard Allen Greene, "Israel military says 2 civilians killed for every Hamas militant is a 'tremendously

this war, Israel has also killed hundreds of aid workers, medical personnel, and journalists,[49] and very possibly hostages.[50] So the assertion that Israel does not engage in massive air-bomb killings of entire populations is wrong. It is a fanciful fantasy.

In addition, the idea that Israel uses ground troops to protect Gazan civilians is only partially true. The real reason is that all those "dumb bombs" don't do the work of catching terrorists or destroying tunnels.[51] Those activities require soldiers on the ground.[52] Even if the IDF engaged in massive air strikes that would flatten Gaza, the terrorist tunnel network would remain unharmed.[53] But it sounds much better

---

positive' ratio given combat challenges," *CNN*, December 6, 2023, https://edition.cnn.com/2023/12/05/middleeast/israel-hamas-military-civilian-ratio-killed-intl-hnk/index.html.

[49] Chris Paterson, "Too many journalists and aid workers are being killed in Gaza despite rules that should keep them safe," *The Conversation*, April 30, 2024, https://theconversation.com/too-many-journalists-and-aid-workers-are-being-killed-in-gaza-despite-rules-that-should-keep-them-safe-227201.

[50] Victoria Bisset, Júlia Ledur, and Leslie Shapiro, "Monitoring the status of hostages still in Gaza after Hamas's attack," *Washington Post*, November 26, 2024, https://www.washingtonpost.com/world/interactive/hamas-hostages-israel-war-gaza/.

[51] Nancy A. Youssef and Jared Malsin, "Israel Struggles to Destroy Hamas's Gaza Tunnel Network," *Wall Street Journal*, January 28, 2024, https://www.wsj.com/world/middle-east/israel-struggles-to-destroy-hamass-gaza-tunnel-network-fb641122; Elana Sztokman, *The War on Women in Israel* (Sourcebooks, 2014).

[52] PBS News, "Military experts discuss Israel's use of unguided bombs and harm to civilians in Gaza," December 15, 2023, video, 7:23, https://www.pbs.org/newshour/show/military-experts-discuss-israels-use-of-unguided-bombs-and-harm-to-civilians-in-gaza; "Two More Reforms to End Housing Discrimination," *The Association for Civil Rights in Israel*, October 13, 2021, https://www.english.acri.org.il/post/_364.

[53] Abuamer, Majd. "Detection, Neutralization, and Destruction: The Limits of Israel's Strategy against Gaza's Tunnels." *Al-Muntaqa: New Perspectives on Arab Studies* 7, no. 1 (2024): 70-79. https://www.jstor.org/stable/48775005.

to say that Israel is "protecting" Gazans, even while killing more than 45,000 people.[54]

Finally, note that people like me who reject this rhetoric are summarily labeled by this writer as"terrorist supporters".

**In a nutshell: The idea that Israel is making the most moral choices and protecting Gazans by not carpet-bombing Gaza reveals troubling fantasies, complete dehumanization of Gazans, and a failure to discriminate between terrorists and civilians. And it is also not true. The IDF continues to engage in very questionable moral choices, such as destroying entire communities, buildings, and neighborhoods. The ground troops are not there to protect Gazans but to do the actual work of reaching terrorist infrastructure, work that carpet-bombing does nothing for.[55] So this entire post can be summarized as wishful thinking to support the idea that Jews are good and the killing they do is just.**

## There is no discrimination/apartheid in Israel

Israel, the "only democracy in the Middle East", is often promoted as an idyllic island of equality and liberal values. This is despite the fact that Israel has no separation of religion and state, discriminatory practices based on religion and gender are legal and practiced regularly — such as the

---

[54] "IDF spokesman says Hamas can't be destroyed, drawing retort from PM: 'That's war's goal'," *The Times of Israel*, June 20, 2024, https://www.timesofisrael.com/idf-spokesman-says-hamas-cant-be-eliminated-will-remain-in-gaza-if-no-alternative/.

[55] For a comprehensive collection and summary of testimonies, CSO reports, and media accounts of IDF's very questionable activities during the post-October 7 war, see this conference by the media outlet *Mekomit* (in Hebrew): https://www.facebook.com/mekomit/videos/1624732265064170. See also the copious reports by the organizations Breaking the Silence, The Seventh Eye, and B'Tselem on these issues.

exclusion of women from political parties or public streets, banning Muslims from moving into certain towns, and the 2018 Nation State Law established Judaism and Hebrew as the official religion and language of Israel.[56] If nothing else, the immense pro-democracy protests that preceded the current war are a striking indication of how fragile Israel's democracy actually is, and how close it is to being broken.[57]

Nevertheless, many supporters of Israel insist that Israel is a perfect picture of democracy and justice. One meme, for example, recites the following list:

**The one thing Israel haters hate the most: The truth.**
**Quick facts:**
**There are over 400 mosques in Israel.**
**77 are located in Jerusalem.**
**The number of mosques in Israel has increased five-fold since 1988 when there were only 80.**
**300 imams receive monetary grants from the Israeli government.**

These "quick facts" may seem interesting and culturally informative on their own. But considering that roughly 20% of Israel's population is Muslim, the existence of mosques and subsidies should not be surprising or "proof" of anything. However, the rest of the meme reveals the agenda:

**Worst. Apartheid. Ever.**

---

[56] "32% of all racist incidents in 2022 were directed at Arab Israelis - Justice Ministry," *The Jerusalem Post*, March 26, 2023, https://www.jpost.com/israel-news/article-735422; Maayan Lubell, "Israel adopts divisive Jewish nation-state law," *Reuters*, July 19, 2018, https://www.reuters.com/article/world/israel-adopts-divisive-jewish-nation-state-law-idUSKBN1K9022/.
[57] Gershom Gorenberg, "Israel's Fragile Democratic Future," *The New York Times*, February 7, 2024, https://www.nytimes.com/2024/02/07/opinion/israel-democracy-netanyahu-war.html.

In other words, these facts are presented as a refutation of something else entirely. The argument it offers is that if there are 400 mosques in Israel, there cannot possibly be discrimination, certainly not anything like apartheid.

There are several major problems with this meme. The most obvious is that the existence of mosques says nothing about segregation or discrimination. If there are seventy-seven mosques in East Jerusalem but their members cannot travel to West Jerusalem on regular "Jewish" roads but only on "Palestinian roads" that are often closed off or require hours of wading through oppressive checkpoints, then you might say that there is apartheid — mosques and all.[58] The roads are just one example of the segregation Israel imposes on Palestinians in the West Bank. Yet, many memes attempt to deny discrimination, segregation, and apartheid by claiming that Israel offers full equality to all its citizens.

One post shared with me reads:

**Apartheid?**
**0 Jews in Gaza.**
**2 million Arabs in Israel, with full equal and civil rights.**
**Numbers don't lie. Antisemites do.**

This text, which completely whitewashes the discriminatory experiences of Muslim and Palestinian Israelis, directly labels those who point out discrimination as "liars" and "antisemites". The meme also tries to reverse claims of apartheid, suggesting that Jews and Israelis are the "real" victims of discrimination, not Palestinians. There are many versions of this argument, such as those showing Arab Israelis as judges, engineers, or doctors — ergo there is no

---

[58] Ben Hubbard et al., "Getting around the West Bank is never easy, but it's a lot harder if you are Palestinian. That's no accident." *The New York Times*, October 13, 2024, https://www.nytimes.com/interactive/2024/10/13/world/middleeast/west-bank-roads.html.

apartheid. Others show elaborate graphs and charts comparing Jewish populations in Arab countries to Muslim populations in Israel, some claiming that the absence of Jews from Arab countries proves that all other countries in the Middle East except Israel are the "real" practitioners of apartheid.

This deflection tactic of "whataboutism" aims to help Israel's defenders avoid a discussion about the status of Palestinians in Israel, the West Bank, and Gaza. By saying "Look over there!", the question of Israel's practices is diverted away from discrimination toward some other shiny object. It avoids addressing factual issues about discrimination in Israel.

Moreover, these memes completely miss the point about apartheid. That is, the apartheid accusation refers to the difference between the status of Jewish citizens of Israel versus the status of Palestinians in *the occupied territories*. As with the practice of separate roads and checkpoints in the occupied territories, the issue of freedom of movement is compounded by a myriad of other rights that Palestinians in the territories struggle with.[59] These include water, electricity, building, and construction, as well as personal status issues, random raids and arrests, and overall statelessness that subjects Palestinians to many very real physical vulnerabilities and dangers with no legal protections.[60] In case there was any doubt, the sign at the entrance to Bat Ayin, a religious settlement in Gush Etzion, reads:

---

[59] See, for example, this clip of the IDF preventing Palestinian farmers from harvesting olives, along with the threat of settler violence: https://www.instagram.com/p/DBWtWzNKQ0t/.
[60] Dana Karam. "The West Bank Apartheid/Separation Wall: Space, Punishment and the Disruption of Social Continuity." *Geopolitics* 22, no. 4 (2017): 887-910; Brooks, Andrew, and Mark Griffiths. "Beyond Apartheid Israel." *Political Geography* 114 (2024): 103193; Raby, Sarah. "The humanitarian crisis of the Israeli occupation and settler colonialism in the West Bank and Gaza." (2023).

**This road leads to the settlement of Bat Ayin which is under Jewish control. Entry for Arabs is forbidden and risks your life. You have been warned!**

The sign shows a skull with a large skullcap and long side curls and crossed swords. So much for no apartheid. Even some Israeli thought leaders have concluded that apartheid in Israel is a real thing and it's bad. Former Prime Minister Ehud Barak said, "If this bloc of millions of Palestinians cannot vote, that will be an apartheid state." Former attorney general Michael Ben-Yair said that "it is with great sadness [...] I must also conclude that my country has sunk to such political and moral depths that it is now an apartheid regime." Former Mossad director Tamir Pardo said that "there is an apartheid state here" featuring "two peoples [who] are judged under two legal systems."[61] These are leaders who have dedicated their life to Israel, who know what is really going on and whose conscience does not allow them to stay silent about it anymore.

---

[61] Li Zhou, "The argument that Israel practices apartheid, explained," *Vox*, October 20, 2023, https://www.vox.com/23924319/israel-palestine-apartheid-meaning-history-debate; Tia Goldenberg, "A former Mossad chief says Israel is enforcing an apartheid system in the West Bank," *AP News*, September 6, 2023, https://apnews.com/article/israel-apartheid-palestinians-occupation-c8137c9e7f33c2cba7b0b5ac7fa8d115; "Former AG of Israel: With great sadness I conclude that my country is now an apartheid regime," *The Journal*, February 10, 2022, https://www.thejournal.ie/readme/israel-apartheid-5678541-Feb2022/.
"Chris McGreal, "Amnesty says Israel is an apartheid state. Many Israeli politicians agree," *The Guardian*, February 5, 2022, https://www.theguardian.com/commentisfree/2022/feb/05/amnesty-israel-apartheid-israeli-politicians-agree.

Thus, stating how many mosques there are in Israel does absolutely nothing to refute the idea that Palestinians in the occupied territories suffer immense discrimination and lack of basic rights which arguably constitutes living under an apartheid regime. One thing has nothing to do with the other. In fact, the Palestinians in the occupied territories may have even more mosques than those in Israel, yet they still cannot move freely the way Israelis do.

There's more. Even in Israel proper, where there are no segregated roads, there is still racial discrimination, despite the 400 mosques. According to the Israel Democracy Institute, Arab schools are poorly funded, which contributes to their graduates "attaining lower levels of education and their reduced employment prospects and earning power compared to Israeli Jews." Palestinian citizens of Israel face much higher rates of poverty than their Jewish counterparts, with more than half of them considered poor in 2020. Palestinian citizens do better in mixed cities than they do in all-Arab cities, although they have less access to municipal services than Jews do in those cities.[62] Another issue is land expropriation. The Israeli government has accorded itself the right to expropriate Arab land, which the government then transfers to the Jewish National Fund whose charter mandates that they are to serve only Jews, and the result is a whitewashed land transfer process from agricultural land in Arab villages to Jewish development towns.[63]

---

[62] Kali Robinson, "What to Know About the Arab Citizens of Israel," *Councill of Foreign Relations*, October 26, 2023, https://www.cfr.org/backgrounder/what-know-about-arab-citizens-israel.
[63] Eljamal Mekarem (2020). "Alienations and Articulations: Tracing Israeli Land Policies Through History," Agora Journal of Urban Planning and Design, 106-119.; Levine-Schnur, Ronit, Constitutional Property Rights in Israel and the West Bank (July 10, 2021). Oxford Handbook on the Israeli Constitution (Aharon Barak, Barak Medina and Yaniv Roznai, eds., Oxford University Press), Available at SSRN: https://ssrn.com/abstract=3884024;

This data masks another reality of life inside Israel: everyday segregation. Although Palestinian citizens of Israel have the same rights of citizenship as Jews — such as the right to vote, study, work, and use all roads — there are nonetheless certain de facto forms of segregation. For example, out of roughly 250 cities and towns in Israel, only eight are mixed.[64] State-funded schools are also segregated, with only a small network of private mixed schools.[65] It is still legal in Israel for landlords and gated towns to refuse to rent or sell property to Palestinians.[66] So while officially Israeli Arabs make up 20% of the population, a de facto segregation dominates real life, which leads to many other forms of discrimination. To wit, Finance Minister Bezalel Smotrich of the radical religious right decided not to transfer funding to Arab municipalities. Just because.[67]

---

Holzman-Gazit, Y. (2016). *Land expropriation in Israel: law, culture and society*. Routledge.

[64] Orbach-Yozgof, Nikola. "Blended cities in Israel." *Israel Affairs* 27, no. 5 (2021): 984-1004; "Israel's mixed cities: Jews still wealthier, but economic gaps may be closing — report," *The Jerusalem Post*, May 23, 2023, https://www.jpost.com/israel-news/article-743914.

[65] Levy, Natalie. "Arabs in segregated vs. mixed Jewish-Arab schools in Israel: their identities and attitudes towards Jews." *Ethnic and Racial Studies* 46, no. 12 (2023): 2720-2746.

[66] Joshua Davidovich, "By allowing towns to segregate, Israel may cross a different kind of red line," *The Times of Israel*, July 13, 2018, https://www.timesofisrael.com/by-allowing-towns-to-segregate-israel-may-cross-a-different-kind-of-red-line/; "The 7 Most Racist Israeli Laws," IMEU Institute for Middle East Understanding, March 6, 2023, https://imeu.org/article/the-7-most-racist-israeli-laws.

[67] Henriette Chacar and Maayan Lubell, "Israeli finance minister suspends funds to Arab towns, East Jerusalem," *Reuters*, August 8, 2023, https://www.reuters.com/world/middle-east/israeli-finance-minister-suspends-funds-arab-towns-east-jerusalem-2023-08-08/.

Yet, Israelis often do not see the segregation, probably because it does not affect them. According to a 2016 Pew Center study about perceptions of discrimination in Israel:

*[M]ost Israeli Jews do not believe that intolerance is a major problem in Israel, even when it comes to their frequently tense relations with the country's Arab population. For example, only about one-in-five Israeli Jews (21%) say there is a lot of discrimination in Israeli society against Muslims, who make up the vast majority of Israeli Arabs. By contrast, roughly four-in-five Israeli Arabs (79%) say there is a lot of discrimination against Muslims [...] Arabs also are more likely than Jews to perceive Israeli society as discriminatory toward a variety of other social and demographic groups. For instance, about a third of Israeli Arabs (34%) say there is a lot of discrimination against gay men and lesbians in Israel, compared with 20% of Jews who say the same. And four-in-ten Arabs (versus a quarter of Jews) say there is a lot of discrimination against women. Indeed, Israeli Arabs are more likely than Jews even to say there is a lot of discrimination against secular (Hiloni) Jews (21% vs. 9%), Mizrahi Jews of Middle Eastern or Mediterranean descent (33% vs. 21%) and Ethiopian Jews (44% vs. 36%) in Israeli society.*[68]

For Palestinian citizens of Israel, discrimination is visible because they live it daily. For many Jewish Israelis, if you don't see it, then it must not exist. (This thinking forms one of the express purposes of the security wall).[69] But discrimination in Israel is real. An apartheid system is in place in the West

---

[68] Michael Lipka, "Israeli Jews, Arabs have different perspectives on discrimination in their society," Pew Research Center, May 25, 2016, https://www.pewresearch.org/short-reads/2016/05/25/most-israeli-jews-do-not-see-a-lot-of-discrimination-in-their-society/.

[69] Zureik, E., Lyon, D., & Abu-Laban, Y. (2010). Surveillance and control in Israel/Palestine. *Population Territory and Power. London: Routledge.*

Bank. And all the attempts at pretending it doesn't exist because there are mosques in Israel cannot change these facts.

**In a nutshell: Memes aimed at proving that there is equality in Israel because Muslims live, work, and worship in Israel do not negate the existence of discrimination in Israel. They certainly do not negate the existence of apartheid practices in the occupied territories, which are well-documented and described even by some Israeli leaders who have been part of creating this system. These memes are deflections and attempts to deny the very real experiences of Palestinians, especially those in the occupied territories.**

## Occupation is a lie / doesn't exist

The attempt to describe the life experiences of Palestinians in the West Bank and Gaza faces a further challenge: the word "occupation". Many of Israel's advocates deny that occupation exists, and express entrenched resistance to facing the realities of Palestinian lives.

I encounter this resistance frequently, both online and in real life. I can see people literally squirm when the word "occupation" is uttered. For example, when I interviewed the mother of a college student about antisemitism on college campuses in the U.S. for a story I was writing for the Jewish Telegraphic Agency (JTA), she described with horror that some students on her daughter's campus talked about "the occupation". To her, the use of the word "occupation" was an example of campus antisemitism. She told me, "I can't even say the word; it's so horrible."

In Israel, too, there is intense resistance to using the word occupation even in left-of-the-center circles. The anti-government protest movement has been at times very aggressive in ensuring that "the occupation" would not be part of the protests, so as to not "offend" people.[70]

One popular graphic aimed at "proving" that there is no such thing as occupation shows a map of the Middle East from Libya in the west, to Sudan and Yemen in the south, to Turkey in the north-west, Uzbekistan in the north-east, and Pakistan in the far east. On this scale, Israel is the size of a sesame seed, not even big enough to hold the letters of its own name. The caption reads:

**End the occupation????!!!!!!**

In another variation of this graphic, the caption reads:

**Israel is the tiny blue spot.... Arab world in green. Tell me more how Israel is "colonizing" Arab land.**

Another version of that map with the title "Israel the 'OCCUPATION'" (sic) includes the following table:

| Arab | Jewish State |
|---|---|
| Arab member countries 22 | Jewish State 1 |
| Total population 481 million | Jewish population 7.2 million |
| Square miles of land 5.08 million | Square miles of land 0.00855 |

---

[70] Tia Goldenberg, "Israelis are protesting for democracy but Palestinians say occupation ignored," *PBS*, August 3, 2023, https://www.pbs.org/newshour/world/israelis-are-protesting-for-democracy-but-palestinians-say-occupation-ignored; Adam Sella, "The Fight Within the Fight: Where Does the Occupation Fit in the Judicial Overhaul Protests?" *Haaretz*, July 6, 2023, https://www.haaretz.com/israel-news/2023-07-06/ty-article/.premium/the-fight-within-the-fight-where-does-the-occupation-fit-in-judicial-overhaul-protests/00000189-2abb-dcb5-a5df-6fff82320000; Ben Reiff, "'No democracy with apartheid': Inside the radical bloc at Israel's anti-gov't protests," *+972 Magazine*, January 25, 2023, https://www.972mag.com/radical-bloc-israel-protests-tel-aviv/.

These graphics are examples of both denial and deflection. Like so many other memes in the genre of proving that Israel does nothing wrong, this set of graphics is diverting away from the issues by pointing at irrelevant issues elsewhere.

To be clear, Israel's occupation of the West Bank has nothing to do with how many countries in the world are Muslim or part of the Arab League. Nor does the relatively small size of Israel compared to the sum total of the land of twenty-two Arab countries absolve Israel of all wrongdoing vis-à-vis the people living on that small strip of land. It is deeply wrong to suggest that Palestinians are fine because there are countries thousands of miles away that are Muslim. I would add that it is shocking for Jews to even suggest that — we who take deep offense when people suggest that we "go back to Poland". Palestinians living in Gaza or in the West Bank do not call Libya or Uzbekistan home any more than I call Poland home.

The occupation of the West Bank is real, despite all attempts at denial or deflection. The occupation is the condition in which Israel is controlling the lives of three million Palestinians who have limited rights. They have no country, no government, and no freedom of movement, and live under military rule that mostly answers only to itself despite the violation of international law. Palestinians under military occupation can be invaded, arrested, or have their homes demolished without a moment's warning and without due process or rule of law.[71] Even children can be detained without seeing an indictment or a lawyer for months[72] Israel

---

[71] Statistics on Palestinian minors in Israeli custody, *B'Tselem*, September 2, 2024
https://www.btselem.org/statistics/minors_in_custody.
[72] Armani Syed, "What Palestinian Children Face in Israeli Prisons," *Time*, December 15, 2023,
https://time.com/6548068/palestinian-children-israeli-prison-arrested/; Statistics on Palestinian minors in Israeli custody,

controls an entire people who are living under conditions that Israelis would never be willing to tolerate themselves. It's illegal and it's immoral, and it is destroying not only the lives of the Palestinians living under occupation, but also the souls of the people — our children — who are tasked with enforcing this untenable and inhumane violence.

> **In a nutshell: The occupation is real, and it is bad. Attempts to deny it by calling the word offensive or antisemitic, or by false comparisons, are deflections aimed at absolving Israel of responsibility for any wrongdoing, for being an illegal occupier and of conducting military rule over three million people in violation of international law. Avoiding the word "occupation" will never absolve Israel of moral responsibility for these acts.**

---

*B'Tselem*, September 2, 2024; AP and Jeremy Sharon, "UN report says Palestinian detainees in Israel subjected to torture, mistreatment," *The Times of Israel*, July 31, 2024, https://www.timesofisrael.com/un-report-says-palestinian-detainees-in-israel-subjected-to-torture-mistreatment/; Wyre Davies, "'I had to bulldoze my house' - Palestinians face spike in Israeli demolition orders in East Jerusalem," *BBC*, October 17, 2024, https://www.bbc.com/news/articles/c01wpg9xrxdo; Bethan McKernan, "A precious resource: how Israel uses water to control the West Bank," *BBC*, May 17, 2023, https://www.theguardian.com/world/2023/may/17/how-israel-uses-water-to-control-west-bank-palestine.

# (2) Palestinians Are Bad and Completely at Fault

In contrast to the first theme — that Israelis are all good — the second theme portrays Palestinians as bad. Jews are often juxtaposed against Palestinians (or Muslims or Arabs) in absolute generalized terms of good and bad. There are many variations of this theme.

## There are no innocent Palestinians

One of the most popular and egregious dictums used in Israel advocacy is the idea that "there are no innocent Palestinians", or "no innocent Gazans". This line has been repeated by Israeli leaders[73] and journalists,[74] and even used in videos by official Israeli social media sites.[75]

When advocates of Israel talk about destroying Gaza instead of rooting out terrorism, they often reveal this belief. Similarly, when pro-Israel advocates respond to criticism about the loss of life in Gaza — which includes at least 12,000

---

[73] Tovah Lazaroff, "'There are no innocents in Gaza,' says Israeli defense minister," *The Jerusalem Post*, April 8, 2018, https://www.jpost.com/arab-israeli-conflict/there-are-no-innocents-in-gaza-says-israeli-defense-minister-549173.
[74] Ruthie Blum, "The myth of Gaza's 'innocent' majority," *JNS*, May 31, 2024, https://www.jns.org/the-myth-of-gazas-innocent-majority/.
[75] David Ingram, "Israeli government sparks outcry with X videos saying 'there are no innocent civilians' in Gaza," *NBC News*, June 14, 2024, https://www.nbcnews.com/tech/social-media/israel-posts-video-saying-are-no-innocent-civilians-gaza-rcna157111; See, for example, this X account (downloaded September 1, 2024) https://x.com/3lfares/status/1800531260315672854/photo/1.

babies and children and, by Israel's own admission, at least 20,000 innocent or "uninvolved" people, which the IDF considers a "tremendously positive" ratio[76] — the response is often a form of "they deserve it" because "they" are all terrorists. Again and again, I see and hear people asserting that "nobody in Gaza is innocent." It is an immense exercise in dehumanizing an entire population in order to justify this mass killing of innocent people.

Similarly, Israeli leaders have called Palestinians "animals" and used that language to justify the goal of "erasing Gaza". In the first month of the war, according to an investigation by *The New York Times*:

> *Inflammatory language has also been used by journalists, retired generals, celebrities, and social media influencers, according to experts who track the statements. Calls for Gaza to be "flattened," "erased" or "destroyed" had been mentioned about 18,000 times since Oct. 7 in Hebrew posts on X, the site formerly known as Twitter, said FakeReporter, an Israeli group that monitors disinformation and hate speech. The phrases were only mentioned 16 times in the month and a half before the war.*

> *The cumulative effect, experts say, has been to normalize public discussion of ideas that would have been considered off limits before Oct. 7: talk of "erasing" the people of Gaza, ethnic cleansing, and the nuclear annihilation of the territory.[77]*

---

[76] Mitchell McCluskey and Richard Allen Greene, "Israel military says 2 civilians killed for every Hamas militant is a 'tremendously positive' ratio given combat challenges," *CNN*, December 6, 2023, https://edition.cnn.com/2023/12/05/middleeast/israel-hamas-military-civilian-ratio-killed-intl-hnk/index.html.

[77] Mark Landler, "'Erase Gaza': War Unleashes Incendiary Rhetoric in Israel," *The New York Times*, November 15, 2023, https://www.nytimes.com/2023/11/15/world/middleeast/israel-gaza-war-rhetoric.html.

The grotesqueness of this language, which should be obvious to anyone but is so ubiquitous that it needed to be explicitly denounced by President Joe Biden,[78] has a very clear purpose. If Israel declares all 2.2 million Palestinians in Gaza "guilty", ergo they all deserve to be killed.

I have had this argument many times on social media with people making this monstrous claim. I have often pointed out that, at the very least, we cannot say that the 12,000 babies and children killed by the IDF were anything other than innocent. Astonishingly, I have yet to witness anybody retracting their claim, even against this reality.

> **In a nutshell: Calling Palestinians "animals" or saying that there are no innocent Gazans or Palestinians is a call for ghastly inhumanity. It is a statement that completely dehumanizes an entire population and is used to justify mass killing of that population, babies and all, with no justice system, no reckoning, and no humanity.**

## Palestinians don't value life (but Jews do)

Another version of the idea that Palestinians are all bad and deserve to die depicts Palestinians as having no basic humanity. This includes the common belief that Palestinians don't "value life" — as opposed to Jews, of course.

One meme shared during this war shows a photo of a Palestinian mother dressing her child in a costume or outfit of a keffiyeh headscarf, an ammunition belt, and a gun, alongside a photo of a Jewish mother crouching on the ground over her child in the protective pose assumed under rocket fire. The caption reads:

**Brave Arab mom. Brave Jewish mom.**
**Which side are YOU on?**

---

[78] U.S. Department of State, October 18, 2023, https://www.facebook.com/photo.php?fbid=732426938916574&id=100064478242854&set=a.226110142881592.

This meme is meant to imply that Jewish mothers value life while Palestinian mothers value death. If such an assertion were true, it would work to justify random killings of unarmed Palestinian mothers — and perhaps even children — since they are all inherently murder-loving.

There are several problems with this meme. For one thing, it's obviously not true, and implying that all Palestinian mothers want their children to kill is a revolting dehumanizing stereotype. Moreover, the leap from the image to the generalization involves dangerous logic. To wit, dressing up a child in a costume — even one that includes a gun — does not mean that an entire population condones murder. Consider, for example, how many Halloween costumes in the U.S. include guns: police officers, soldiers, superheroes.[79] Does this mean that kids dressed up with toy guns are violence lovers whose mothers are happy for them to kill or be killed?

Similarly, at the risk of engaging in a form of "whataboutism", I would also point out that it is extremely popular for Israeli children to dress up as IDF soldiers for the holiday of Purim.[80] In this line of thinking, how would such an image be shared among Palestinians? As proof that Israeli mothers train their children to be killers? Just saying.

---

[79] "Parents create 'Goodies Not Guns' to discourage violent Halloween costumes for kids," *ABC News*, October 22, 2017, https://abcnews.go.com/Lifestyle/parents-create-goodies-guns-discourage-violent-halloween-costumes/story?id=50634572; "Are gun-related Halloween costumes falling out of favor?" *Montana Right Now*, October 6, 2017, https://www.montanarightnow.com/news/are-gun-related-halloween-costumes-falling-out-of-favor/article_bc275b81-b6b0-5d06-8380-59a499440268.html.
[80] "Guns and Purim", Tova in Israel, March 21, 2016, http://tovainisrael.com/blog-posts/guns-and-purim/; " Middle East Eye, "Clip resurfaces of Israeli MK encouraging her son to say he wants to 'kill Arabs'", August 9, 2023, YouTube video, 1:00, https://www.youtube.com/watch?v=emWISZ_k4BM&ab_channel=MiddleEastEye.

Beyond dress-up games, consider cultures that *actually* glorify children holding weapons.[81] The United States comes to mind, as roughly half the country continues to vehemently reject gun control while taking cutesy Christmas photos with their children holding guns.[82] Ironically, that same political bloc of American gun lovers includes some of the fiercest defenders of Israel's actions, those expressing outrage about a Palestinian mother dressing up her child with a toy gun. The hypocrisy is mind-bending.

Another problem with this meme is the idea that Palestinian mothers are not interested in protecting their children. Considering that this war has flooded us with images of Palestinian families mourning their children — as at least 12,000 babies and children were estimated to have been killed in Gaza during this war — this meme takes on repulsive messaging. Israel kills Palestinian babies and children and argues that Palestinian mothers do not protect their children. It's sickening, really.

---

**In a nutshell: It is not true that only Israeli mothers protect their children while all Palestinian mothers send their children to die. Of course Palestinian mothers love their children and want them to live. We shouldn't be making grand generalizations and dehumanizing entire populations based on children's costumes. Such flawed logic would implicate many groups of gun lovers.**

---

[81] Sam Wollaston, "Kids and Guns review — a terrifying look at the heart of American culture," *The Guardian*, July 31, 2014, https://www.theguardian.com/tv-and-radio/2014/jul/31/kids-and-guns-tv-review-francine-shaw; Walter Johnson, "Guns in the Family," *Boston Review*, March 23, 2018, https://www.bostonreview.net/articles/walter-johnson-guns-family/.

[82] Gustaf Kilander, "Lauren Boebert poses her children with guns in Christmas photo," *Independent*, December 8, 2021, https://www.independent.co.uk/news/world/americas/us-politics/lauren-boebert-guns-children-christmas-b1972033.html.

## Palestinians have no culture or history other than murder

Many memes compare Israelis to Palestinians with the aim of branding Israelis/Jews as "good" and Palestinians as "bad". One meme shared during this war shows two columns, "Israel" and "Palestine":

| Israel | Palestine |
|--------|-----------|
| Abraham<br>Isaac<br>Jacob<br>Joseph<br>Moses<br>Joshua<br>David<br>Solomon<br>Jesus | Yasser Arafat |

The aim here is to portray Israel as having a rich history of great cultural/religious heroes while Palestinians have only one guy, a terrorist. In addition, Jewish history goes back 3,000 years, whereas Muslim history seems to have begun in the twentieth century.

There are several problems with this meme. One is that this table completely erases Muslim history and culture. For the record, Islam has a rich cultural history that includes major contributions to math, music, astronomy, zoology, architecture, medicine, geography, poetry, philosophy, horticulture, and calligraphy.[83]

This meme is problematic in other ways, too: it only includes men, it somehow includes Jesus even though Jews reject his leadership, and the Israeli figures are all religious. The point seems to be that Jews have a legitimate, ancient

---

[83] "Arab Contributions to Civilization," ADC, https://adc.org/arab-contributions-to-civilization/.

religious Jewish (or Judeo-Christian) claim to the land, while Palestinians have none, although this point is not entirely clear. Is it about having a state, or existing as a religion at all, or whether the religion is moral? This is open to interpretation. In any case, it is meant to juxtapose Judaism as good and worthy against Islam which is bad and unworthy.

I would like to add one more point about why this meme is disturbing, a point that some people may have difficulty with. That table implies that Arafat was not an acceptable leader of his people. Those of us who grew up in the shadow of PLO (Palestine Liberation Organization) terror attacks in the 1970s and 1980s know this argument well. However, Arafat did in fact sign a peace treaty with Israel that could have brought about a different reality. Former head of Shin Bet Ami Ayalon, who was in charge of working with Arafat to implement that agreement, writes in his memoir, *Friendly Fire: How Israel Became Its Own Worst Enemy and the Hope for Its Future*, that Arafat was a complicated man who tried to serve his people. It is patently dismissive of Arafat's work to cast him as having no value as a human being or as a leader of his people. I highly recommend reading Ayalon's book to gain some perspective on this point.[84]

The table comparing Abraham/Isaac/Jacob to Arafat represents a broader theme of pro-Israel advocacy — that Palestinians have no history at all. (This is also twisted in the sense that Islam honors most of the same biblical fathers that Judaism does, especially Abraham/Ibrahim. The Exodus and *Akedah* are both in the Koran.) In one meme, for example, an Israeli flag and a Palestinian flag are planted side by side; the Israeli flag has deep, rich, healthy roots, while the Palestinian flag has none. The metaphor is clear: Palestinians have no history, but Jewish Israelis do.

---

[84] Ami Ayalon, *Friendly Fire: How Israel Became Its Own Worst Enemy and the Hope for Its Future* (Steerforth, 2020).

Similarly, a cartoon shows an ultra-Orthodox Jewish *Haredi* man (black hat, long black coat) standing on top of a pile of books titled science, history, technology, culture, philosophy, and economics, with the caption "3300 years". Next to him is an Arab man (keffiyeh, robe) holding a long sword and standing atop a pile of skulls, with the caption "1400 years". The message is that Jews (or the Jewish religion) have a wealth of culture, literature, and ideas as their legacy, while Islam (or Arabs) is nothing other than killing and murder.

This caricature is all wrong for several reasons. First, the idea that all Muslims throughout history are violent while *Haredi* Jews are all enlightened and cultural is a twisted reading of history. It is in fact ridiculous to see a *Haredi* man on top of books of Western civilization considering that *Haredi* culture is completely averse to the subjects listed. *Haredi* children in Israel barely study basic math, certainly not philosophy or science. The image is a grotesque failure of accurate representation. Furthermore, the idea that Islam is just violence is an outrageous erasure of the entire Muslim/Arab/Palestinian culture. It is racist, obnoxious, and dehumanizing.

This meme is also linked to the idea that all Jews are good and all Arabs are bad; that Jews do not hold weapons or kill, but all Arabs do. Such caricatures dehumanize Arabs by turning them into murderers and help Israelis and Jews deny any wrongdoing, even when Jews are the ones doing the killing.

There are many variations of this idea on social media. A similar cartoon shows two images. On the left is a man clad in Muslim garb genuflecting in prayer with the caption "Muslims send 1.8 billion prayers to destroy Israel." On the right is a scientist in a white coat looking into a microscope with the caption "15 million Jews have 187 Science Nobel prizes." At the bottom is another caption, "Calculate who is making a difference for humanity." At least this meme, as opposed to the previous one, uses an image of a scientist to represent scientific study as opposed to trying to paint a *Haredi* man as a master of enlightenment. Nevertheless, this meme reflects the same skewed message that Islam is all about murdering Jews while Judaism is pure because Jews are too busy in science labs to hold guns.

A similar meme compares Nobel Prizes to "prove" that Jews have more inherent worth than Palestinians:

**2 billion Muslims have 15 Nobel prizes.**
**15 million Jews have 214 Nobel prizes.**

Another one is about Olympic medals:

**Olympic medal count**
**22 Arab states: Total 2**
**Israel: Total 6**

These memes attempt to use prestigious prizes to show which group is more worthy, and therefore who is more deserving of land, more deserving of autonomy and freedom, more destined to be in control, and perhaps even more deserving to live.

All this can be characterized as a massive branding exercise: Arabs are culture-less, uneducated killers, while Israelis are enlightened, pure-minded, peace-loving scientists.

The dehumanization process goes even further at times. In some memes, Palestine and Palestinians don't exist — just like Golda Meir said about Palestinians, and just as Tomer taught us in ninth grade. One meme that has been shared during this war shows a medieval-looking map with names such as "Fantasia", "Middle Earth" and "Terabithia". The word "Palestine" is circled on the map with the caption:

**The real location of Palestine**

The graphic includes a picture of two people laughing. As if to say, the idea that Palestine even exists is a joke.

> **In a nutshell: Palestinians are human beings who want to live, who love their children, and who value life. Islam also has a long history and rich culture, Arabs have many leaders and role-models and deserve the same rights to live as everyone else. They should not be reduced to caricatures, or be branded as uneducated, uncivilized, or inhumane killers. Oversimplifying a culture or people to a simplistic image of "killers" is a manipulative attempt to dehumanize the Other and justify the destruction of that culture and the people associated with it.**

## All Palestinians are terrorists

Linked to the theme portraying Palestinians, Muslims, and Arabs as having no culture or roots or history other than a Jew-hating bloodlust is the assertion that all Palestinians are basically terrorists. This idea is present in some of the memes discussed above, and it is an undercurrent in almost the entire spectrum of pro-Israel rhetoric as well as the reality on the ground driving the worst aspects of the war.[85]

The idea that Palestinians only value terrorism finds expression in many different memes. One that keeps appearing in my feed reads:

> **How are Palestinians always out of water,**
> **but never out of rockets?**
> **Make it make sense!**

As if to say, Palestinians do not value their own lives. They obviously just want to be terrorists and don't care about

---

[85] Yaniv Kubovich, "'No Civilians. Everyone's a Terrorist': IDF Soldiers Expose Arbitrary Killings and Rampant Lawlessness in Gaza's Netzarim Corridor," *Haaretz*, Dec 18, 2024, https://www.haaretz.com/israel-news/2024-12-18/ty-article-magazine/.premium/idf-soldiers-expose-arbitrary-killings-and-rampant-lawlessness-in-gazas-netzarim-corridor/00000193-da7f-de86-a9f3-fefff2e50000

their basic needs. Another popular meme aims to make the same point with different images:

**Over the past 7 years, 16.3 Billion [sic] has been donated to the Palestinian cause. Your generous donations have made such a difference.**

This post, with its dubious data (what currency? Who is the "you" doing the donating? To which "cause" exactly?) goes on to show three photos of guns, fighters, and tunnels, with the captions "Education", "Healthcare", and "Housing". As if to say, Palestinians do not care about their own life and only care about killing.

Obviously, this premise is untrue. Palestinians, like most human beings, care about education, healthcare, and housing. The meme is an attempt to portray Palestinians not as normal human beings but as killers. This meme also skews and over-simplifies many complex issues. To wit, there are multiple causes of poverty among Palestinians, Israel has played a troubling role in monitoring the incoming and outgoing resources in Gaza, and Bibi Netanyahu's governments funded the terror activities of Hamas for many years in an attempt to prevent the Palestinian Authority from establishing a proper state and governance.[86] Again, this is the same branding

---

[86] Abu-Ras, Wahiba, and Rozena A. Mohamed. "Child poverty and youth unemployment in Palestine." *Poverty & Public Policy* 10, no. 3 (2018): 354-370; Easton, Scott D., Najwa Sado Safadi, and Robert G. Hasson III. ""We Deal With Symptoms Rather Than Causes": Antipoverty Policy Making in Occupied Palestinian Territories." *Journal of Loss and Trauma* 22, no. 8 (2017): 631-645; Joronen, Mikko, and Mark Griffiths. "Ungovernability and ungovernable life in Palestine." *Political Geography* 98 (2022): 102734; for a three-part documentary series exposing the history of Netanyahu bolstering Hamas, see "Chapter 1 in the series Calculated Risk - The Policy that Led to October 7th (Not Accidental)," YouTube video, October 2, 2024, 32:01, https://www.youtube.com/watch?v=0r4Y0DEeGCw&ab_c hannel=%D7%96%D7%94_%D7%91%D7%90%D7%95%D7%95 %D7%99%D7%A8.

exercise, intended to paint all Palestinians as uneducated, cultureless terrorists. It attempts to dehumanize all Palestinians, a necessary prerequisite for justifying ongoing killing and other atrocities.

A similar stab at depicting all Palestinians as hostage-abducting terrorists reads:

**If you don't want the IDF in your home,
then don't keep the hostages in it.**

This meme is problematic for many reasons. On the most obvious level, the overwhelming majority of Gazans do not have hostages in their homes. There are roughly 2.235 million Gazans before the war, and there were 250 hostages. Doing the math for a moment, even if every hostage were being held by, say, ten people — even if it were 100 people per hostage, and 2,500 Gazans were participating in some way in holding the hostages — that would still leave 2.233 million Gazans who are *not* holding hostages. The idea that all Gazans should be treated as hostage captors devoid of humanity is grotesque. (And killing 45,000 people as collective punishment is abhorrent from this perspective.)

What's worse is that we know that the IDF's actions were never really about rescuing the hostages. Netanyahu repeatedly places other priorities ahead of hostage rescue; in fact, his own negotiating team has asserted that he overtly sabotages the negotiation talks.[87] The families of hostages

---

[87] Jacob Magid, "Netanyahu issues list of 4 'nonnegotiable' demands as hostage talks slated to restart," *The Times of Israel*, July 7, 2024, https://www.timesofisrael.com/netanyahu-issues-list-of-non-negotiable-demands-as-hostage-talks-slated-to-restart/; Lorenzo Tondo, "Israeli government accused of trying to sabotage Gaza ceasefire proposal," *The Guardian*, July 7, 2024, https://www.theguardian.com/world/article/2024/jul/07/israeli-government-accused-of-trying-to-sabotage-gaza-ceasefire-proposal; Mick Krever et al., "Netanyahu derailed a potential Gaza hostage deal in July, Israeli newspaper reports," *CNN*, September 4, 2024, https://edition.cnn.com/2024/09/04/middleeast/netanyahu-

especially complain that rescuing their loved ones is nowhere on the government's agenda. To wit, when IDF soldiers accidentally came across three hostages who were shirtless, unarmed, and screaming in Hebrew that they were hostages, the soldiers shot them.[88] This is painfully clear evidence that rescuing hostages was nowhere on the soldiers' minds or missions. The preposterous (and false) notion that all Gazans are holding hostages is just a clever ruse to justify a policy of random home invasions and collective punishment of all Gazans — even the innocent, even the children.

This assertion that all Palestinians are terrorists is disguised in many cleverish rhetorical devices. In one meme, for example, a woman says to her friend:

**Israel cares more about the lives of Israelis than about people trying to kill Israelis. That's apartheid!**

As if to say, all 45,000 Gazans who were killed, including children, were trying to kill Israelis, and therefore Israel is under no obligation to care about them. A similar post declares:

**I wish people cared about Jewish babies being murdered as much as they do for the rights of those responsible for their deaths.**

Again, the assertion is that all those who are killed by the IDF are responsible for the deaths of Jewish babies and

---

derailed-hostage-deal-in-july-intl/index.html; "Members of Israel's negotiating team accuse Netanyahu of intentionally sabotaging hostage deal talks — report," *The Times of Israel*, August 20, 2024, https://www.timesofisrael.com/liveblog_entry/members-of-israels-negotiating-team-accuse-netanyahu-of-intentionally-sabotaging-hostage-deal-talks-report/.

[88] Emily Rose, "Israeli troops killed hostages, mistaking their cries for help as ambush -military," *Reuters*, December 28, 2023, https://www.reuters.com/world/middle-east/israeli-troops-killed-hostages-mistaking-their-cries-help-ambush-military-2023-12-28/.

therefore Israel has the right to not care about them. Even the Gazan babies and children.

These memes conflate a few twisted arguments. One notion is that Gazans caught in Israel's crossfire are all "people trying to kill Israelis", which is not true. As we know, the majority of people Israel has killed were innocent, by Israel's own admission. Moreover, killing 12,000 children is *not* killing terrorists. Yet, when I try to have this discussion with people on social media, and point out that babies are by definition not terrorists, it usually does not go well. I have heard responses such as, "Well, their family are Hamas", or "Well, they will grow up to become terrorists". These views are chilling beyond description. I continue to be surprised at how entrenched this idea is — that all Gazans deserve to die, even babies. I am deeply disturbed by how deeply some people are invested in the justification of Israel's actions, to the extent that they will find any argument that helps defend the killing of babies — "their" babies, of course, not ours. The madness of these exchanges continues to astound me.

Furthermore, these memes about Gazans all deserving to die are also used to try to refute arguments of apartheid. The above meme tries to "prove" that apartheid doesn't exist while denying that Israel kills innocent Palestinian. As if to say, both killings and apartheid are justified because there are Palestinian terrorists who try to kill Jews. This argument makes no sense and lacks all moral and reasonable logic.

Following the events of October 7, many Palestinian leaders expressed pain, anger, and outrage over Hamas's actions.[89] Yet, they were never heard, respected, or believed.[90]

[89] Mohammad Shukri Khalaf, "The position of Arab Israelis on the events of October 7, 2023," *Zeitgeschichte Online*, October 6, 2024, https://zeitgeschichte-online.de/themen/position-arab-israelis-events-october-7-2023.
[90] Jacob Magid, "Abbas denouncing Hamas, but criticism kept private due to IDF 'aggression' — top aide," *The Times of Israel*, December 7, 2023, https://www.timesofisrael.com/abbas-

Israel's Minister of National Security Ben-Gvir immediately called on the police to prepare for violence, as if the Palestinian community would immediately express support for Hamas.[91] That never happened. But Palestinian citizens of Israel continue to be equated with terrorists, even as they do everything to express non-violence and sympathy with the victims. As one Palestinian peace activist wrote on her Twitter page (my translation from Hebrew):

> *It doesn't matter what we do, how much we contribute, how much we volunteer or support the people of the south. It doesn't matter how much we denounce Hamas, how many funerals we attend or, shiva houses we visit. People still attack us, conduct lynches, call us terrorists.*

> **In a nutshell: The rhetorical defense of Israel that casts all Palestinians/Arabs/Muslims as terrorists — even babies killed by the IDF — dehumanizes Palestinians and ignores their pain, experiences, and real lives. It also ignores efforts to empathize with Israelis following October 7. Ultimately it functions to justify the most appalling military actions and the worst forms of discrimination. It is also very wrong. It seems absurd to have to say this, but Palestinians are human beings, and nothing – not even October 7 -- justifies condemning an entire group to death.**

## Palestinians are not normal humans

Once people are labeled "terrorists" — even if they are babies — they are dehumanized, a process that paves the way for atrocities.

---

denouncing-hamas-but-criticism-kept-private-due-to-idf-aggression-top-aide/.

[91] Jeremy Sharon and Michael Bachner, "Ben Gvir widely panned for warning of renewed Jewish-Arab intercommunal riots," *The Times of Israel*, October 11, 2023, https://www.timesofisrael.com/ben-gvir-widely-panned-for-warning-of-renewed-jewish-arab-intercommunal-riots/.

The dehumanization process takes many forms, some of which are subtle. For example, some memes that show Palestinians in Gaza doing "normal" human activities are used as "proof" that something is wrong with them. In one popular post, a photo of masses of Gazans on the beach in the middle of the war was shared with the caption:

**This is the beach in Deir al Balah, Gaza, taken today. You won't see this picture in the media because it's exactly the story they don't want you to see.**

In other words, in order for us to believe Palestinians when they talk about their suffering, they cannot ever do normal human things, like go to the beach.

There are several manipulative components in this post. One is around the idea that people can seek refuge in the midst of an awful war. Of course, Israelis also seek out normalcy during the war, but when Gazans do it, clearly something is off about their life stories. A second, related issue, is that Palestinians are lying. Because how dare Palestinians live "normal" life! Even if they've been to hell and back. This photo must prove that there is no humanitarian crisis, no starvation, no bombing of hospitals, no thousands of people dead. They're making it all up.

A similar post shared around the beginning of the war shows a photo of a beautiful hotel. The caption reads:

**This is a picture of the Al Mashtal hotel. It is located in Gaza City. It's one of the numerous 4 or 5 star hotels in the Gaza strip. Feel free to check on the website, or the excellent reviews on Trip Advisor. Strange for what's being described as an 'open-air prison', a 'concentration camp'.**

Again, this post punishes Gazans for having any semblance of normalcy. And it casts them as liars, as if the border crossings that forbid Gazans from leaving are imaginary. And by the way, this hotel was bombed by Israel in February 2024.

> **In a nutshell: Palestinians are dehumanized by being punished for engaging in normal life. This dehumanization process, which is connected to the idea that Palestinians are all liars, helps justify inhumane treatment. This line of thinking works to flatten human experiences and cast Palestinians as liars.**

## Palestinians are liars and hypocrites

I shared my experience of being hired to "prove" that Palestinians are liars as one of my first wake-up calls about the toxic Israel advocacy culture I had inhabited for most of my life. The moment I relinquished the idea that all Palestinians are unreliable liars opened my eyes and led me on the path that eventually got me to this place of unpacking all the propaganda and indoctrination. I discovered that this stance of "they are all liars" forms a core process of dehumanization and justification of violence against Palestinians.

The need to "prove" that Palestinians are liars can reach extreme and even absurd levels. One manufactured photo of two women in hijabs holding a Palestinian flag and a rifle while walking on a surface with the earth behind them reads:

### Palestinians were on the moon before 1948.

As if to say, Palestinians lie about all of human history.

A related assertion is that Palestinians and their allies are hypocrites. They cannot be trusted, they don't mean what they say, and they don't actually want what they say they want. It is all a ruse to hide the murderous antisemitism that drives them.

One meme that is a typical example of this theme shows two stands with signs that read "SUPPORT"; one with a Palestinian flag that says "Palestinians" and one with a Uyghur flag that says "Uyghurs". The Palestinian stand has a long line of people queueing, while the Uyghur one is empty. The point is to show that the world is full of hypocrites. If people truly cared about human rights, they wouldn't be so radically upset *only* about Palestinians. The point being, it's not that Israel has done anything wrong to Palestinians; it's that the world is obsessed with the Palestinian issue (while remaining unmoved by other issues). It is also worth pointing out that this meme is a classic example of "whataboutism".

Of course, human rights activists are not concerned only about Palestinians. This is a classic deflection tactic that avoids accountability by trying to pin blame on the victims and their allies, as if there is something very wrong with them. In this case, they care too much about one issue, which apparently means they must be wrong.

Palestinians and their allies that are cast as hypocrites with the entire Arab world. This is hinted in some of the memes mentioned above that suggest that the Arab world does not actually care about Palestinian rights or independence, but just wants to attack Israel. Another popular post reads:

**22 Arab states**
**57 Muslim countries**
**refuse entry to Gazans.**
**And the world demands that**
**1 Jewish state care for these Nazis.**
**Fuck off.**

A glaring issue with this meme is that it refers to all Gazans as Nazis. This points to another core theme in pro-Israel advocacy that seeks to turn the entire conflict into something else entirely: a type of Holocaust in which Jews are victims and Palestinians are Nazis. This line deserves its own analysis, which is the subject of the next section.

There are many variations of this post. For example, one cartoon shows a UN speaker asking a crowd, "Who wants to free Palestine?" as everyone raises their hands; in the next cel he asks, "Who wants to host Palestinians?" and all hands go down.

Notice that these posts combine several themes. The first one describes all Gazans as "Nazis", which erases their culture, dehumanizes an entire people, and justifies whatever actions are taken against them. These posts also deflect away from Israel's actions by blaming the rest of the Arab world for the mistreatment of Gazans, as if Saudi Arabia is the one launching rockets over Gaza and destroying entire communities. The main point of both posts is that the entire Arab world is full of liars and hypocrites and therefore deserves no sympathy or consideration. A corollary is that if the Arab nations don't care about Palestinians, then Israel has no obligation to care about them either. Dehumanization process complete. No need to care.

> **In a nutshell: The theme of Palestinians being uncultured, uncivilized, lesser-human deviant terrorists is wrapped up in the underlying idea that Palestinians are liars. Thus, even if Palestinians protest and try to "prove" their humanity, this is rendered impossible. Branded as liars who cannot be trusted completes the dehumanization process, thus justifying anything that happens to Palestinians because they are not deserving of even being heard.**

# (3) Israel/Jews Are the Real Victims

If Israelis/Jews are all good and Muslims/Arabs/Palestinians are all bad, then this entire conflict is one in which Jews are the real victims. In one example of this theme, a map shows Israel as a tiny country in the region with red arrows pointing at it from Lebanon, Syria, Yemen, Iran, Iraq, Gaza, and the West Bank, with the caption:

**Only Israel can be attacked on seven sides and still be considered the aggressor.**

In other words, Israel is cast as the real victim. Anything that Israel does towards Palestinians is thus rendered moot because, well, look at Iran threatening Israel. It's a classic diversion tactic. Israel can do no wrong because it's surrounded by enemies wanting to attack it.

The idea that Israel is the real victim finds expression in several related ideas. The most glaring theme is antisemitism. In fact, the documentary film *Israelism* that explores the pro-Israel advocacy movement in the United States — a film with very similar ideas to those I present here and a must-watch, in my opinion — focuses quite a bit on the role of antisemitism in deflecting criticism of Israel.[92] Watching that film made me think that perhaps the antisemitism deflection is the whole story. Indeed, I often find that since October 7, pro-Israel

---

[92] *Israelism*, https://www.israelismfilm.com/.

advocacy deflecting to antisemitism seems to dominate our communal discourse. I compiled several themes that revolve in large part around antisemitism.

## All criticism of Israel is antisemitism

The primary construct of Jewish victimhood is antisemitism. This idea is old, and it's powerful. Indeed, the idea that Palestinians are fakers or liars leads to another conclusion, one that Tomer taught us back in the 1980s. And that is: The real motive behind all actions of all Palestinians is nothing more than old-fashioned antisemitism. In Tomer's class, we learned that "Palestinian self-determination" is fake — that it is just a smokescreen for the desire to see all Jews die. We learned that opposition to West Bank settlements is a lie — that Palestinians are opposed to *all* Jews living *anywhere*.

This line of reasoning has been amplified during this war. Netanyahu talks about it, government representatives talk about it, and Jews around the world talk about it. This war has been so enmeshed with themes of antisemitism that for many people they have become inseparable. Even American politicians get in on this. Ron DeSantis, for example, said that the U.S. should have no sympathy for Palestinians or let them into America "because they are all antisemites".[93]

One meme, for example, shows two photos, one of KKK-clad people burning a cross and the other of keffiyeh-clad protesters, with the caption:

**Spot the difference.**

As if to say, Palestinians are the KKK, end of story. One Jewish professor with a large following said:

---

[93] Stephen Groves, "DeSantis says US shouldn't take in Palestinian refugees from Gaza because they're 'all antisemitic'," *AP News*, October 15, 2023, https://apnews.com/article/desantis-israel-hamas-gaza-palestinian-refugees-water-73a468f8d030e083844d16e82684c406.

**If you're still wondering how and why antisemitism is acceptable in academia, remember that more than half of the Nazis who organized the 'Final Solution' had doctorates. Having a PhD doesn't make you a good person. Just a highly paid one.**

This text, in addition to casting all sympathy with Palestinians as antisemitism, also vilifies the entire academia as one big cesspool of antisemites or potential antisemites.

Some of the memes around antisemitism combine many rhetorical tactics. A T-shirt labeled "Antisemite International" reads:

**I'm not that interested in the repression and human rights abuses in Syria, Togo, Iran, Crimea, Turkey, Somalia, Venezuela, Eritrea, Bangladesh, Saudi Arabia, Cameroon, Libya, Sudan, Zimbabwe, Equatorial Guinea, North Korean, and Russia because there are no Jews involved.**

This is a classic deflection tactic of "Look over there!" or "whataboutism". Its purpose is to suggest that Israel does not have to answer to critics because there are other people doing bad stuff, too. A similar post reads:

**Genocide? Putin has massacred
half a million Ukrainians.
Not one march.
No campus riots.
No outrage.
Israel defends itself against Hamas terrorists
who butchered 1400 children and women
and took 200 hostages.
Suddenly everyone is a human rights activist.**

This, too, combines several tactics. For one thing, it boasts a lie. It is absolutely not true that the world expresses no outrage against Putin and what he is doing in Ukraine. That war has been one of the top news stories since its onset, sparked protests around the world, has dramatically impacted American political events, and is often discussed in the same sentence as the war in Gaza. Moreover, this post is, again, a classic deflection tactic aimed at drawing attention away from Israel's actions. This meme alludes to an antisemitic undercurrent in order to justify Israel's actions by asserting that they are all "defense" against the killing of 1,400 people including children, ignoring the irony that Israel's actions have killed 12,000 children. And in the process, it also completely dismisses "human rights activists", as if they are all insincere, hypocritical antisemites.

Labeling academics, leftists, and human rights activists as antisemites reveals a hidden political agenda. The underlying drive is to cast anyone on the political left as antisemitic, thus strengthening the right. This has many variations — attacks on so-called "wokeness" as if empathy is a character flaw, attacks on feminists as if women seeking equality hate Jewish men, attacks on the entire college experience because opening up to new ideas threatens the old order. Often, these groups are bunched together under the title "antisemitism" as a way to delegitimize an entire political ideology.

One cartoon combines these themes with some Holocaust-themed imagery aimed to portray human rights activists as Jew haters. The first cel shows a flock of sheep with an angry wolf behind them as a man is yelling to the sheep, "A wolf behind you!"; in the second cel, the sheep are chasing the man away screaming "No to wolf haters! No to wolfphobia!" as the wolf salivates gleefully over the sheep. The story here seems to be that the sheep are Jews or Israelis, the wolf is Hamas, and the man represents "reasonable" people who want to see Jews defend themselves but are instead chased away by, say, human rights activists afraid of being seen as Islamophobic. This cartoon insinuates that Islamophobia is fake because the threat Islam poses for Jews is real, and the Jews are all about to die.

This cartoon also combines different tactics. It portrays all Arabs as "wolves" intent on destroying Jews. It casts human rights activists as naïve idiots whose only concern is being politically correct and who are going to get the Jews killed. It does not distinguish between Hamas (the wolf, supposedly) and Palestinians, and makes Israelis look innocent (as if the IDF only kills in self-defense and doesn't kill anyone but terrorists). It also turns Israelis into sheep, suggesting that those criticizing Israel's actions or saying that Israel shouldn't kill innocent Palestinians are in fact antisemites eager to send sheep to the slaughter. Like the Nazis did to the Jews.

A sharp and telling meme in bold all-caps white text on a black background with a Jewish Yellow Star (reminiscent of Holocaust imagery) that reads simply:

**WE'RE DONE EXPLAINING OUR RIGHT TO EXIST**

As if to say, everything Israel is doing is necessary to keep Jews from being eradicated as a people. We can kill whomever we want, displace whomever we want, even kill 12,000 children. It is all for the purpose of Israel's survival.

Many advocates insist that all pro-Palestinian protests are antisemitic. Adam Milstein wrote in *The Jerusalem Post* that: "It's almost impossible to find a 'pro-Palestinian' rally that isn't drenched in antisemitic rhetoric, anti-Jewish venom, or stereotypical tropes." I am aware that there have been some unsavory antisemitic incidents in pro-Palestinian rallies in the U.S., such as calls to "Go back to Poland" or to kill all Zionists. Those are truly disturbing and even scary. But not all pro-Palestinian chants or beliefs are antisemitic. For Milstein, the mere use of the words "genocide" and "apartheid" is an act of antisemitism. Palestinians' references to Israel as "home" or "stolen land" are also antisemitic, as if to say that Palestinians have no right to express pain, anger, or longing. Their entire history is illegitimate. He writes:

*Representative Ilhan Omar has infamously and repeatedly used antisemitic rhetoric. Her daughter was among the Columbia students arrested for their illegal encampment, flaunted her antisemitic bona fides. In an attempt to defend the protesters against claims that they're antisemitic, she said "…we should not have to tolerate antisemitism or bigotry for all Jewish students, whether they're pro-genocide or anti-genocide." Rep. Omar was implying that Jews who support Israel are de facto "pro-genocide". The ADL called out Omar's comments for what they are, a "blood libel" against Jews. To combat this troubling trend, media outlets and leaders must acknowledge that these pro-Palestinian activists are antisemitic. The onslaught of protests, boycott demands, divestment campaigns, and slogans must be referred to as "antisemitic efforts".[94]*

Astoundingly, even when Rep. Ilhan Omar was denouncing antisemitism she was called antisemitic, because of her use of the word genocide. Even as this writer and others like him are effectively doing what she is accusing them of — demanding an absolute defense of Israel's actions, even when Israel's actions can easily be seen as genocidal, given the realities on the ground in Gaza as well as the difficult history of the Palestinians in Israel since 1948 — he calls Omar antisemitic for daring to criticize Israel. Rather than engaging in an honest and authentic conversation about Israel's actions, rather than acknowledging the importance of Omar's condemnation of antisemitism and her insistence that even Jews with whom she fiercely disagrees deserve respect, this writer continues to attack her and call her an antisemite. This could have been a great moment for reconciliation, in which Omar and the Zionist community come together to talk about hate speech and find shared values and humanity. Instead, it

---

[94] Adam Milstein, "Exposing the vile antisemitism of the 'Pro-Palestinian' activists," *The Jerusalem Post*, June 23, 2024, https://www.jpost.com/opinion/article-807374.

was used as an opportunity to create further division and perpetuate the process of dehumanizing the other side.

The "antisemite" accusation quashes any meaningful dialogue and attempts to protect Israel from criticism. Unfortunately, it does not help Israel and only further fans the flames of hatred.

> **In a nutshell: The introduction of antisemitism into discussions about the conflict shifts attention away from Israel's actions and rewrites the entire narrative. The antisemitism claim frees Israel from accountability and turns the discussion on its head so that Israel is deemed the victim, even when it is the aggressor. Unfortunately, 45,000 dead Gazans, including 12,000 children, cannot explain how they were driven by antisemitism. More to the point, Israel is an autonomous state with a powerful army. And its actions cannot be excused by claims of antisemitism.**

## Antisemitism drives all political discourse

The antisemitism argument often goes a step further and rewrites all current political discourse through this lens.

There are plenty of memes, graphics, and tweets that make this point. One typical example reads:

**Harvard Law admissions essay prompt this year: "Describe a challenging experience you have had in your life, and why it is Israel's fault."**

This is a classic overdramatic self-victimization response to being accused of wrongdoing. It's a kind of eyerolling "Everything is always my fault", a response in which the speaker avoids accountability by making grandiose claims of being "blamed for everything".

Another college-centric post shows parents sitting at a table with a young guy dressed like Hitler wearing a T-shirt that says "I love Hamas". The father is saying:

**Son, your mother and I are concerned about how college has changed you.**

This cartoon conflates several points. One is that Hamas is equal to the Nazis, which also frames the entire conflict as being about antisemitism. This framing, again, enables Israel to avoid accountability or even a response to criticism about its actions against Palestinians, as the entire conflict is framed as being about antisemitism, a continuation of the Holocaust. This cartoon, like many other posts, particularly targets colleges, which are seen as aligned with Hamas/Nazis/Palestinians who are equated with human rights activists and antisemites. All these caricatures are conflated as one being.

A similarly themed graphic shows a "Verify that you're human" window with the text "I support Israel" to click on. As if to say, anyone who doesn't support Israel couldn't possibly be human.

The expansion of the antisemitism frame sometimes goes way back to encompass the entire history of Israel, Palestine, and Zionism. One meme reads:

**73% of the British mandate of Palestine is now Jordan. Why not "free Palestine from Jordan"? Because they can't blame the Jews.**

This post takes me directly back to my class with Tomer, when we learned that "Jordan is the real Palestine". Redirecting attention to Jordan is a deflection tactic used to avoid accountability, an example of "whataboutism". In this case it expands the antisemitism argument and argues that any accusations aimed at Israel are nothing more than a centuries-old form of antisemitism.

One last point about blaming the entire world for Israel's reprehensible behavior. This practice has been extended to blaming the world even for Israel's unconscionable actions

against its own people. One particularly infuriating post that
was shared with me dozens of times reads:

**May your family never be kidnapped while the world
demands you cease fighting for them.
I stand with Israel.**

The assertions here are all wrong. It's not *the world* that
doesn't care about the hostages. In fact, the world seems to
care deeply. Public displays featuring the hostages can be
found all over the world, millions of people and dozens of
foundations support the families of the hostages, all the major
news outlets cover the issue with compassion and regularly
interview families of hostages, the White House and other
government officials regularly hold conversations and
meetings with the families, many world actors are heavily
involved in pressuring the parties to make a deal, families of
hostages speak all over the world, including at the United
Nations and the Democratic National Convention, and even
A-list celebrities are in on it and wear hostage paraphernalia
at major events like the Oscars.[95]

---

[95] Ruby Kraner-Tucci, "Art attack: Creative campaigns to ensure
hostages are not forgotten," *The Jewish Independent*, January 29,
2024, https://thejewishindependent.com.au/public-art-takes-
hostage-crisis-to-the-streets-in-many-forms; Anna Rahmanan, "The
Artists Behind the 'Kidnapped' Posters Plastered Around the
World," *Observer*, October 23, 2023,
https://observer.com/2023/10/the-artists-behind-the-missing-
posters-plastered-around-the-world/; Ilana Goodman, "NBC4:
Largest poster in the world features 173 Israeli hostages," *Israel
National News*, December 20, 2023,
https://www.israelnationalnews.com/news/382256; Agam
Goldstein, Almog, "I was a captive of Hamas. After I was freed, I
was imprisoned by online trolls." *Washington Post*, August 21,
2024,
https://www.washingtonpost.com/opinions/2024/08/21/hamas-
israel-hostages-antisemitism/; "Background Press Call on Efforts
to Secure the Release of Hostages in Gaza," The White House,
September 4, 2024, https://www.whitehouse.gov/briefing-
room/press-briefings/2024/09/04/background-press-call-on-

It's simply not true that the world doesn't care about the hostages. And it's extremely dismissive of all those efforts to suggest it. The world cares. You know who doesn't care? *The Israeli government*. That post should read:

**Imagine being captive for almost a year with a government that cares more about itself than about you.**

Israeli Prime Minister Benjamin Netanyahu is the one who most emphatically does not care about the hostages. He regularly sabotages the negotiation talks and moves the goalposts in order to avoid a ceasefire/hostage deal. His own negotiating team and top brass have been saying this for months. The families of the hostages, along with throngs of Israelis, protest and beg and plead for a deal every day, while Bibi ignores them. He talks about a "long war", as if to prepare us for a war that will never end. He talks about "sacrifices", as if laying the groundwork for his plan that all hostages will die. He talks about a "complete victory", as if that's even a thing. As if there is anything more important than bringing the hostages home.[96]

---

efforts-to-secure-the-release-of-hostages-in-gaza/; Mathilda Heller, "Gwyneth Paltrow, Gal Gadot, other celebrities express outrage, grief at murdered hostages," *The Jerusalem Post*, September 2, 2024,https://www.jpost.com/israel-hamas-war/article-817348.
[96] Gideon Allon, "'No doubt' Netanyahu preventing hostage deal, charges ex-spokesman of Families Forum," *The Times of Israel*, April 26, 2024, https://www.timesofisrael.com/no-doubt-netanyahu-preventing-hostage-deal-charges-ex-spokesman-of-families-forum/; Yonah Jeremy Bob and Tovah Lazaroff, "Netanyahu actively sabotaging hostage deal, sources say," *The Jerusalem Post*, July 16, 2024, https://www.jpost.com/israel-hamas-war/article-810551; "Former IDF chief of staff blames Netanyahu of sacrificing remaining hostages," *The Jerusalem Post*, September 22, 2024, https://www.jpost.com/breaking-news/article-821255; Elana Sztokman, "The problem is not antisemitism; It's Bibi," *The Roar*, Substack, September 27, 2024, https://elanasztokman.substack.com/p/the-problem-is-not-antisemitism-its.

And yet, this lie that it is "the world" that is keeping the hostages in tunnels — rather than the Israeli government — continues to take hold. It aligns with a favorite longstanding Jewish narrative that whatever bad thing is happening to us is due to antisemitism.

But it's simply not true. The problem here is not antisemitism. The problem is Israeli leadership. This false narrative that Israel's problem today is antisemitism is a deflection tactic that effectively supports Bibi and his corrupt government. The narrative of "it's the world's fault" forcefully undermines the real efforts to bring back the hostages. Also, it's just a lie.

> **In a nutshell: Although it is convenient to respond to accusations of wrongdoing by accusing others of antisemitism and arguing that antisemitism drives all political discourse in the world — including, apparently, the entire human rights movement and college culture — that is just an avoidance tactic. It is a classic example of whataboutist deflection, intended to avoid all accountability for Israel's actions.**

## The war/conflict is just like the Holocaust

The Holocaust theme has already reared its ugly head in many posts I cited above. We already encountered ideas such as that Hamas are Nazis, that the world wants Israel to act like sheep ready for slaughter, and that accusations of Israel's wrongdoing are nothing more than centuries-old antisemitism. Many examples of this are making the rounds:

**Don't forget to turn your clocks back to 1938 Germany time this weekend.**

Or another one:

**If you've ever asked yourself what you would do in the 1930s and 1940s, you're doing it now.**

Or this one:

**Next time someone tells you
Jihad simply means 'My Struggle',
remind them that is also the meaning of
'Mein Kampf'.**

Framing the Israel/Palestine war as a new Holocaust serves a few purposes. It casts all Palestinians as guilty Nazis, it casts Jews and Israelis as victims, and ultimately shifts the narrative away from the idea that Israel has done anything wrong. It is the ultimate deflective blame-shifting tactic to avoid accountability.

This tactic is also one of the favorite tactics used by the current Israeli government. Because another by-product of framing this as a Holocaust-related series of events is that it enables the government to cast Israel as a country facing an existential crisis. This allows the government to operate in emergency mode and avoid their own accountability with voters. Thus far, this tactic has worked. Despite the disaster of October 7 and all that has followed, the government has kept itself in power, avoiding inquiries and elections.

In some cases, the entire world is cast as Nazis or antisemites. One graphic shows the Red Cross as a piece of a swastika. The caption reads:

**Hide when needed.**

As if the Red Cross are Nazis because they care for Palestinians.

Similarly, when France decided to stop sending weapons to Israel in protest of how Israel uses their weapons in Gaza, a response on social media implied that the French president is a Nazi and a supporter of terrorism over the past century:

**Next time French President Macron wants to lecture
Israel on how to handle this war, remind him that:**

- His country collaborated with the Nazis and went above and beyond in delivering Jews.

- France offered asylum to dictator Khomeini in 1978 before he took control of Iran.

- France sheltered Bin Laden's son before he was expelled in 2023 for glorifying terrorism.

- Macron still has yet to help the two French hostages that Hamas has held in Gaza for over a year.

**Maybe a little less judgment and a little more introspection is necessary**

Here, the narrative portraying Israel's critics as Nazis is conflated with randomly selected tidbits of history, even those not connected to Macron at all. It is an exercise in broad-brush branding as evil anyone who dares to call on Israel to stop bombing Gazan civilians.

**In a nutshell: Framing actions in Gaza in Holocaust terms is the ultimate Jewish avoidance tactic. In this line of thinking, Israel can do no wrong because the entire world is out to kill us. But this is wrong. Palestinians are not Nazis and are not all supporters of violent terrorism, Israel is a powerful country with a massive army that is not heading like sheep to the slaughter, and there are many legitimate reasons for Palestinians to demand accountability and justice from Israel. These topics should not be avoided or evaded.**

# (4) Everything Israel Does Is Justified

Seen together, the arguments that Jews are good and Palestinians are bad, that Jews are the real victims in the Israel/Palestine conflict, that accusations against Israel are nothing more than rehashed antisemitism that has taken over the world — especially among human rights activists — and that Israel has done no wrong, have clear implications. In this rendering, everything that Israel does becomes justifiable and correct.

This is not surprising. After all, asserting Israel's absolute correctness is the ultimate goal of Israel advocacy. Laid out this way, however, the toxicity of this stance emerges. In this stance of absolute correctness, there is no room for compromise, discourse, negotiation, self-criticism, listening, change, empathy, or even awareness of other perspectives. There is only one side being unequivocally right and the other side being completely wrong. Reality on the ground, tragedies borne by the "enemy", and endless bloodshed on the "other side", become invisible and irrelevant.

This absolutist justification of Israel's actions is also bolstered by additional forms of rhetorical manipulation aimed at further entrenching the idea of Israel's absolute righteousness.

## Inevitability: Israel has no choice

The theme of inevitability is frequently invoked by Netanyahu's government and IDF spokesman. We often hear them defending Israel's actions as "this is a war of no choice".

Many of Israel's advocates invoke quotes by the late Prime Minister Golda Meir with this theme. One popular Golda Meir quote is:

**We Israelis have a secret weapon. We have no place else to go.**

As if to say, Israel will fight tooth and nail and do whatever it takes because there is no other choice. The fact that Jews live safely and are thriving in dozens of countries around the world seems irrelevant to this point.

Another famous Golda Meir quote justifies an absolutist stance and the absence of negotiability:

**We want to live. Our neighbors want us dead. It leaves not much room for compromise.**

Again, this dramatic oversimplification rests on the ideas that all Palestinians are murderous, all Jews are innocent, and antisemitism is at the root of the conflict, and therefore Israel is free from the need to compromise or even acknowledge another perspective. There is no admission of oppression, discrimination, or occupation. In this absolutist rendering, Meir said that Israel has no choice. This position is eagerly adopted by many of Israel's advocates today. It enables Israel to act without any self-awareness or acknowledgment of wrongdoing.

Similarly, this idea of "no choice" or inevitability creates a bravado that enables Israel and its advocates to ignore international criticism.

One telling social media interaction demonstrates how all these ideas are intertwined — that Israel is all good, Palestinians are all bad, and that Israel does not want the war but has no choice. One woman asked her followers a classic Israel advocacy question: "What is one thing you wish people understood about Israel?" The question itself implies that the world misunderstands Israel and is unfairly judging Israel, and therefore Israel needs advocates to go out and "explain" Israel's stance. Here are a few of the 59 responses:

- That we're a tiny tiny country.

- That we want to live in peace with our neighbors.

- That we're not looking to expand our territory.

- Israel has a secret weapon. We the Jews do not have any other place to go. Golda Meir

- It's filled with life-loving people, living ordinary lives; people who don't hate anyone who isn't trying to kill us.

- How many rockets have been aimed at Israel and how busy Iron Dome has been shooting them down. I talked to a very close non-Jewish friend yesterday. She had no idea Hezbollah has fired 1000s of rockets or that places like Sderot were under constant bombardment by Hamas. She says that not knowing this makes Israel's actions look disproportionate rather than the reasonable reactions they are....

- Nothing. I'm done "explaining" Israel.

- That we have the right to live without apologizing to anybody

- When we said "Never Again" we meant it.

- That we are a people of love

- I'm so so tired of the world thinking we want war.

- That we are willing to make peace with anyone who is willing to make peace with us. We can be really good neighbors.

- That we are the key to a wonderful world

This thread combines many of the themes described above: Israel is a peaceful, well-intentioned, tiny, powerless little nation that does not want war. But Israel is faced with a Holocaust-type existential threat and therefore can do whatever it needs to do without apologizing. If there is no peace, it's the fault of the other side. Israel is all good.

This stance is a kind of "all clear" permission for Israel to do whatever it wants with impunity. As encapsulated in this popular Golda Meir quote that's making the rounds on social media:

**If we have to choose between being dead and pitied, and being alive with a bad image, we'd rather be alive and have a bad image. – Golda Meir**

All criticism of Israel is reduced to "a bad image". As if there is no substance to anything negative anyone says about Israel. Netanyahu supporters love this tough bravado. It gives Israel permission to ignore the entire world. This stance, according to which Israel does no wrong and is *forced* to engage in military violence against its own loving nature, is used by the government as well, especially in international relations. In fact, many cabinet members as well as right-wing and religious pundits regularly encourage Netanyahu to ignore the world — even allies like the United States — and do what he wants.[97] This has been a theme of his entire career. For example, when Ben-Gvir promoted the expulsion of all Palestinians from Gaza and received a public reprimand from the American government for this, he responded by saying, "We are not another star in the American flag".[98] In other

---

[97] Dr. Yagil Henkin, "A new security doctrine is needed, even if the price is perpetual war," *Israel Hayom*, October 24, 2024, https://www.israelhayom.com/2024/10/24/a-new-security-doctrine-is-needed-even-if-the-price-is-perpetual-war/.

[98] Jacob Magid, "US slams 'irresponsible' calls by Smotrich and Ben Gvir for emigration of Gazans," *The Times of Israel*, January 3,

words, defiance and rejection of international pressure is part of this entire pro-Israel posture as it is defined in the Netanyahu orbit. It is an expression of the entire "We do no wrong" and "We don't care if our actions give us a bad image in the world" rhetoric. It is a complete rejection of human dialogue and international relations.

> **In a nutshell: The idea that Israel has "no choice" implies that Israel's hands are tied, that the war is someone else's fault, and that Israel has done no wrong. This of course is not true. Israel has had many choices. The incessant escalation of violence is merely a reflection of Netanyahu's choices.[99]**

## It's their own fault

Netanyahu's own negotiators have described his repeated sabotage of ceasefire talks with endless acts of moving the goalposts.[100] Like an abuser saying to their victim, "You made me do it", the language of "no choice" is just another tactic of avoiding responsibility for one's actions. Indeed, as with dynamics of emotional and physical abuse, the natural extension of "I have no choice" is "You made me do it".

2024, https://www.timesofisrael.com/us-slams-irresponsible-calls-by-smotrich-and-ben-gvir-for-emigration-of-gazans/.

[99] Noam Sheizaf, "This is a war of choice. Netanyahu's choice," *+972 Magazine*, July 16, 2014, https://www.972mag.com/this-is-a-war-of-choice-netanyahus-choice/.

[100] Yonah Jeremy Bob and Tovah Lazaroff, "Netanyahu actively sabotaging hostage deal, sources say," *The Jerusalem Post*, July 16, 2024, https://www.jpost.com/israel-hamas-war/article-810551; Elana Sztokman, "The problem is not antisemitism, it's Bibi," *The Times of Israel*, September 27, 2024, https://blogs.timesofisrael.com/the-problem-is-not-antisemitism-its-bibi/; Elana Sztokman, "3 myths about the war in Gaza," *The Roar*, Substack, September 12, 2024, https://elanasztokman.substack.com/p/3-myths-about-the-war-in-gaza.

*New York Times* columnist Bret Stephens, for example, wrote an op-ed with the title "Hamas bears the blame for every death in this war".[101] He draws this conclusion despite his own admission of the following:

> *Reasonable people can criticize Israel for not allowing enough time for civilians to get out of harm's way: There are, especially, elderly, disabled and sick Gazans — and those who help them — who may be effectively homebound.*
>
> *Reasonable people can also oppose other measures that Israelis have taken in response to the deadliest massacre of Jews since the Holocaust. It seems neither right nor smart for Israel to cut off water and electricity to Gaza until Hamas's hostages are returned — not because Israel shouldn't do whatever it takes to obtain their release but because the people who suffer most from the action are the ones who have the least say over the fate of the hostages. Hamas's leaders, I'm sure, have amply supplied themselves and their forces with fuel, generators, potable water and other essentials.*

Even with this understanding, Stephens still places all the blame on Hamas because of their tactics of pressuring Gazans to stay put and not offering them any protections.

Similarly, a headline in *Mosaic* magazine asks the following question:

**Why does the Palestinian movement always fail?**

It was shared on social media with the following tweet:

**The Palestinians are enduring yet another tragedy. But once again, it is of their own making.**

---

[101] Bret Stephens, "Hamas Bears the Blame for Every Death in This War," *The New York Times*, October 15, 2023, https://www.nytimes.com/2023/10/15/opinion/columnists/hamas-war-israel-gaza.html.

But it is Israel that drops bombs on civilians, that shoots into civilian crowds in the belief that Hamas terrorists hide there, that attacks hospitals, kindergartens, and tent encampments. Israel makes these choices, not Hamas. To blame Palestinians for their own suffering — is if to say, if Hamas is among them, then they all deserve to die — is a sick and immoral attempt to justify murderous choices.

When I hear this kind of argument, I often ask, "What would you do if you were a Gazan?" Meaning, if terrorists lived among you, what would you do to stop them? If you were a kindergarten teacher and terrorists decided to use your storage closet to hide guns, what exactly would you do to stop them? Is there anything you *could* do without possibly being killed yourself? And if you were not able to stop them, do you think you and your children would deserve to die for that?

This notion that Gazans deserve to die because Hamas exists there is horrendous. But it is deeply entrenched in the rhetoric of Israel's defense. As if to say, *we may be pulling the trigger on innocent people, even children, but don't blame us for it. It's their own fault.* It is a complete dehumanization of the Other intended to enable some of the worst actions.

Israel's advocates indeed have many twisted ways to blame Palestinians for their situation, many of which reflect profound cruelty. I have frequent conversations about this point on social media. For example, my Facebook friend Leah (not her real name) wrote this comment on my timeline:

**We are \*not\* inflicting all this misery on the Gazans. They brought and continue to bring it on themselves every day. I have sympathy for the Gazans like I have sympathy for the Germans during World War II and the Holocaust their Nazis perpetrated. I now have a lot of respect for Germans. I hope once the Palestinians surrender and stop their terrorism, they can rebuild Gaza like Germany rebuilt itself after the complete defeat of the Nazis.**

Here, not only are Palestinians all cast as Nazis, but Gazans are also directly blamed for their own experiences of starvation, displacement, and all their suffering — even as Israel is the one dropping the bombs. I tried to explain my point to Leah. I wrote:

*"They are doing it to themselves" is a callous, toxic, blame-the-victim approach that seeks to absolve us of our responsibilities here. WE are dropping the bombs. WE are destroying entire neighborhoods and entire families. WE are making those awful choices. WE are. Nobody is forcing us to do that. And the tens of thousands of innocent people who have died -- their blood is on our hands, nobody else's.*

But Leah was unmoved. She doubled down on blaming Palestinians, and continued the Nazi references, terminology that justifies "complete defeat" of Gaza, with all that implies.

**In a nutshell: Palestinians are human beings. Gazans are not Nazis. The overwhelming majority of Gazans did not carry out the events of October 7. It is wrong to condemn the entire population of Gaza to death. (Just as it is wrong to blame all Israelis for the actions of its government!) Even if the ruling party carries out terror attacks, that still does not give anyone the right to kill entire civilian populations. Blaming 2.2 million Gazans for the acts of terrorists — who also terrorize innocent civilians, including children — is classic victim blaming.[102] Justifying the killing of non-involved parties by blaming them for their own deaths is a position of immense cruelty. Furthermore, acts based on this kind of thinking — that an entire population deserves to die — can readily be classified as ethnic cleansing.**

[102] Felice Friedson and Giorgia Valente, "Most Palestinians support West Bank groups but don't back Hamas, researcher says," *The Jerusalem Post*, August 23, 2024, https://www.jpost.com/israel-hamas-war/article-815996.

## Israel's actions are justified by God

In a related trend that's on the rise in the current religiously dominated right-wing Israeli government, justification of Israel's actions takes on a religious tint: they are justified by God.

Indeed, in my religious high school too, biblical texts were used to explain Zionism. We learned about Jewish history on the land, the twelve tribes, the temples and the expulsions, and the 2,000-year-old prayers for Jewish autonomy in Jerusalem. These ideas have been reawakened — or maybe they were always there — and have become amplified on social media. As if to say, Jews are right because God says so.

One popular meme that frequently appears on my feed shows a map of Israel designated as "1948 CE" being peeled back in many layers to reveal the words "13th century BCE". The text appears on an Israeli flag design, and the peeling back of the layers matches a blue Star of David against a white background. The message is clear: The current State of Israel is a continuation of events that began when the Israelites were nomads wandering in the desert.

Ancient maps are a popular backdrop for this kind of messaging. One graphic being shared shows a map of the region from the First Temple period when the twelve Israelite tribes dwelled on the land, based on borders described in the book of Joshua. Significantly, this rendering of ancient Israel includes parts of Lebanon, Syria, Jordan, and Egypt. In one share of this graphic, the accompanying text reads:

**Never. Ever. Forget. Where the children of Israel
Jewish Israelite Hebrew Nation come from.
And whose land it is and has always been.
Since Hashem's blessing.
Protect our inheritance in every way, every day.
Be proud.
From every tribe and for every Jew.**

The idea that all this land should automatically belong to Jews based on a reality that existed 3,000 years ago, an ancient text, and "God's promise" is clearly absurd. Many things have happened since then, including the tragic disappearance of ten of those twelve tribes and the scattering of the rest into countries around the world.

I am not suggesting that Jews don't have strong ties to the land. I'm saying that ancient history, or graphics like this map, are practically irrelevant in the current reality. This map does nothing to provide credibility in the twenty-first century. What the map does is try to paint Jews as legitimate citizens and Palestinians as non-existent. A popular Zionist slogan used to be, "A land with no people for a people with no land". This slogan, which completely erases Palestinian existence, aims to do the same thing as this map. That is, justify the idea that Jews of the world have every right to live in Israel in any location under any conditions while Palestinians do not. Or as another version of this ancient map reads:

**IT'S CALLED ISRAEL. NOT PALESTINE.**

The intention is clear. Palestine doesn't exist, it never has, and Palestinians have zero right to live there. Even if their families have been there for generations.

Another meme reads:

**Many of my dearest friends live between the river and the sea: IT HAS ALWAYS BEEN OUR LAND.**

As if two thousand years of scattering did not exist. As if there was never anyone else living on that land while the Jews were mainly elsewhere.

Another meme that has appeared on my feed many times shows a photograph of the Jerusalem skyline with the Dome of the Rock at the center, with the caption:

**Israel doesn't occupy the land. They OWN it.**
**Genesis 15;18–21**

Thus, according to the referenced biblical text, God promised Abraham this land, and therefore Israel "owns" it.

This language of "ownership" is used by government ministers as well. Ben-Gvir often talks about being the "*ba'al habayit*", (landlord or owner). His campaign slogan was "Who are the landlords here? Time for Ben Gvir".[103] Orthodox Jews in my hometown have expressed elation at this idea.[104]

This language of Jews as the "landlords" is particularly painful to many Palestinians. It aggravates the feeling among many Palestinians that they are second-class citizens in Israel, a feeling exacerbated by the Nation State Law.[105]

A graphic that summarizes this theme shows a portrait of Moses holding the tablets at Mount Sinai with the caption:

### God stands with Israel.

> **In a nutshell: Biblical references from thousands of years ago that claim to be the word of God are not a legitimate justification for claims today. They should certainly not be used to erase the real lives and histories of others whose ancestors settled on this land more recently. And most alarmingly, we should be questioning how these texts are used to justify a religious mission.**

---

[103] Al Jazeera English, "Israel's Itamar Ben-Gvir calls police 'landlords' of Jerusalem," May 21, 2023, YouTube video, 0:29, https://youtube.com/shorts/CJFUAw8o40Y?si=icsYE3KJAUt-4zgK.

[104] Rabbi Yehuda L Oppenheimer, "Who Is The Baal HaBayit?" *Jewish Press*, November 16, 2022, https://www.jewishpress.com/judaism/torah/who-is-the-baal-habayit/2022/11/16/.

[105] This issue of the language of "mastery" was discussed at some length in one of my podcast episodes with Dr. Fakhira Halloun, "Women Ending War S1 E5: The everyday work of peace building, w/Dr. Fakhira Halloun and Yael Treidel," August 5, 2024, YouTube video, 46:21, https://www.youtube.com/watch?v=3W-HNBU_sQI&list=PLyw9ntxS-kikAUsI-XvSeqSm7-i_pMCB2&index=15&ab_channel=ElanaSztokman.

## War is a religious mission

Linked to the seemingly increasingly prevalent view that all of Israel's action are justified by God is the idea that the war is a religious mission.

Aside from the fact that the government waging this war is dominated by an unprecedented number of religious ministers and legislators, many of whom openly espouse messianic thinking and theocratic ambitions for Israel,[106] there are other troubling indications of increased God-thinking behind the deadly weapons of war. This finds expression in a range of trends and phenomena. Rabbis frequently describe combat duty as a religious sacrifice – while, in a head-spinning twist, some rabbis ardently fight for continued army exemptions for the "most religious" yeshivah students.[107] In addition, this war ushered in new religious missives. I frequently receive text messages like this one:

**What are you doing on behalf of soldiers?**
**1.  Lay tefillin**
**2.  Light Shabbat candles**

The anniversary of October 7 was marked in some communities as a "Day of Modesty" in which women were urged to cover their bodies in order to protect soldiers. Leaving aside the gendered aspect of this dictate and similar others, which deserve their own lengthy analysis (see my book *Conversations with my Body* for further reference)[108], the

---

[106] Bernard Avishai, "Netanyahu's Government Takes a Turn Toward Theocracy," *The New Yorker*, January 7, 2023, https://www.newyorker.com/news/daily-comment/netanyahus-government-takes-a-turn-toward-theocracy.

[107] Jonathan Lieberman, "Being an Israeli right now means making the ultimate sacrifice — opinion," *The Jerusalem Post*, January 6, 2024, https://www.jpost.com/opinion/article-780828.

[108] Elana Sztokman, *Conversations with My Body: Essays on My Life as a Jewish Woman* (Lioness Books, 2022)

underlying premise of these messages is that fighting the war is a religious mission.

Indeed, the war is often likened to ancient religious wars in Jewish history. On the holiday of Purim, for example, when mass protests calling for a ceasefire and the release of the hostages were being held around Israel, I received the following message:

**On this day of Purim, let's never forget, no matter how the diabolical nations try to twist the truth, it is Israel alone which is the moral guiding light in the world and will always be protected by the awesome power of Hashem [God].**

This text combines many themes already mentioned here — Israel is all good, the whole world is against Israel, and those criticizing Israel are liars and "diabolical" — and adds a whole other God (*Hashem*) component. It emboldens defenders of Israel as acting with God's protection, following the 2,500-year-old Purim story when the Jews, threatened with extermination, fought back and won (while incidentally killing tens of thousands of Persians).

Similarly, the Passover story also evokes the "God protecting Jews throughout history" theme to justify Israel's actions. One cartoon showing Pharoah grabbing Hamas leader Yahya Sinwar by the shoulders reads:

**"Believe me, you better let them go."**

As if to say, this war is akin to the Exodus from Egypt, and Hamas is like the ancient Egyptians holding Israelis as slaves. The fact that Israel is a fully independent state with its own very powerful army seems to have eluded the cartoonist. Moreover, the power relations in the case of Israelis and Palestinians is in fact reversed (it is actually the Palestinians who live in what has been described as an open-air prison who could be seen as "enslaved".[109]

Even among secular Israelis, there is the sentiment that fighting in Gaza is just another event in Jewish history. One photo of utter destruction in Gaza has been shared with the text:

**We are not doing it to teach them a lesson. We are doing it because we learned ours.**

In other words, this war is not about Gazans but about the Egyptians, the Persians, the Romans, the Crusades, the Spanish, and the German Nazis. The fact that Palestinians have no connection to any of these historical groups is of no importance to the posters. The story claiming 3,000 years of Jewish victimhood renders the current facts irrelevant to the current reality. It allows Israel to do what it wants with impunity because for Israel, the enemy is not the Palestinians but 3,000 years' worth of enemies.

This generalizing of Jewish history supports the idea of the war as a religious mission, an idea that is now intrinsic to IDF activity. Rabbis in the IDF rabbinate have been leading prayer and singing sessions with soldiers about to enter Gaza, singing the Passover song "*V'Hi She'amda*", a song about God standing with Jewish ancestors to save the Jews. The underlying idea is the same: This war is akin to the Exodus and every other historical moment of danger for the Jewish people and fighting in Gaza is a religious mission. Member of the Knesset Zvi Sukkot, a religious radical whose ideas are considered so violent that the IDF rejected him from service, is an official lecturer at the College of National Security to army recruits and commanders in training. One image that went viral epitomizes this religious grandiosity of combat: A

---

[109] Jamal, Amal. "Jewish sovereignty and the inclusive exclusion of Palestinians: Shifting the conceptual understanding of politics in Israel/Palestine." *Frontiers in Political Science* 4 (2022): 995371.

soldier in uniform reads from the Torah using a sword the Torah (instead of the traditional '*yad*' hand pointer) to guide his reading.

Meanwhile, soldiers are encouraged to pen letters to their families in case they die, in which they frequently glorify death in service of God and the nation.

> **In a nutshell: Religious rhetoric provides zealots with a warped sense of a divine mission, and is often used to dehumanize the Other — a tactic Jews ought to recognize from having frequently been on the other side of it. The use of religious rhetoric to provide absolute justification for Israel's actions — including murder and destruction of homes — is deeply disturbing.**

## Palestinians deserve to die

With God on your side, everything you do is justified. Seen from another angle, the corresponding idea is that all Palestinians deserve to die.

We have already seen this idea rear its ugly head in various memes, graphics, and exchanges. In some cases, this theme is even more overt, with a very specific and explicit justification for wanton destruction of Palestinian lives.

For example, one meme juxtaposes a photo of a thriving Gaza beach under the word "Before" with a photo of the same spot showing complete destruction under the word "After", with the caption:

**Mess with the best. Die like the rest.**

This chilling, nausea-inducing meme doesn't even bother to mention God, but simply asserts that Israel is "the best" and therefore all Palestinians deserve to die (like "the rest" who deservingly died). In a similar vein, another meme reads:

**We are not asking you to understand us. We are not asking you to love us. We are now simply warning you: Don't mess with us. Signed, The Jewish People.**

For me, this exceedingly threatening meme has echoes of listening to Meir Kahane's JDL rhetoric in my youth. It is a way to justify Jewish violence in any form, couched in a perpetually circumspect stance. As if anyone Israel attacks is out to get us — a Nazi, an antisemite, a Palestinian, or just "the world".

In a nutshell: The religious mission, coupled with language of antisemitism, superimposed on a generalized dehumanization of Palestinians, aims to give Israel the right to do whatever it wants to whoever it wants with absolute impunity.

# The Toxic Tactics in Short

To summarize the rhetorical flow of the memes presented here, pro-Israel advocacy rests on the following ideas:

## (1)    Israelis/Jews are good, do no wrong

- Jews are good/righteous
- The IDF is the most moral army in the world
- There is no discrimination/apartheid in Israel
- Occupation is a lie/doesn't exist

## (2)    Palestinians are bad and at fault

- There are no innocent Palestinians
- Palestinians don't value life (but Jews do)
- Palestinians have no culture other than murder
- All Palestinians are terrorists
- Palestinians are not normal humans
- Palestinians are liars and hypocrites

## (3)    Israel/Jews are the real victims

- All criticism of Israel is antisemitism
- Antisemitism drives all political discourse
- The war/conflict is just like the Holocaust

## (4)    Everything Israel does is justified

- Inevitability: Israel has no choice
- It's their own fault
- Israel's actions are justified by God
- War is a religious mission
- Palestinians deserve to die

The rhetorical tactics used by Israel's advocates share many characteristics with tactics used by narcissistic abusers. I say this as someone who spent seven years researching tactics of emotional abuse, bullying, and sexual abuse. Before that, I spent over a decade working in organizations addressing domestic abuse. That work sensitized me to tactics of verbal violence, and I became hyperaware of these types of verbal exchanges in my surroundings.

During a seemingly unrelated chapter of my life, I worked as a Media Chair for Democrats Abroad-Israel. I spent the years of the (first) Trump presidency doing many media spots on panels sitting opposite Trump supporters, which meant that I was exposed to toxic forms of political discourse in very public spaces where the toxicity was tolerated and at times even encouraged.[110] It often took me quite some time to recover from those spots, as if I had just been beaten up verbally. For a few years I wrote a blog called *Toxic Tactics* in which I collected and cited some examples of the toxicity I had witnessed, read about, and/or experienced.

Given this history, it is impossible for me not to see the similarities between emotional abuse on the personal level and rhetorical manipulation on the systemic level in the world of Israel advocacy. Based on my analysis of themes in Israel advocacy, I think it is worthwhile to point out some of the toxic tactics that are part of the work of Israel advocacy:

- Lying
- Whitewashing actions or rewriting history
- Deflecting
- Whataboutism

---

[110] Elana Sztokman, "Tackling Trump in the Israeli media," *A Jewish Feminist*, November 9, 2019, http://jewfem.com/index.php?option=com_easyblog&view=entry&id=668&Itemid=497.

- Generalizing the Other
- Erasing culture and history
- Victim blaming
- "You made me do it"
- Dehumanizing the Other
- Vilifying all leftists / human rights activists / academics Arabs / Palestinians
- Claiming that God is on your side
- Collective punishment

All these themes and practices are integral parts of Israel advocacy that I have analyzed here.

There is one more thing: Overall, engaging in incessant debating is also toxic. This type of badgering that Israel's advocates at times engage in constitutes its own tactic of abuse and harassment.

Life is not the debating team. As much as I loved Tomer's class, it was bad education to train us to always prove that we are right. We don't have to always be better, smarter, wittier, more "clever" and morally superior. We don't always have to have the last word. Life is much better when we stop and listen to the Other. Especially when that Other is trying to tell us that we are hurting them.

With this understanding, and a resolute decision to let go of my past, I set out to figure out for myself what I really believe about the place I have called home for the past thirty years.

# Part III: Where to From Here

# The Search for Empathy

Yussuf Abu Rabia Shizam, a 24-year-old agricultural engineer from Beit Lahia in Gaza, was so disturbed by the food shortages in his community that he dedicated himself to growing food locally and ensuring food security for his community. A report about his work from August 2024 showed him growing acres of beautiful green plants amid bombed out buildings. He was determined.[111]

Then, on October 21, 2024, he was killed by an IDF bombing of his home.

You will not find this story anywhere in the Israeli media. I learned about this from a WhatsApp group I belong to called "Gaza updates". The group is in Hebrew, aimed at an Israeli audience, to fill in the gaps about what we don't see happening on the ground in Gaza. The Israeli media is notoriously pro-IDF and rarely shows Palestinians' perspectives or the real impacts of Israeli actions on the ground.[112] The group has fewer than 1,000 members despite the importance of the information shared. The posts are often firsthand accounts, stories, videos, and updates about the people in Gaza — their lives, their homes, their families, and their tragic and bloody experiences in this awful war. The death of children. The flattening of buildings and neighborhoods. The search for bodies under rubble. The starved search for food. The

---

[111] Instagram account of "Whispering Olive Trees", downloaded August 4, 2024, https://www.instagram.com/reel/C-NBqolxH43.
[112] Edo Konrad, "The 'pact of silence' between Israelis and their media," *+972 Magazine*, October 16, 2024, https://www.972mag.com/israeli-media-pact-of-silence-gaza/.

crumbling hospitals with the wounded and dead on the floor. The harrowing screams of survivors.

The story of Yussuf Abu Rabia Shizam stayed with me. The photos of his beautiful greenery and the love in his eyes as his fingers dug into the rich soil filled me with hope — only for a brief moment, as it turned out. Very brief. I was inspired to know that someone, somewhere, had a vision for the future that was full of life, and was succeeding to bring back life amid the destruction. And then in an instant, even that was gone.

I showed the video about him to a friend who also loves digging their fingers into soil and growing food from the ground. I thought they would relate to the young man and find a common joy. My friend watched the video without reaction. I said, "This man was killed yesterday in his home in Gaza." My friend continued to stare blankly. In addition to being an avid gardener, my friend is also a reserve soldier and a Zionist immigrant. I said, "No reaction?" They continued to stare blankly.

I thought to myself, this facial expression, or lack thereof, shows the depth of numbness that results from the dehumanization of the Other. My friend was unable or unwilling to see this person as a kindred spirit. Only as the "enemy". It was crushing.

I encounter this every day. In the supermarket, in the media, on Facebook, and pretty much everywhere I wander in my life in Israel, I find expressions that demonstrate the dehumanization of the Other. People I love sat on my couch laughing about flattening Gaza. When I said I don't accept that kind of language in my house, they stopped, but no doubt, only around me. The owner of my local grocery store, who I chat with often, once said to me as he was stocking broccoli in the freezer, "Kill them all." I looked at him in shock. He said, "Say 'Amen'! Why aren't you saying 'Amen'?" I asked, "Who is 'they'?" He turned away, with a barely hidden look of disgust, having discovered that I was, in his mind, siding with the enemy. A traitor. My doctor, too, is an enthusiastic

Bibi supporter, despite everything that has happened and everything we know. She is smart, kind, empathetic with her patients, and well-educated, and we have been friends for years. But when the conversation moves to politics, I feel like she becomes a different person. The endless compassion she shows her patients does not extend to Palestinians.

This is my life in Israel. We are all stuck in a discourse we did not create and that we are often unaware of being engulfed in. Signs throughout Israel read "Together we will win", even though there is no such thing as "together" or "we" or "winning". It's all a lie. A parking garage sign reads, "Only 47 spots left. 35 NIS per hour. Together we will win!". A billboard reads, "Our bank offers a special interest rate to new customers. Together we will win!". Driving on the highway, the overpass has photos of the hostages, signs calling for Bibi to resign, and an electronic sign that reads, "Light traffic ahead. Together we will win!". I wonder who pays for all these "Together we will win!" signs that effectively urge us to support an endless war. The Ministry of Transport? The local municipalities? The commerce office? I ponder this question as I listen to the news obsessively, wondering what disaster is happening right now as I walk or drive through this country. The headlines share names and details of the dead — dead Israelis, never dead Palestinians.

I often feel powerless against these forces. I go to rallies, I participate in communal conversations, I attend meetings and events, I engage in difficult and painful exchanges on social media, I share news and facts and perspectives, and I write incessantly. There is something profoundly demoralizing and deflating about going to protests week after week with hundreds of thousands of people and feeling like it has no impact. The government persistently ignores protesters, because the system allows it to. They answer only to themselves, to the need to keep coalition members happy. They do not have to answer to the citizens — the protesters are not their constituents, so they don't matter. The disempowerment is crushing.

For me, as an anthropologist who spends her life analyzing language and power, my greatest tool is my writing. I am intent on sharing and amplifying different words, an alternative set of linguistic tools to describe our world. I'm determined to reject the hierarchies imposed on us by those who hold power, and offer the world a language of compassion and humanity.

But that is not enough. As I've been learning.

# Women Mobilizing for War and Peace

Within days after October 7, I received a message from my friend Lola Rokni asking for urgent help.

Lola, a vivacious and gentle-spoken business consultant and coach, is an impressive woman. Barely a year earlier, Lola founded the Modi'in branch of the organization *Bonot Alternativa*, "Women Building an Alternative". Bonot was one of the leading groups in the pro-democracy camp that had cropped up in early 2023 right after the fifth round of Israeli elections that until then had led to prolonged lawlessness, the first one to result in a government coalition albeit a terrifying one. Bonot, along with a slew of other outraged groups, immediately began protesting the new Netanyahu government's plans to install authoritarian measures and radical religious practice into Israeli governance that threaten the long-term sustainability of Israel democracy, such as it was.[113] Every Saturday night since the government formation, the groups would gather on Kaplan Street in Tel Aviv as well in a dozen smaller locations around the country, demanding that the government abandon its obnoxious plans.[114] Bonot,

---

[113] Patrick Kingsley and Isabel Kershner, "The Israeli Government's Plan to Overhaul the Judiciary: What to Know", *The New York Times*, March 29, 2023, https://www.nytimes.com/article/israel-judiciary-crisis-explainer.html.

[114] Patrick Kingsley, "Mass Protests Over Government's Court Plans Sweep Israel", *The New York Times*, March 9, 2023,

as opposed to the other groups, presented a feminist approach to the threats posed by the government, emphasizing religious aspirations to control women's bodies and personal status.[115] The Bonot signature protest was the handmaiden's tale march – that is, women would line up wearing the red robes and white caps made famous by author Margaret Atwood and would march silently through the street during the weekly Saturday night anti-government rallies.[116] These artistic demonstrations gained national and even international attention – and Margaret Atwood herself tweeted about this, calling it "astonishing".[117]

Bonot very quickly amassed a following of tens of thousands of women across Israel, in large part due to the jarring visibility of the red-robe marches, and also in large part due to the hard work of women like Lola who took it upon herself to establish a local branch of Bonot.[118] Bonot counts

---

https://www.nytimes.com/2023/03/09/world/middleeast/israel-judicial-protests-netanyahu.html?s .

[115] TOI Staff, "Anti-overhaul protesters rally for women's rights outside religious courts", *Times of Israel,* July 18, 2023, https://www.timesofisrael.com/anti-overhaul-protesters-rally-for-womens-rights-outside-religious-courts/.

[116] Naama Riba, "Why Are These Israeli Protesters Dressed Up Like 'The Handmaid's Tale?'", *Haaretz,* March 1, 2023, https://www.haaretz.com/israel-news/2023-03-01/ty-article/.premium/why-are-these-israeli-protesters-dressed-up-like-the-handmaids-tale/00000186-9d65-df48-ab96-bd65cc790000.

[117] Haaretz Staff, 'Astonishing': Atwood Responds to 'The Handmaid's Tale' Becoming Israeli Protest Symbol, *Haaretz,* Mar 18, 2023, https://www.haaretz.com/israel-news/2023-03-18/ty-article/.premium/astonishing-atwood-responds-to-the-handmaids-tale-becoming-israeli-protest-symbol/00000186-f5ae-dd8e-a7d7-f7ef02e90000.

[118] In case you're curious about this: Yes, I did once don the red-robe costume and cap and march with the group. But I found it very difficult to place myself in that posture of the submissive, silent, faceless religious woman. I feel like I've lived bits of that character in real life, not in a dystopian future, and have spent so much of my life undoing it all that I could not bring myself to do it again, even as a theatrical protest. (You can read more about that

dozens of branches around Israel – all since early 2023. The Modi'in branch, which was so successful that it was reported in the *Washington Post*[119] and which the national organization sees as its prototype for local organization, is a result of Lola's tirelessness and leadership skills.

One pre-war highlight of Bonot's work took place On International Women's Day, March 8, 2023, when an estimated 20,000 women created a human chain in dozens of cities all around Israel, all of us wearing red t-shirts that had become the symbol of the movement.[120] I had never seen so many feminist women turn out in Modi'in – at least 5,000 women lines the streets in red that day – and couldn't help wondering where they had been hiding all these years! From my experience of having been an active feminist protester since the late 1990s. I am fairly certain that this was the largest ever Women's Day protest in Israel, by leaps and bounds.[121] It was, frankly, a moment.[122]

---

in my book, *Conversations with my Body*.) After that experience, I continued to protest, but not as one of the Bonot performers. Indeed, many feminists have criticized the organization's tactics for turning women into something we are not and do not aspire to be, as if the red robes send the wrong message. Nevertheless, the protest clearly had its intended effect. The red robe protests made headlines for months and undoubtedly kept the issues of democracy and women's rights in the public discourse.

[119] Steve Hendrix, "Israel's massive democracy movement is ready for war", *Washington Post,* October 24, 2023, https://www.washingtonpost.com/world/2023/10/24/israel-democracy-protesters-war-aid/.

[120] Reuters, "Israeli women form human chains to protest planned judicial overhaul," March 8, 2023, *Ynetnews,* https://www.ynetnews.com/article/hy1smwl1n .

[121] Tal Meidan, "Women Are Leading Israel's Biggest-ever Protest Movement," *Haaretz,* Mar 22, 2023, https://www.haaretz.com/opinion/2023-03-22/ty-article-opinion/.premium/women-are-leading-israels-biggest-ever-protest-movement/00000187-09f8-d1cf-a7af-fdf8d66f0000.

[122] To be fair the Women's Day protest in March 2023 was not the largest feminist protest in Israel's history. That distinction goes to the protest in December 2018 when 100,000 people – women and

And then, eleven months after these protests began – at the height of anti-government momentum in which approximately half a million Israelis were showing up to Kaplan Street in Tel Aviv every Saturday night – the war broke out.

I am not sure if the world outside of Kaplan fully appreciates what a relief this war was for Bibi. Within moments, the protest movement dissipated.[123] In fact, a large portion of protesters quickly donned their army uniforms and scooted off to battle.[124] Even Bibi's most die-hard opponents on the street stood down from their positions and reported for duty.[125] The soldiers did this despite incessant attacks by members of Netanyahu's government calling them traitors and anarchists, and in some cases called for them to be thrown in jail.[126] General Yair Golan, for example, one of the protest

---

men – went on a single day strike on behalf of victims of sexual assault and domestic violence. That event was a response to the government's years-long delay in transferring an allocated 250 million NIS to organizations working on this issue. That protest was impressive for sure; the fact that many companies had given permission to their workers to participate helped. But it did not lead to any kind of movement or mass mobilization that way the work of Bonot did. Also, it took yet another few years for that funding to eventually get transferred.

[123] Adam Sella, "Large Antigovernment Protest Returns to Tel Aviv, as Criticism of Netanyahu Mounts." *The New York Times*, Feb. 17, 2024, https://www.nytimes.com/2024/02/17/world/middleeast/tel-aviv-protest-netanyahu-israel.html.

[124] Isabel Kershner, "Back From War, Reserve Soldiers Set Their Sights on Israel's Politics as Usual," *The New York Times*, Feb. 28, 2024, https://www.nytimes.com/2024/02/28/world/middleeast/israel-reserve-soldiers-gaza.html .

[125] Eetta Prince-Gibson, "Israel's protest movement caught between anger and solidarity," *Jewish Independent*, March 9, 2024, https://thejewishindependent.com.au/israels-protest-movement-caught-between-anger-and-solidarity.

[126] Shira Rubin, "Politicians called them 'traitors.' Now they're manning Israel's home front," *Washington Post*, October 15, 2023,

movement leaders who has since become the head of the Labor Party which then merged with Meretz to become the Democratic Party, immediately went into action and drove down to rescue party-goers from the Nova festival.[127] Picture this: Only weeks early, hundreds of reservists led by an organization called Brothers in Arms had signed a petition declaring that they would refuse to serve under this administration. And then, right after October 7, the organization declared a pause to its protest activity and urged all the signatories to report for duty – which, apparently, most did without hesitation.[128] This war was such good news for Bibi's political position that in his very first public statement following the October 7 attack, his first comments were an almost gleeful emphasis on, "solidarity." As if to say, we're all okay now because criticism is gone. *Everyone is now behind me as I lead this war.* It was code for: All those protests are finished.[129] And then, by the way, the war slogan actually became "Together we will win", words plastered all over Israel. Ending public opposition to the government was at

---

https://www.washingtonpost.com/world/2023/10/14/israel-brothers-in-arms-gaza-border/ .

[127] Mary Louise Kelly, Erika Ryan, Linah Mohammad, and Courtney Dorning, "For this Israeli general, the horror of Oct. 7 meant a return to the battlefield," *NPR*, November 7, 2023, https://www.npr.org/2023/11/07/1211329918/for-this-israeli-general-the-horror-of-oct-7-meant-a-return-to-the-battlefield.

[128] Steven Erlanger and Natan Odenheimer, "They Refused to Serve. Now They're Supporting Israel's War Effort," *The New York Times,* Oct. 29, 2023, https://www.nytimes.com/2023/10/29/world/europe/israel-reservists-hamas-war.html.

[129] Herb Keinon, "Israeli solidarity stays strong one month after Hamas-Israel war," *Jerusalem Post*, November 11, 2023, https://www.jpost.com/arab-israeli-conflict/gaza-news/article-772568.

least as important – perhaps even moreso – that "winning", whatever that even means.[130]

Back to my friend Lola. Like so many others in Israel, Bonot quickly pivoted away from its political activity towards the war. Within two days, Lola was mobilizing support for families displaced from the south, many of whom had landed in Modi'in. Lola wrote to me and to many others asking for assistance collecting food, clothing, baby supplies, furniture, linens, medications, and more. By the end of October, Lola had secured the donation of an empty house (the family had temporarily relocated pending renovations) and had transformed the house into Bonot Modi'in Command Central. A team of volunteers went into full gear organization supplies and equipment, and making rosters for volunteers. I found myself spending hours cleaning out closets and sending my husband on trips back and forth to the Bonot house, depending on the request of the day. One day it may have been school supplies; another day there was a request for dolls; another day it was plus-size clothing. Like everyone else in the country, I was on the home front, mobilized to take care of civilians left behind.

Some of those civilians were my children and grandchildren, by the way, who had also been displaced from their homes in the south. We were extremely fortunate to be able to take care of them all, though we had support from dear friends for whom I am eternally grateful. My husband and I found ourselves running a "Grandparents day care center" for two months, as were countless others in Modi'in and elsewhere. We used to make jokes with the other grandparents we regularly met in the parks about how the country was now dependent on us for daily functioning. This was apparently such a common situation that a local Whatsapp group formed

---

[130] Joel Carmel, "'Together We Will'...Speak the Truth. Only Then Can We 'Win.'" *Jewschool,* April 11, 2024, https://jewschool.com/together-we-will-speak-the-truth-only-then-can-we-win-174196.

of Grandparents on the Front. (You know it's a real trend when there is a Whatsapp group for it.)

During those first one or two months, almost everyone we knew in Israel was in a state of shocked-mobilization. We were all trying to recover from the horrendous attack – especially those who personally knew people who were killed, injured, displaced, or taken hostage – and at the same time many of us also had loved ones in army service. There was very little criticism of the war in those early days, even as some of knew exactly where we were headed. Even if we were feeling wrong about the war, we weren't saying it out loud. At least not at first.

And then something started to shift. A few months into the war, I was invited to a group called *Imahot Zoakot*, Mothers Screaming Out. This was a group of mothers of IDF soldiers who were starting to speak openly about their doubts about the war and its unclear goals. Many soldiers were being killed and injured, included a large number from "accidents" or so-called "friendly fire".[131] Reports were coming out about sloppiness, bad decision making, and a lack of proper equipment.[132] Tens of millions of dollars were being raised from around the world for IDF equipment – including basics, such as helmets and bulletproof vests, which should have needed to be supplied via philanthropic donations.[133] Israeli

---

[131] Fatma Tanis, "Friendly fire and accidents have killed a lot of Israeli soldiers in Gaza. Here's why." *NPR* January 26, 2024 https://www.npr.org/2024/01/26/1226977365/israel-idf-gaza-middle-east-deaths.

[132] Emanuel Fabian, "IDF: Deaths of 29 of 170 soldiers in Gaza op were so-called friendly fire, accidents," *Times of Israel*, January 1, 2024 https://www.timesofisrael.com/idf-deaths-of-29-of-170-soldiers-in-gaza-op-were-so-called-friendly-fire-accidents/.

[133] Judah Ari Gross, "Does the IDF need donations of equipment? It's complicated. The military is unequivocal that there are no major shortages, so why are units still asking for gear?" *EJewish Philanthropy*, October 12, 2023, https://ejewishphilanthropy.com/does-the-idf-need-donations-of-equipment-its-complicated/.

soldier mothers, who are typically relegated to a role of silent acquiescence, were angry, frustrated, and terrified for their children – and breaking their silence.[134]

This was new. And it also went against the grain. After all, the purpose of the donations to IDF soldiers was not only to supply equipment but to mobilize world Jewry in support of the war. Fundraising campaigns played on old fears and language of existential threats to get the world behind Bibi. Together we will win. The slogan was showing up everywhere – on street signs, on massive highway banners, on parking garages, on buildings, on malls, and in dozens if not hundreds of global fundraising campaigns. The messages were emotional pleas for unquestioning and unwavering support.[135]

*Give money and also, don't criticize Israel.*[136]

And this evolved into a massive worldwide campaign of supporting Israel against all attack.

The mothers of soldiers were fighting against all that. It was a hard battle to win, even if our children were on the line. Still they grew.

That was just the beginning. Over the course of the next six months, a whole slew of women's organiztations – especially mothers' organizations -- were created. *Ima Era* ("Mother Awake"),[137] *Za'akat Ha'imahot* (Mothers' Cries),[138]

---

[134] Elana Sztokman, "Israeli mothers like me are fed up with having our children used as cannon fodder," *JTA*, May 29, 2024, https://www.jta.org/2024/05/29/ideas/israeli-mothers-like-me-are-fed-up-with-having-our-children-used-as-cannon-fodder .

[135] Roy Schwartz, "Israelis Need to Update Their Mantra 'Together We Will Win'", *Haaretz*, Jan 25, 2024, https://www.haaretz.com/opinion/2024-01-25/ty-article-opinion/.premium/can-israelis-win-together-against-dangers-lurking-at-home/0000018d-3ca3-d35c-a39f-befbb1d50000.

[136] Mickey Gitzin, "Buying into 'Together We Win' Means We All Lose," *NIF*, Jul 30, 2024, https://nifcan.org/buying-into-together-we-win-means-we-all-lose/.

[137] https://www.imaera.org.il/

[138] https://www.facebook.com/groups/crymothers/

*Imahot Bahazit* (Mothers on the Front),[139] *Horim Zoakim Dai* ("Parents Screaming Enough),[140] *Imahot Neged Alimut*,[141] and others. I found myself in so many Whatsapp groups that my phone was on fire all day long.

The groups started to overlap. Messages and conversations fed into each other. People started to wonder if there was a need for so many groups. Then some differences began to emerge. While one group emphatically called for an immediate ceasefire and return of hostages, another dedicated its energies to ensuring that ultra-Orthodox young men would be forced into the draft so that Israel would have enough manpower to "win". Some groups included men (hence the name "parents" that was changed from its original "mothers"), while others did not. Some groups encouraged all women to join, not just mothers, while others had strict entry rules about "soldier mothers only". While "Mothers against nonviolence", for example, is for both Jewish and Palestinian women, many others were formed for Jewish mothers only. And while many organizations are open and flexible and eager to include women who are not mothers as well as men and non-binary participants, others are stricter about their intended membership.

The diversity of definitions around "women's organizating" is not always easy to navigate – which should perhaps be obvious. Women, like all other humans, are complex and dynamic and being one does not automatically dictate a predictable political outlook. Still, this reality can be hard. To wit, I had a difficult experience trying to recruit help for Arab single mothers in Jaffa. One of the immediate byproducts of the war was discrimination against Arab

---

[139] https://www.imahot.org/
[140] https://zoha.org.il/
[141] https://www.mavisrael.com/

workers throughout Israel.[142] Several mayors announced on October 8 that they would fire all Arab municipal workers – without any self-consciousness about the racism involved, not to mention the illegality of such measures.[143] Certainly legal aid organizations went into high gear to fight this reality, but this, too, was an uphill battle given all that was going on.[144] A particular group of Arab women were especially vulnerable to these measures: that is, women wearing hijab. Their visibility often made women in hijab an immediate target. My friend, Maha, a lifelong peace activist and resident of Jaffa who continues to fight for justice and shared society despite having experienced many traumas in her life, was physically attacked right near her house by a group of yeshivah students shouting Ben Gvir-esque slogans. The threats to Palestinian and Muslim women following the war were very real – and very far from any kind of larger cultural consciousness or national agenda.[145]

One day, I was approached by another Muslim friend, Liza, whose organization offered assistance for single mothers in Jaffa who were struggling due to the war. Liza, herself a mother of seven, the youngest of whom was born on October

---

[142] Adam Asad, "What's it like being an Arab-Israeli after October 7", *Ynetnews*, November 15, 2023, https://www.ynetnews.com/article/rjkpezg4p.

[143] Hilo Glazer and Itay Mashiach, "'Systematic Witch Hunt:' What Persecution of Arab-Israelis Looks Like Amid Gaza War," *Haaretz*, Nov 2, 2023, https://www.haaretz.com/israel-news/2023-11-02/ty-article-magazine/.highlight/systematic-witch-hunt-what-persecution-of-israeli-arabs-looks-like-amid-gaza-war/0000018b-90db-db7e-af9b-fbdb254e0000 .

[144] Layla Gantus, "The Many Civil and Human Rights Challenges Facing Israel's Palestinian Citizens," *Carnegie Foundation*, February 28, 2024, https://carnegieendowment.org/posts/2024/02/the-many-civil-and-human-rights-challenges-facing-israels-palestinian-citizens?lang=en.

[145] Joanie Margulies, "Increased tensions, identity struggles: How Givat Haviva helped Arab Israelis cope post Oct. 7," *Jerusalem Post*, October 24, 2024, https://www.jpost.com/israel-news/article-825666 .

7 itself, is also a firebrand. While Lola was mobilizing the community of Modi'in to support displaced women and families, Liza was mobilizing her own community in Jaffa to support struggling mothers. When Liza approached me, I began to make calls. Lola was very supportive of Liza's efforts while noting that there are no non-Jews living in Modi'in and thus helping Jaffa women was not likely on the community's radar. I raised some money and kept making calls. But unlike Lola, many Israeli women's organizations were not interested in supporting Palestinian women at the time. It was too far from their "agenda" at the time. It was also partially an issue of capacity. As more than one woman said to me, "I don't have any energy or bandwidth to even think about Arab women in Israel."

Those were the better responses. Others wondered why I would even care about Arab women in Israel. "They're all terrorists", was not an uncommon sentiment. Things like that.

Over the course of this war, these sentiments seem to be shifting and going in waves and at times in opposing pulls, like a tug of war over our views and sympathies.

I would argue that there are two concurrent trends happening in Israel. On the one hand, the war turned many people "two steps to the right", as common wisdom has it. Even many of my longtime peace activist friends seemed to be struggling at times. Some criticized Palestinian citizens of Israel weren't speaking out about the horrors of October 7 (ignoring the fact that many were, and that pro-Israel sentiment among Palestinian citizens of Israel had *increased* since October 7).[146] Other Israelis expressed feelings of being uncomfortable in mixed groups, as if to suggest that solidarity with Palestinians is no longer an option for them.

---

[146] Adam Asad, "What's it like being an Arab-Israeli after October 7", *Ynetnews*, November 15, 2023, https://www.ynetnews.com/article/rjkpezg4p

Certainly, Israeli political leaders seem to be validating the sense that the country is moving not only two steps the right but much further in that direction. We have witnessed many disturbing expressions of racism from even the highest locations of power. The International Court of Justice at the Hague chronicled many of these for the world to see and hear during deliberations over whether Israel has legally committed genocide against the Palestinians in Gaza.[147] That was an intensely shaming moment for the Jewish people and for Israel, even as the government tried to deny that these things were said, or as President Herzog tried to claim, that racist statements or calls for ethnic cleansing were merely "pulled out of context". Those are hard claims to maintain considering that the government is actively pursuing plans to settle Gaza with Jewish towns, after having completely razed Palestinian cities. These are chilling realities happening as this book goes to print.

At the same time, many groups are challenging these trends with opposing actions. The organization Standing Together organizes aid convoys for Gaza in which hundreds of trucks are loaded with supplies donated by Israelis who are deeply concerned about the people of Gaza. My friend Rabbi Haviva Ner David regularly participates in these donation campaigns, which she chronicles on social media and elsewhere.[148] She optimistically reports that everyone involved

---

[147] Tia Goldenberg, "Harsh Israeli rhetoric against Palestinians becomes central to South Africa's genocide case," *AP News,* January 18, 2024, https://apnews.com/article/israel-palestinians-south-africa-genocide-hate-speech-97a9e4a84a3a6bebeddfb80f8a030724.; "Database of Israeli Incitement to Genocide," *Law for Palestine,* January 15, 2024, https://law4palestine.org/wp-content/uploads/2024/02/Database-of-Israeli-Incitement-to-Genocide-including-after-ICJ-order-27th-February-2024-.pdf.
[148] Haviva Ner-David, "Jews and Arabs hoped to fill a truck with aid for Gaza civilians. We ended up filling 300," *JTA,* August 26, 2024, https://www.jta.org/2024/08/26/ideas/jews-and-arabs-

is overwhelmed by the sheer mass of support demonstrated for the people of Gaza. So that is happening. Similarly, while I was helping my friend Liza gather support for the women of Jaffa and encountering mixed reactions, a mixed group of Jews and Palestinians were actively organizing in the southern Bedouin town of Rahat, collecting aid for both Jews and Palestinians who were struggling with displacement, injury, and trauma. The Rahat headquarters for those activities was established as a direct result of reflective conversations around the country about the need for shared society.[149] Calls for a new vision emerging from all corners urged forth collaborative, creative efforts towards real change.

I would also like to point out that some of my Palestinian friends take issue with these accusations. "We were also mourning October 7," one dear friend from the north has said to me numerous times. "It was a horrible massacre. We felt it, too. But before we could even take a breath, Gaza was already under attack. We were in this terrible situation, mourning losses from all sides. And against that backdrop, Israelis are looking at us as if we are terrorists. We are in an impossible position." I have also heard Palestinian citizens of Israel complain that no matter how often or how loudly they condemned the Hamas acts of October 7, it never seems to be enough.[150]

So that is happening too.

Meanwhile, there is also movement in the other direction. While most people believe that the country has taken two

---

hoped-to-fill-a-truck-with-aid-for-gaza-civilians-we-ended-up-filling-300.

[149] Carole Nuriel, "Arab sraeli mobilization and solidarity in response to the Hamas massacre," *Times of Israel Blogs,* Nov 21, 2023, https://blogs.timesofisrael.com/arab-israeli-mobilization-and-solidarity-in-response-to-the-hamas-massacre/.

[150] Dr. Adam Asad, Yaron Kaplan, "Most Arab Israelis: October 7 Attack Does Not Reflect Islamic, Palestinian, or Arab Society Values," *Israel Democracy Institute,* December 26, 2023, https://en.idi.org.il/articles/52016 .

steps to the right, I think that many of us have taken two steps to the left. I know I have. My peace activism has never felt more urgent. And I know I'm not alone. The half a dozen or so women-led peace initiatives are growing. Nearly every week I read about a new initiative, and I am added to a new Whatsapp group. In July, a new coalition of some fifty organizations held a massive gathering in Tel Aviv to revive the peace movement and establish a positive vision.[151] Also, more and more groups are conscious of the need to have Palestinians and Jews together in leadership roles, and to see equal representation around the table. Itach Maaki – Women Lawyers for Social Justice[152], an organization I have been involved with for over a decade, recently turned to a co-leadership model with two directors, one Jewish and one Palestinian. Other groups are now running on similar models: A Land for All,[153] Standing Together,[154] and Combatants for Peace,[155] for example, all have co-leadership models, and five out of six of the co-directors in those three organizations are women. I'm sure there are more.

That said, on the national level, women are still far from being at the center of decision making. Certainly, feminist women who believe in shared society, non-violence, and democracy, are not yet having the kind of impact that they should.

That's where the work of the Forum 1325 comes in.

---

[151] Charlie Summers, "At Tel Aviv confab, Israel's embattled peace camp seeks to revive itself post-Oct. 7," *Times of Israel*, July 2, 2024, https://www.timesofisrael.com/at-tel-aviv-confab-israels-embattled-peace-camp-seeks-to-revive-itself-post-oct-7/.
[152] https://www.itach.org.il
[153] https://www.alandforall.org/english/?d=ltr
[154] https://www.standing-together.org/en
[155] https://cfpeace.org/

# Partnering With Eva

Eva Dalak is a Palestinian citizen of Israel born in Jaffa to a family that lived there for generations. In April 1948, after the Deir Yassin massacre in which Jewish forces killed over 100 Palestinian residents in cold blood in one of hundreds of "depopulated" villages,[156] her family was terrified of being attacked as well. They got on a boat to escape — temporarily, they hoped — heading to Gaza and Nablus. All except her grandmother, who was nine months pregnant at the time. As her grandmother got onto the boat, she went into labor. She got off the boat, turned back to Jaffa, and gave birth to Eva's mother on May 5, 1948. As luck would have it, that is how Eva, born 26 years later, came to be born in Jaffa as a citizen of Israel while most of her mother's family were refugees living in Gaza.

Eva's family is Muslim, but she attended a French Jesuit school in Israel, then studied political science at a university in Paris. She worked for the United Nations and lived around the world before settling in Costa Rica with her spouse and two children. Eva has been working in conflict transformation for twenty-five years, has been to twenty-two conflict zones, speaks many languages, and is a big believer in the importance of women's leadership. She travels back and forth to Israel/Palestine to continue her work as a consultant and a proponent of peace activation.

I have heard Eva tell this story several times. She often shares it on the podcast we started together during this war.

---

[156] Noga Kadman, *Erased from Space and Consciousness: Israel and the Depopulated Palestinian Villages of 1948* (Indiana University Press, 2015).

The podcast, called "Women Ending War", is a determined effort to change our reality and end this violence.

Eva and I met on Zoom in February 2024. She was consulting for a women's coalition I am active in called Forum 1325 for Political Agreement,[157] a group working to advance systemic solutions to the ongoing conflict while advancing women's leadership and perspectives. The group is built on the premise of United Nations Security Council Resolution 1325 (UNSCR 1325) that calls for women's leadership and involvement in all areas of peace and negotiation, as well as the insistence on gendered perspectives about issues such as definitions of security.[158] Our group sought Eva's guidance about getting women a seat at the table in decision-making about this war in an effort to create a different reality. I found Eva to be amazing, insightful, wise, articulate, and broad-minded.

For a long time, I wanted to host a podcast to share my ideas, mostly about gender but also about politics, culture, and language. My plans kept getting derailed by events around me. But as this war progressed, and all the "Together we will win" signs engulfed me and obfuscated the truth about the bloodshed and violence, I decided it was time for me to focus on the war. I asked Eva to partner with me, and she agreed. I also approached a donor who generously funded us, and off we went. We began recording Season 1 in June and July of 2024, and Season 2 in September and October.

A core aspect of what we are trying to accomplish is to always incorporate diverse voices. We try to have Palestinian and Jewish women in every episode, though it does not always work out that way. I definitely do not want to be in a situation where we only have Israeli Jews in the studio. That

---

[157] https://www.youtube.com/@1325forum

[158] https://www.un.org/womenwatch/osagi/wps/; United States Institute of Peace, *What is UNSCR 1325?* https://www.usip.org/gender_peacebuilding/about_UNSCR_132 5 .

feels like it would defeat the purpose, or put me in a patronizing position of telling someone else's story on their behalf. Perhaps this might have certain value as well — creating allies, putting myself in someone else's shoes — but as a woman who fought my whole life to be heard, I really don't want to block someone else from speaking their own truth in their own way. So that's the setting we try to create.

We also try to create an atmosphere of holding space, even when it's hard. This means allowing people to tell their life stories without arguing or correcting them. Palestinians on the podcast may use words like "genocide", "ethnic cleansing", and "colonialism", and I never challenge or try to "correct" the usage of these terms, despite all that Zionist upbringing that trained me to do exactly that. I practice what I learned from my friends in Nonviolent Communication: *connect before you correct*. It's a radical concept though it shouldn't be, about letting another person tell their story and just listening. By holding that space, I am actively rejecting that Bibi-esque and Tomer-like behavior that expects us to debate and badger until we "win". I am letting go of that entire persona, the one that is supposed to have the last word and school everyone around me in the sound bites about Jewish moral superiority, Zionist righteousness, and the need to quash all criticism. Just sitting there and listening is a kind of corrective measure — for me and possibly for others around the table.

This is not always easy. There are moments that shake me. Sometimes Palestinians say things that make me wonder if they think all Jews should leave. (I wonder what the people holding "Free Palestine" signs thought about what to do with eight million Israeli Jews). As a mother of IDF soldiers, I find it difficult to hear Palestinians' particular hatred of soldiers, even as I understand their pain. Israelis have mandatory conscription, and average soldiers have very little say in what they are expected to do. Opting out of that service in Israel is complicated and comes with serious social, cultural, and economic consequences. Also, many soldiers are motivated by values of service, honor, protection, and devotion to their people. Generalizations about IDFsoldiers are just as problematic as generalizations about any other group. Just as I would not accept anyone saying, "All Gazans are.....", I also don't accept statements that "All IDF soldiers are...." And I especially don't like hearing that so many people in the world consider them to be monsters. *Those are my kids we're talking about.* Despite everything happening, it feels like an unhelpful, grandiose, radical position that does not promote peace.

Still, some women refuse to sit at a table with mothers of soldiers. A Palestinian woman named Amal from East Jerusalem told me at my woman's dialogue group a few years ago that if her family knew that she was sitting around the table with soldiers' mothers, they would disown her. That was very hard. Even as I reject my indoctrination, I still live in my real world with real people whom I refuse to classify as bad. Israelis do not deserve to be generalized, stereotyped, or dehumanized any more than Palestinians do. Sometimes, it's a tightrope walk for me.

But these exchanges are also encouraging, because, after all, Amal showed up. Eva shows up. We are all still talking. And if I can be fully present in the process of reversing the dehumanization of Palestinians, maybe I'll get lucky and the world will stop dehumanizing my children.

There are other tough moments for me. Many interviewees take for granted that the history of the region can be defined as one of colonialism and ethnic cleansing, that the current war is undeniably a form of genocide, that Palestinians are the real indigenous people, and that this entire land is Palestine. Even though I still struggle with some of this — for example, I think the word "colonialism" is a misnomer; Jews are not the British Empire and we are actually arguably indigenous, even if we were mostly absent for 2,000 years — I usually take a position of listening. I understand why Palestinians use the term "colonialism" to describe Zionist actions of taking over entire villages and replacing them with

Jewish settlements. The Zionist takeover of Palestinian land has been violent and appalling, and the Israeli government is still doing it. I drive through Israel looking at signs of towns and cities and think about how many Palestinians were driven out of those places in order for Israel to exist. Maybe I am a colonialist, too. Maybe I *should* go back to Brooklyn, I sometimes think. But I can't and won't advocate for that kind of Jewish population transfer as a remedy to accusations of colonialism. A solution has to deal with the reality, and the people whose lives are here right now. There has to be another way. But it's painful. And I know I am complicit in Palestinians' pain. If the word "colonialism" is hard for me to hear, I need to deal with it and face the troubling truth about our history.

And there's the genocide thing. In our very first exchange in our very first episode, Eva used the word "genocide". I knew it would make many Jews cringe, or worse — yell and call me names and cluster me with antisemites and terrorists. I did not argue with Eva's use of the word, say it's not true, or defend Israel. I sat with it, held space, and listened. Eva has lost many family members in Gaza, as have other guests on our podcast. And I am certainly not going to tell Palestinians whose families are being relentlessly bombed that they are not experiencing ethnic cleansing or genocide. We've had several conversations and posts about the use of the word genocide in which I explain why I believe it is so important for Jews and Israelis to listen to this and to understand why Palestinians are calling their experiences genocide. What Israel is doing in Gaza is appalling and we should be acknowledging that, period, with whatever language works to express the awfulness of it.

The entire exercise with Eva is an experiment in shared society and shared humanity. Can we sit and be present with each other's truths and life stories, and still share the space or even live on the same land without violence? Despite our vastly different experiences, can we have a conversation in which both our lived experiences are valid? Is that possible? Our studio is a microcosm where we attempt to answer these questions.

# Revisiting October 7

On the first anniversary of October 7, Eva and I went on a field trip to the Gaza rim. I wanted to talk about that day and face it head on. Eva wanted to talk about the history that led to that day. She always says that October 7 did not start anything but rather brought a history dating back to 1947 into the living rooms of Israelis. I understand the importance of context. After all, Seyla Benhabib writes in her book *Situating the Self* about the importance of context in humanizing the Other.[159] Her theory about the generalized other and the concrete other describes how the people with whom we identify merit details such as names, history, and context in order to receive our empathy, while the people with whom we do not want to identify are generalized without any details or individuality. Thus, context is an important part of humanizing the Other, which is why I appreciate Eva's insistence on context. (It is worth noting that when the UN Secretary General said that there is a "context" to October 7, he was chastised by Israel and the pro-Israel community.[160] It is also worth noting that every time Israel is criticized for its actions in Gaza, Israel insists on bringing up the "context" of October 7.[161] Let's call that the "politics of context").

---

[159] Seyla Benhabib, *Situating the Self: Gender, Community, and Postmodernism in Contemporary Ethics* (Routledge, 1992).
[160] Patrick Wintour, "UN chief 'shocked' by 'misrepresentation' of comments in row with Israel," *The Guardian*, October 26, 2023, https://www.theguardian.com/world/2023/oct/25/israel-says-it-will-ban-un-staff-after-secretary-generals-comments.
[161] Dov Waxman, "Jewish response to Hamas war criticism comes from deep sense of trauma, active grief and fear," *The Conversation*, October 30, 2023, https://theconversation.com/jewish-response-

While I fully appreciate Eva's need to remind us of context, part of me also really wants October 7 to stand on its own. I think Israelis need a moment of mourning. Just as I want to take a moment to mourn the Palestinian experiences of 1947-48, I think that Israelis also deserve that in this moment. October 7 was too big of an event to be automatically lumped in with seventy-five years of regional history.

We went to the Gaza rim in search of both these things — my need for the Israeli pain of October 7 to be seen, and Eva's need to underline the context leading up to October 7. Could we do both these things at the same time, in the same moment?

We went to the Nova festival memorial site, where 364 party-goers were massacred. We walked through the memorial, taking it all in. Eva had an herbal remedy she brought with her specifically for this ritual and she sprinkled it on the ground. "The land is screaming out for peace," she said. We spent a moment just feeling the pain of the massacre. It was an important moment of connection for us, of mutual empathy and shared humanity. This was Eva's first time in the region since she was a child, and perhaps she was reluctant to go there. But she did it and faced it. We were both present with the enormity of what happened there.

And then, *boom*.

Literally, *boom*. As we stood there talking about the dream of peace, we heard the shattering blasts behind us. I told Eva what they were. "That's us bombing Gaza." She had no idea. She had never actually been to the Gaza rim during a war. I have, many times, and I was familiar with the experience of hearing the IDF bombing Gaza. We stood there for a moment taking it in.

Then, another boom. Those booms were so loud. They shook your bones, your skull, the earth beneath your feet. And they masked what we don't want to see. Right now, lives are being utterly destroyed.

We did that. Israel. The IDF. The 3,000-year-old Jewish people. Whatever. We are still doing it. A year after the Nova massacre, Israel is still killing in Gaza. More than 45,000 deaths later.

Oh, and the hostages. As I write this, there are still 100 hostages in Gaza. Also under those blasts. With nobody saving them.

We wanted Nova to be a memorial, as if this is something from the past that must be grappled with. But it's not in the *past*. It is all still in the *present*. Very much in the present.

If I think about it too much, I may find myself completely crumbling. Instead, I take note, take it in, take a breath, and move on.

We got into the car to drive to our next stop. Eva was saying something to me, but I couldn't hear her. I needed some time for my bones to settle back into their sockets.

We drove fifteen kilometers north of the Nova festival memorial to meet Roni Keidar, an 80-year-old Jewish peace activist from Netiv HaAsara, one of the villages on the Gaza rim that was badly hit on October 7. Roni lost friends, family, and neighbors that day, as well as her home of fifty years. We met her in her latest temporary shelter where she had been living for a month.

Roni shared her life story with us. Born in the UK in 1944, she moved to Israel in 1951 and considers it her only home. She married an Egyptian Jewish man, moved to Sinai, then moved to Netiv HaAsara in 1981 after the Sinai Peninsula was given to Egypt in exchange for peace. Her family spent a few years in Egypt on behalf of the Israeli government, where she became involved in interfaith peace work. Back in Israel, she worked with Palestinians in Rafah and made many friends in Gaza whom she trusted. Although one friend turned on her on October 7, the rest did not. Many of her neighbors described feeling betrayed by Gazans they worked with, but Roni said she did not. Her friends are not terrorists, she said.

Curious to know her thoughts about Palestinian experiences and narratives, we asked Roni what she thought about what was going on in Gaza. She replied, "Well, some people talk about the question of proportionality…"

This answer was unexpected. After all, after 45,000 killings, what might be "proportional"? Only 30,000? Only 20,000? Maybe only 5,000 babies and children instead of 12,000? I was taken aback by this. It was hard to hear Roni's answer, even in my space of "connect before you correct".

Still, I did that. I held space.

Eva, on the other hand, could not sit still. She decided to interrupt Roni and tell her own life story. She began to share her family's experiences since 1947. This visibly changed Roni's posture. She fell silent, leaned in a bit, and mostly stopped sharing her own story. It was a tense moment. Clearly Roni was struggling with Eva's story and wasn't expecting the conversation to go there. Weren't we talking about October 7, not all that "context"? At the same time, Eva was struggling with Roni's narrative, which did not make room for Gazans' experiences since October 7, nor for Palestinians' experiences of Diaspora Jews making Israel their home in the first years of statehood, as Roni did in 1951. It was challenging.

Still, we got through it. Just barely. I reached out to Roni after the interview, and she was clearly shaken, not ready to engage with someone else's trauma while she was still so embroiled in her own. I think she may still be angry at me, feeling like I somehow ambushed her. I didn't mean to, but I understand why it could have felt that way. The conversation was supposed to be about Roni and October 7, yet we ended up centering it elsewhere. And Eva — well, I think she may not be so happy with me either. Roni's ideas weren't what she was expecting. Eva listened for as long as she could, until she couldn't anymore. Once again, she felt she was facing a situation in which her family was rendered invisible, a sidenote of sorts in someone else's narrative.

Still, we ended the day with smiles and kindnesses, resting on our shared belief in peace and a deep desire to create an alternative reality in which we are all free to live as human beings, though the path toward that reality remains unclear.

# Women's Inclusion and Leadership

And the war rages on.

Three facts stand out about the post-October 7 war: It is the longest war in Israel's history, it is the bloodiest, and there are no women in decision-making positions anywhere in anything having to do with it.

The frequent correlation between prolonged bloodshed and the absence of women in power has been noted around the world. It has led to the creation of an entire movement of women around the world advocating for conflict resolution and peace through advancing women's leadership in negotiations and issues of security. This movement is bolstered by UN Security Council Resolution 1325, that calls for women's inclusion around the table. The premise of UNSCR 1325 is that when women have a seat at the table, peace is more likely to be achieved and to last. Anecdotal proof of this premise can be seen in places like Ireland, Rwanda, and elsewhere.

Still, some people may say it's merely coincidental. After all, who says that women are the answer and would miraculously bring peace? Indeed, if the current Israeli government is any indication, women can be just as bad as men when it comes to racism, violence, and narcissistic corruption. The few women scattered in Netanyahu's government are the worst. Homophobic messianic Minister of Settlements and National Missions Orit Strock is vociferously against returning the hostages.[162] Racist MK Limor Son Har-Melech openly advocates for killing Palestinians and for a complete Jewish takeover of Gaza.[163] Minister for Social Equality (formerly Gender Equality, until this government canceled that mission entirely), and self-described "proud racist"(!) May Golan has spent much of the war demonizing feminism, and also promotes the Judaization of Gaza.[164] Minister of Transport Miri Regev is apparently as corrupt as they come, using her entire budget to hand out projects as prizes to Likud loyalists.[165] To name but a few.[166] This is a very

---

[162] Sam Sokol, "Far-right minister: Hostage deal throws war goals in trash to save only 22-33 hostages," *The Times of Israel*, May 1, 2024, https://www.timesofisrael.com/far-right-minister-claims-hostage-deal-throws-war-goals-in-trash-to-save-hostages/.

[163] Patrick Kingsley and Isabel Kershner, "Revenge Attacks After Killing of Israeli Settlers Leave West Bank in Turmoil," *The New York Times*, February 27, 2023, https://www.nytimes.com/2023/02/27/world/middleeast/israel-palestinians-west-bank.html; Jeremy Sharon, "'It is doable': 10 Likud MKs to attend conference calling for 'resettling Gaza'," *The Times of Israel*, October 16, 2024, https://www.timesofisrael.com/it-is-doable-10-likud-mks-to-attend-conference-calling-for-resettling-gaza/.

[164] Yoana Gonen, "May Golan: Minister for Rolling Back the Status of Women," *Haaretz*, April 9, 2023, https://www.haaretz.com/opinion/2023-04-09/ty-article-opinion/.premium/may-golan-minister-for-rolling-back-the-status-of-women/00000187-6233-dde0-afb7-7e3320a50000.

[165] Rachel Fink, "Israeli TV Exposé Uncovers Alleged Deep Corruption of Key Netanyahu Minister," *Haaretz*, May 27, 2024, https://www.haaretz.com/israel-news/2024-05-27/ty-article/.premium/israeli-tv-expose-uncovers-alleged-deep-corruption-of-key-netanyahu-minister/0000018f-bab5-d0b7-abdf-feb7c40f0000.

[166] For more about the anti-feminist, anti-Palestinian, anti-peace, and anti-humanity women occupying spaces in Israel's government, see my periodic round-ups on my Substack, such as this one: "The problem with women," *The Roar*, December 28, 2022, https://elanasztokman.substack.com/p/the-problem-with-women?utm_medium=reader2.

painful reality that at times makes me want to pull my hair out. Or at least write about it.[167]

This phenomenon of awful women leaders brings the premise of UNSCR 1325 into question. Do we even know for certain that women are more moral than men as leaders? Are women more peace-seeking than men, more compassionate than men, better than men at managing war? My friend, investigative science journalist Josie Glausiusz, asked this question in an article for *Aeon* titled, "Would the world be more peaceful if there were more women leaders?"[168] After scouring all the available research on the subject, she concluded that we have no idea, because there have not been enough women leaders to amass any reliable macro data on the subject.

Nevertheless, despite the depressing state of Israel and of gender equality generally, many people believe that women's participation in leadership does lead to more conflict resolution. The UN has collected some compelling findings on women and peace. A global study of forty peace processes since the end of the Cold War found that:

> *Women's participation increases the probability of a peace agreement lasting at least two years by 20 percent, and by 35 percent the probability of a peace agreement lasting 15 years. [...] In cases where women were able to exercise a strong influence on the negotiation process, there was a much higher chance that an agreement would be reached than when women's*

---

[167] Elana Sztokman, "Amy Coney Barrett and the Women Who Uphold the Patriarchy," *Lilith*, October 27, 2020, https://lilith.org/2020/10/amy-coney-barrett-and-the-women-who-uphold-the-patriarchy/.

[168] Josie Glausiusz, "Would the world be more peaceful if there were more women leaders?" *Aeon*, October 27, 2017, https://aeon.co/ideas/would-the-world-be-more-peaceful-if-there-were-more-women-leaders.

*groups exercised weak or no influence. In cases of strong influence of women an agreement was almost always reached.*

These findings are encouraging. But they also reveal a distressing reality. Out of sixteen current conflicts where dialogue is taking place, the study found that in fifteen of them, decision-making was left to a small group of male leaders.[169] These issues do seem to be inversely correlated — fewer women involved seems to mean more bloodshed.

In addition, the role of women in grassroots activity also seems to play an important role in advancing women's vision in leadership. The same UN study found that peace was 64% more likely when civil society representatives were involved, as opposed to only military and political actors. A George Washington University study also found that it's not enough to include women, but also crucial to advance diverse gender perspectives and women's experiences in peace, war, and security.[170]

The UN Women analysis concludes that, in order to advance peace and security,

*All actors involved in official peace processes should make quantifiable, time-sensitive commitments to ensure women's direct and meaningful participation during specific phases of the process, to include women's perspectives and gender-responsive provisions in all meetings, consultations, and agreements, to train all parties on their gender-responsive obligations within their area of expertise, and to acknowledge and provide holistic support for women's groups. [...] Women should not be on the*

---

[169] "A Global Study of UN Security Council Resolution 1325," UN Women, https://wps.unwomen.org/resources/.
[170] Clara Fisher et al., "UN SecurityCouncil Resolution 1325 in Peacekeeping: Challenges and Opportunities," The Elliott School of International Affairs, The George Washington University and Women in International Security (WIIS), August 2016, https://wiisglobal.org/wp-content/uploads/UN-Security-Council-Resolution-1325-in-Peacekeeping-Challenges-and-Opportunities.pdf.

*sidelines observing, but an integral part of negotiations and decision-making on the future of their country.*[171]

To that end, a group of women trained in leadership, negotiation, and conflict resolution by the Israeli-Palestinian women's rights organization Itach-Ma'aki, led by Dora Bender, got together around the beginning of the war and created Forum 1325. Dora and I met in January 2024, and she invited me to join the group even though I had not been officially trained by Itach-Ma'aki. (I did participate in a related training with Itach-Ma'aki in 2018 called "Women Building Bridges", after which I led a Jewish-Palestinian women's dialogue group for four years). Dora invited me to help with strategic planning for the group, which I gladly did. The group consists of Jewish and Palestinian citizens of Israel with diverse identities and professional backgrounds, all of whom are leaders in their fields and committed to advancing systemic solutions to the conflict. This goal could not be more urgent. The surrounding bloodshed and male-macho intransigence driving this war have already destroyed too many lives.

This is so important. Whenever I call for a different outlook or for an end to the violence in my writing, I often receive this response: *What other choice do we have?* Despite my deep offense at the suggestion that killing thousands of innocent people is "our only choice", I also have another response. I roll out the materials created by Forum 1325 about the many potential solutions to this seemingly intractable conflict. And I remind people that, if they could achieve peace in places like Ireland and Rwanda, we can achieve peace in Israel/Palestine as well.

---

[171] "Fact Sheet The Global Study of UN Security Council Resolution 1325: Key Messages, Findings, and Recommendations," UN Women, https://wps.unwomen.org/resources/fact-sheets/Fact-Sheet-and-Key-messages-Global-Study-EN.pdf.

# Solutions

I would like to point out that axioms such as "there are no alternatives", or "there are no solutions", or even "there is no negotiating partner" are toxic talking points. They are related to the "we have no choice" dictum which is intended to absolve Israel from all responsibility and to enable the government to conduct any bloody actions they wish with impunity.

Ironically, I also hear Palestinian peace activists claiming that their communities feel that "there is no partner" to engage in negotiation. They say this in response to the Israeli obduracy when it comes to negotiations, ceasefires, and even hostage deals.[172]

This tells us that those grandiose claims about "the other side" are all manufactured. On all sides, there are people who want peace, and there are people who want to spill blood. Once we recognize that we are engaging in spin and talking points, we can put those sayings aside and get to work.

Because there definitely are solutions based on values of humanity, human rights, freedom, and security. And there are people on all sides of the conflict ready to negotiate and implement any or all of those solutions. In fact, the Alliance for Middle East Peace (ALLMEP) has a coalition of 164 organizations working toward solutions. We interviewed

---

[172] See, for example, the episode of our podcast "S1E9 A Plethora of partners: Nivine Sandouka of ALLMEP & Naomi Sternberg of Geneva Institute," Elana Sztokman, September 3, 2024, YouTube video, 56:12,
https://www.youtube.com/watch?v=76bZ0h6Fui8&list=PLyw9n txS-kikAUsI-XvSeqSm7-
i_pMCB2&index=24&t=7s&ab_channel=ElanaSztokman.

ALLMEP Regional Director Nivine Sandouka, who shared insights and a vision of resolutions, despite her own personal struggles as a mother living under occupation and with a family suffering in Gaza.[173]

Forum 1325 has been working to identify solutions and make them clear and presentable. In one of the Forum's webinars, Professor Shosh Shor outlines the benefits and challenges of four primary solutions: the two-state solution, the binational state solution, the federation model, and the confederation model.[174]

## Two-State Solution

The two-state solution has been the only potential solution on the agendas of most international actors for several decades, arguably since the 1947 partition plans. Many organizations and diplomats see it as the only solution available. Over the years, American and other governments have worked intensively on implementing variations of a two-state solution, even as the parties have always found ways to reject it.[175]

The challenges in negotiating this solution include, among others, jurisdictions, borders, Jerusalem, settlements, rights of return, economics, water, and travel.

The Geneva Initiative, a Jewish-Palestinian initiative to end the conflict and a member of Forum 1325, advances a detailed proposal for a two-state solution. As described in its Mission Statement, the Geneva Initiative "provides realistic

---

[173] Ibid.

[174] Forum 1325 for Political Agreement, "An Introduction to Diplomatic Solutions (Hebrew)," January 2, 2024, YouTube video, 1:28:35, https://www.youtube.com/watch?v=w9uISKe9c94&ab_channel=Forum1325forPoliticalAgreement.

[175] Shalom, Zaki. "The Controversy Surrounding Prime Minister Netanyahu's Position Regarding the Two-State Solution—Background and Implications." In *Polarization and Consensus-Building in Israel*, pp. 240-260. Routledge, 2023.

and achievable solutions on all issues, based on previous official negotiations, international resolutions, the Quartet Roadmap, Clinton Parameters, Bush Vision, and Arab Peace Initiative."[176] The basic components of the accord are described below:

---

### 1. Mutual recognition

*As part of the accord, the Palestinians recognize the right of the Jewish people to their own state and recognize the State of Israel as their national home. Conversely, the Israelis recognize the Palestinian state as the national home of the Palestinian people.*

### 2. Borders and settlements

*The border marked on a detailed map is final and indisputable. According to the accord and maps, the extended borders of the State of Israel will include Jewish settlements currently beyond the Green Line, Jewish neighborhoods in East Jerusalem, and territories with significance for security surrounding Ben Gurion International Airport. These territories will be annexed to Israel on agreement and will become inseparable from it.*

*In return for the annexation of land beyond the 1967 border, Israel will hand over alternative land to the Palestinians, based on a 1:1 ratio. The lands annexed to the Palestinian State will be of equal quality and quantity.*

### 3. Jerusalem

*The parties shall have their mutually recognized capitals in the areas of Jerusalem under their respective sovereignty.*

---

[176] Mission Statement, Geneva Initiative, Downloaded October 30, 2024 https://geneva-accord.org/mission-statement/.

*The Jewish neighborhoods of Jerusalem will be under Israeli sovereignty, and the Arab neighborhoods of Jerusalem will be under Palestinian sovereignty.*

*The parties will commit to safeguarding the character, holiness, and freedom of worship in the city.*

*The parties view the Old City as one whole enjoying a unique character. Movement within the Old City shall be free and unimpeded subject to the provisions of this article and rules and regulations pertaining to the various holy sites.*

*There shall be no digging, excavation, or construction on al-Haram al-Sharif / the Temple Mount, unless approved by the two parties.*

*A visible color-coding scheme shall be used in the Old City to denote the sovereign areas of the respective Parties.*

*4. International Supervision*

*An Implementation and Verification Group (IVG) shall be established to facilitate, assist in, guarantee, monitor, and resolve disputes relating to the implementation of the agreement. As part of the IVG, a Multinational Force (MF) shall be established to provide security guarantees to the parties. To perform the functions specified in this agreement, the MF shall be deployed in the state of Palestine.*

*5. Refugees*

*The agreement provides for the permanent and complete resolution of the Palestinian refugee problem, under which refugees will be entitled to compensation for their refugee status and for loss of property, and will have the right to return to the State of Palestine. The refugees could also elect to remain in their present host countries, or relocate to third countries, among them Israel, at the sovereign discretion of third countries.*

*6. Security*

*Palestine and Israel shall each recognize and respect the other's right to live in peace within secure and recognized boundaries free from the threat or acts of war, terrorism and violence. Both sides shall prevent the formation of irregular forces or armed bands, and combat terrorism and incitement. Palestine shall be a non-militarized state, with a strong security force.*[177]

## Binational State

Many analysts believe that the type of two-state solution promoted by the Geneva Initiative is no longer viable.[178] Many believe that the land cannot be broken down into puzzle pieces and that all parties feel belonging to the whole land. Others see the two-state solution as too difficult, or as an idea whose time has come and gone.[179]

Instead of a two-state solution, the idea of one binational state would turn the entire land "from the river to the sea" including Israel, the West Bank, and Gaza into one entity in which all people are equal citizens with equal rights. This includes the approximately two million Palestinians in Gaza and the three million Palestinians in the West Bank, as well as the eight million Jewish citizens of Israel and the two million Palestinian citizens of Israel. Doing the math, this would result in a country of roughly eight million Jews and seven million Palestinians.

---

[177] "Geneva Initiative: The Accord," Geneva Accord, https://geneva-accord.org/the-accord/.

[178] Nimni, Ephraim. "The twilight of the two-state solution in Israel-Palestine: Shared sovereignty and nonterritorial autonomy as the new dawn." *Nationalities Papers* 48, no. 2 (2020): 339-356; Falah, Ghazi-Walid. "The (im) possibility of achieving a peaceful solution to the Israeli-Palestinian conflict." *Human Geography* 14, no. 3 (2021): 333-345.

[179] Nimni, Ephraim. "The twilight of the two-state solution in Israel-Palestine: Shared sovereignty and nonterritorial autonomy as the new dawn." *Nationalities Papers* 48, no. 2 (2020): 339-356.

For many Palestinians, this is an ideal solution, perhaps the only solution, as it reflects a kind of "normalcy" in which people who live in a place are all equal citizens of that place.

For some Jews, the binational state is a terrifying concept. One fear concerning this solution has to do with security, and the notion that all Palestinians are potential terrorists and it is therefore impossible to live together without walls, blockades, checkpoints, and the like. But the bigger fear is that this would mean the end of the Jewish state. Indeed, some proponents of the binational state do in fact envision the end of Israel and Zionism altogether.[180] Even without that element that invokes in some Jews the fear of being exterminated (again), the binational state is a re-envisioning of the Jewish state such that Jews would lose the much-coveted Jewish majority that ensures the country's Jewish character.[181]

However, this is perhaps the point. That is, one of the most commonly heard justifications for the current situation of military rule in the West Bank is the fear of this so-called "demographic problem". That is, for some Israelis, it's better to systematically repress three million Palestinians than take the risk that Jews will no longer be a majority in the Jewish state.[182] Of course, deciding that three million people do not count as citizens or even as human beings who deserve basic rights is an inhumane and undemocratic stance. Israelis and Jews need to do better than this, or accept the label of an apartheid state.

The binational state is in some ways the most direct response to the de facto reality on the ground. In practice, the

---

[180] Halper, Jeff. "Decolonizing Israel, Liberating Palestine." *London: Pluto. doi* 10 (2021).

[181] Elitsoy, Z. Ash. "A "Jewish State" or a "State for All Its Citizens?": Palestinian Demands for Redefining the Boundaries of the Israeli National Identity and the Jewish Response." *İsrailiyat* 7 (2021): 4-17.

[182] Lustick, Ian S. "Annexation in right-wing Israeli discourse—The case of Ribonut." *Frontiers in Political Science* 4 (2022): 963682.

creation of a binational state would need to address a series of challenges, such as the system of government and elections, daily security, water, education, joint economies, and the right of return. But the biggest challenge in my opinion is this: Is it possible to create a binational state in which all citizens have equal rights, and *also* ensure that the state will always be a safe haven for Jews, where Jews are secure and protected? If this is possible, and I think it is, then the follow-up challenge would be convincing Jewish Israelis — especially religious Zionist and right-wing Zionist Israelis — that it is indeed possible. Not only is it possible, but it may actually be ideal.

That conversation would require a redefinition of the idea of a Jewish state. That is, rather than conceive of Israel as a state primarily for Jews with everyone else as an inconvenient afterthought, this arrangement would mean that the country would be for all its inhabitants equally, no matter whose religion or ethnicity happens to be in the majority.

This outlook is, in my opinion, the only moral approach. However, it can *potentially* erase a very real need for Jews of the world to have a safe haven. But I do not think that it *must necessarily* erase that need. I believe that it is very possible to have a state where Jews' rights, needs, freedoms, and cultural expressiosn are fully protected whether or not Jews are a demographic majority. If those needs are sewn into the fabric of the country, they can be protected *without* having to trample on anyone else's basic human rights.

In fact, I would argue that it is possible – and perhaps most desireable – to create a state in which Jews' needs for safety, protection, freedom, and cultural expressions are met along with with needs for safety, protection, freedom, and cultural expressions for all other inhabitants of the land.

I am imagining such a possibility, and it brings me joy and hope. But it requires Jewish Israelis and Jews of the world to be willing to reconfigure long-held views about what "Jewish State" means. I'm hoping that communal conversation will happen, and soon.

## Federalism

Not everyone has given up on the idea of a two-state solution. Several groups are working on variations of the two-state solution that adjust for the criticisms of the original one. The adjusted-two-state-solution concept can be categorized under the umbrella of "federalism", which reflects the notion of separate state entities that are loosely connected.

Dora Bender, the initiator of Forum 1325, heads the Federal Forum (originally hosted by the organization Challenge-Etgar). According to the group, Federalism "combines a central or 'federal' government, with other autonomous governments in a single political system, dividing the powers between the two," such as the systems in the United States, Switzerland, and Belgium. They argue that this is the ideal system for Israel/Palestine because it offers "a just, sustainable, equitable and democratic resolution to the Israeli-Palestinian conflict [...] [and] enables both of the national groups to enjoy self-determination, autonomy and cooperation, with the benefit of interdependent economies."[183]

The underlying justification for the Federalism proposal is that "the emphasis on simple territorial division (an issue of 'real estate')" guiding most two-state solution plans "ignores the deep identification of both nations to the whole land, and the lack of mutual recognition of the national identity and thus the right of national self-determination of the other side [...] Even when Israelis and Palestinians maintain, often in a haze of ambiguity, that they are satisfied with or agreeable to a partition of the land, unilateral visions lurk under the discourse, emerging periodically and violently [...] Jews and Palestinians can never effectively separate: they are, in fact, interlocked. Any peace process built on partition is doomed to fail." They also argue that the binational state solution is

---

[183] Federal Forum, "Building a Shared Future for Israel-Palestine," Challenge, https://challenge.org.il/federal-forum/.

problematic because it will enable violence and thus lead to instability.[184]

The Federalism system is comprised of "systems of small, semi-autonomous districts (states/provinces/cantons) united by an overarching federal government that avoid territorial partition." They argue that this is an ideal solution, because it:

> *Offers the flexibility to engineer a tailor-made, unique model for the region's particular challenges [...] account for security, respect for identities and holy/cultural sites, reduction of economic and political inequalities, migration policies, and other key issues [...] provide a grassroots effort to reduce fear, mistrust, and resentment [...] [and] simultaneously provide for both people's pursuit of national character and attachment to the 'whole, undivided land' [...] [I]t permits the establishment of small, semi-autonomous districts (states) than can have distinct national or cultural characteristics, demarcated based on population clusters. This replaces the zero-sum dynamics which have prevailed in mainstream solutions and opens up new possibilities through negotiation of levels of devolution between federal and regional governments, providing more robust self-determination to a wider variety of groups.*

> *Moreover, adding a regional level of government provides an additional level for expression of national identities and their internal sub-groups: one can imagine a secular-Zionist province of Tel Aviv, Haredi or Hasidic enclaves, and Bedouin, Druze, or Christian polities. However, the overarching federal state would provide the land and its citizens with geographic continuity, cooperation, freedom of movement, and democratic representation in an entity that can arbitrate authoritatively between the states and decide on universal laws.*[185]

---

[184] Ibid.
[185] Ibid.

The Federalism idea, then, is an adaptation of the two-state solution into a possibly multi-state solution that allows people to identify with the land as well as with their cultural or ethnic group while still being part of a loosely connected whole. Basing this model on the success of the United States sounds convincing. If America can unite fifty very different states, Israel should be able to unite a few. However, American political culture may cast some doubts on whether America has indeed succeeded in overcoming internal fissures. That history is still playing out.

## Confederation

Finally, a federalist solution that rests between the two-state solution and the federalism idea is the confederation. This is similar to a federalist system but with looser ties between entities, more like the European Union than the United States. The EU model is attractive because it successfully ended centuries of warfare between many states in a peaceful entity; it allows each body to fully retain its cultural identity, and has, for the most part, remained steady (Brexit notwithstanding). This solution also separates the issues of citizenship and residency, allowing both Israeli settlers and Palestinian refugees to live where they are and be part of the nation they want to belong to.

According to the Federal Forum, "critics of a confederate solution argue that this model keeps in place most of the shortcomings of the two-state solution which alienate certain sectors of both societies. [...] A confederation of two sovereign states, as opposed to one unitary common state or two completely independent and detached ones, also maintains a competitive dynamic which might lead to it falling prey to the same Achilles' heel that has plagued the previously reviewed models. Having 'rival' two-states while

---

[186] Special thanks to Dora Bender and the scholar of Forum 1325 for patiently explaining these distinctions to me. Errors are my own.

requiring joint decision-making might actually exacerbate the mutual mistrust and grievance that degenerates nation-to-nation cooperation into a political or military struggle."[187]

A main advocate of a confederacy is Dr. Warda Sada, a professor of education and leadership, longtime peace activist, and a Christian Palestinian citizen of Israel from Beit Jala who was fired from her professorship position at the beginning of the war due to a social media post share, Dr. Sada, a member of the All its Citizens party and of Forum 1325, gave a talk on behalf of Forum 1325 about the proposed solution explaining the details of the proposal. She is working on a more comprehensive solution, and many organizations are eagerly awaiting her final paper.[188]

Similarly, A Land for All is a binational organization advocating for a confederation solution (also a member of Forum 1325), headed by joint women co-chairs, the Jewish Israeli May Pundak and the Palestinian citizen of Israel Dr. Rula Hardal. The plan of A Land for All is effectively a two-state solution with flexible borders. The components of the proposal are as follows:

---

### 1. One Land, Two States

*Palestine/the Land of Israel is one historic and geographic unit, stretching from the Jordan River to the sea. In it, two sovereign states will exist — Palestine and Israel, where the two people will realize their right of self-determination. The border between the two states will be drawn according to the June 4, 1967 border, thus bringing a complete end to the occupation.*

---

[187] Ibid.
[188] Forum 1325 for Political Agreement, "The Federal Proposal: Between one nation and two nations, the combining solution" (Hebrew), February 12, 2024, YouTube video, 1:20:06, https://www.youtube.com/watch?v=xQuCDza9ysg&ab_channel =Forum1325forPoliticalAgreement.

## 2. Democracy, Human Rights, Rule of Law

The two states will be democracies; their governments will be founded on the principle of rule of law and recognition of the universality of human rights, as recognized by international law, based on the principles of equality, freedom and the sanctity of human life.

## 3. Migration and Citizenship

Both countries will have the right to determine the nature of immigration into them, and their citizenship laws. Therefore, Palestine will be free to grant citizenship to Palestinian refugees, and the State of Israel will be free to grant citizenship to diaspora Jews, as they see fit.

## 4. Vision of the Open Land

Both states will be bound to the open land vision, where citizens of both countries are free to move and live in all parts of the land. This right will also apply to any person who becomes a citizen of either country, including Palestinians from the Palestinian diaspora in Palestine, and Jews from the Jewish diaspora in Israel. The two countries will work to fully realize this vision in several phases, mutually, and any progress will require both countries' agreement.

In the first stage, the two states will recognize the right of their citizens to move, travel, visit, work and trade in all parts of the land. In addition, in the first phase, the two countries will determine an agreed number of citizens of the other country who will live in their territory and receive permanent resident status, with all entailed rights. Such agreement will allow Israelis, including those who currently live in the territories where Palestine will be established, to live as permanent residents of Palestine, as long as they are willing to live peacefully alongside their neighbors under Palestinian sovereignty.

This agreement will also allow Palestinians, including those who become citizens of Palestine, to become permanent residents of Israel, as long as they are willing to live peacefully alongside their neighbors under Israeli sovereignty.

*These permanent residents, who will live in a country other than their country of citizenship, will be required to respect local laws and abstain from activities which undermine the security of the country in which they live or the security of its citizens. The Israeli permanent residents of Palestine will exercise their voting rights in Israel, and the Palestinian permanent residents of Israel will exercise their voting rights in Palestine.*

### 5. Jerusalem

*Jerusalem will serve as the capital of both states. Palestinian residents will be Palestinian citizens, and Israeli residents will be Israeli citizens. Jerusalem will be a city shared by and open to citizens of both countries within agreed borders. A special municipal government will be established in it, managed jointly and equally by both states. Holy places will be managed with participation of representatives of the different religions and international community, while ensuring freedom of worship to people of all religions.*

### 6. Security

*The two states will solve all their disputes in peaceful ways, and will act against any violence or terror. Each of the two countries will be sovereign on all matters relating to protecting public order within its borders and the personal security of its residents. Armed militias and unauthorized organizations will be disarmed. The two states will enter a mutual defense treaty against external threats; no foreign military power will enter the territory of either country, but only in agreement. A shared supreme security council will be formed to monitor and decide on common security issues. The council may deploy a joint force to protect the external borders, with the agreement of both states.*

## 7. Shared Institutions

*The two states will share the following institutions:*

*Human Rights Court, which will be empowered to serve as the highest instance to rule on the following two matters: Petitions by non-citizen residents against the country of their residence, claiming a violation of their rights; Conflicts between the two states as to the rights of their citizens residing in the other state, and all matters deriving from the one land vision.*

*A shared institution to guarantee a minimum economic safety net for all residents of the land, both Palestinians and Israelis. A special authority to manage and develop the land's economy to include institutions for economic cooperation, coordination of customs, traffic of goods, and labor, work migration, development of infrastructure and local and international investments. The economic institutions will strive to reduce the gaps between different regions and populations. Institutions for cooperating on matters of water, natural resources and the environment, on the basis of a just distribution of resources, out of a commitment to develop the land and its resources to the benefit of all its residents.*

*Any additional shared institution required for the purpose of realizing the Two States, One Homeland solution. All shared institutions will have equal representation of citizens of both states.*

## 8. Palestinian Citizens of Israel

*The Palestinian-Arab citizens of Israel will be granted national minority rights, civil equality, appropriate representation in government institutions in Israel, fair distribution of national resources and appropriate representation in the institutions shared by Israel and Palestine. Insofar as a Jewish minority is created in Palestine, it will receive similar rights.*

## 9. Restitution and Reparation

*A common mechanism will be created to manage the restitution of property lost or confiscated as the result of the conflict, or for reparation in case restitution is impossible.*

*The principles of restitution and reparation will be agreed upon with the purpose of achieving maximum justice to victims of the conflict. Old wrongs will not be amended with new wrongs.*

### 10. Reconciliation

*Common mechanisms will be established to reconcile the two people, including establishment of shared reconciliation councils to allow profound and comprehensive discussion of past wrongs on both sides. Shared plans will be formulated to promote reconciliation on the communal levels, the education systems and cultural institutions.*

### 11. International Framework

*To implement the reconciliation agreement, an international body acceptable to both sides will be formed, representing the following, among others: the Arab League, the European Union and the UN. This body will guarantee the implementation of the Two States, One Homeland plan, and will support it diplomatically, legally and economically. The Two States, One Homeland solution will serve as the basis for integrating two independent states under a comprehensive peace agreement with Middle Eastern countries.*[189]

The political organization A Land for All has developed extensive details about this solution, based on both the reality in the region and success stories from around the world. They believe that "A Land for All is not fantasy. It is rooted in the historical, geographic and emotional realities of the conflict, and it is based on historic precedent. Nor is it a close-ended solution. On the contrary, it invites discussion, comments, corrections and additions. But to work towards it, we also have to be able to dream, and mostly, make dreams a reality. It's in our hands."[190]

---

[189] "Shared and Agreed Founding Principles," A Land for All, https://www.alandforall.org/english-program/?d=ltr.
[190] "From Conflict to Reconciliation: A new vision for Palestinian-Israeli peace Draft for discussion," A Land for All, https://www.alandforall.org/wp-content/uploads/2021/02/booklet-english.pdf.

We interviewed Dr. Hardal on our podcast where she described the negotiation process of focusing on needs. The primary Palestinian need, she said, is freedom, while the primary Israeli need is security. Once the conversation focuses on needs rather than grandiose ideologies, everything is possible.

All these potential solutions contain bits of hope alongside challenges. They are all based on the principle that all human beings matter, we all deserve to live in dignity, freedom, and security, and discussions based on a genuine belief in these core values can yield results. It is not true that this is a "war of no choice". We all have choices, every single day, if we choose to see them.

Most importantly, this brief glance at some of the available solutions and the people dedicating their lives to them makes one thing very clear: There *are* solutions and there *are* partners for peace. We just have to be willing to see them and engage with them.[191]

We are not the first people in the world to be at war. Many other seemingly intractable enemies — Ireland, Rwanda, and others — signed peace agreements. We did, too, by the way: Israel-Egypt, Israel-Jordan, Israel-PLO — we did this. Once we open our minds to the possibility of solutions, the solutions appear. Peace is possible. But we must be willing to do the work ourselves first. We cannot have peace outside unless we create peace within our hearts.

---

[191] "Debunked: Israel has 'no partner for peace'", *MEMO*, November 22, 2023, https://www.middleeastmonitor.com/20231122-debunked-israel-has-no-partner-for-peace/.

# Apologies

Eva and I were invited to participate in a webinar for a group in Denmark called GADIP — Gender and Development in Practice — that works on peace, security, and gender. They wanted to hear from us about our work together, our experiences of advancing a peaceful solution, and our challenges. During that talk, Eva said that Israel was established in 1948 because Jews just wanted to annihilate Palestinians. In that moment, for the first time in our work together, I pushed back at Eva, perhaps a bit aggressively. I said that although our guiding principle is "connect before you correct", in this case I felt the need to correct the notion that all Jews want is to annihilate Palestinians. I said that Israel accepted the 1947 partition plan — unlike the Palestinians — because clearly most Jews were okay with the idea of living side by side with Palestinians. I also said that it's important to understand the Jewish context, which was that we were then three years after the Holocaust where six million of us were killed.

Eva's response was this: *I misspoke.*

That was a crucial moment for me. Eva heard me, and she retracted what she said. That doesn't happen every day, certainly not in conversations about this conflict. It showed me that Eva and I have built a trusting enough relationship, and have spent enough time holding space for each other, that when I need to insist on a point that is important to me, there is room for that in our dynamic. If I don't spend my time pushing back, correcting, and arguing the way I was trained to, I can still have a healthy negotiation over certain ideas that are important to me. As Eva often says, we don't always agree on everything, and we come from radically different places, but we share a deep mutual respect and a powerful desire for resolution, reconciliation, and peace.

Shortly thereafter, a commentator wrote, "What if Elana were to ask Eva, 'What do you need to hear from me right now for real reconciliation?'" So I asked Eva, "What do you need to hear from me right now for real reconciliation?" Eva thought for a moment and said, "An apology."

She said she needed affirmation that "As Palestinians we were here, we existed, and we have the right to live in peace, in freedom, in our own land [...] I as a Palestinian on the personal level and on the collective level, I feel betrayed. I feel I need an apology and an acknowledgement that we have been betrayed."

I listened and thought about this for a moment. I remembered how former Prime Minister Naftali Bennett ran on the platform "Never apologize". I thought about the IDF killing of Shireen Abu Akleh, when Bennett, speaking for Israel, repeatedly denied that Israel did it and blamed Palestinians, and even when the truth finally came out, he never apologized.[192] I thought about how in 2021, Benny Gantz refused to build a coalition with the Arab parties, instead bending to the two MKs on his list who categorically refused to even speak to Palestinian lawmakers, and how as a result we are now in this situation.[193] I thought about how many Palestinians told me that when that happened, they felt betrayed, and as a result there was an uproar in May 2021. It was about betrayal, and how badly Palestinians needed

---

[192] Elana Sztokman, "Bennett responds like an abuser, with gaslighting not compassion," *Jewish Independent*, May 17, 2022, https://thejewishindependent.com.au/bennett-responds-like-an-abuser-with-gaslighting-not-compassion-2 .

[193] i24News, "Gantz says won't form gov't with Arab parties," *i24NEWS*, February 15, 2020, https://www.i24news.tv/en/news/israel/politics/1581795544-gantz-says-won-t-form-gov-t-with-arab-parties.

Gantz, or anyone, to apologize for that utter dehumanization. I thought about so many moments in my life, far from this war, in which I felt the way Palestinians do. I felt the collective sting of millions of hostile exchanges coarsing through my soul in which the other person felt the unrelenting need to explain to me, to fix me, to mold me, to twist my arm and my mind until I gave up, without ever once considering how I felt, without ever acknowledging any of my experiences. So many moments came pouring out of my consciousness as I thought about what Eva was saying to me, what she was asking of me. All those pains, betrayals, and refusals to apologize.

In this moment, I found myself confronting head on the many lessons I have learned along my journey. The hundreds of Palestinian villages lost in 1948. Raja Shehedeh's stories of living under occupation. The detention of Palestinian children. The wall. The home demolitions. And this war, this bloody war. The 45,000 killed, all those babies in body bags. All those craters in the ground where homes used to be. It all washed over me, like an avalanche.

I fully understood why Eva needed an apology. And in that moment, with the portrait of a pained history filling every fiber of my being, wrapped tightly in a toxic rhetoric that I was born into, a political discourse in both personal and collective arenas swirling in my brain that I have been desperately trying to wipe out of my soul, I understood unequivocally. I knew what I had to do. There wasn't even a shred of doubt.

I needed to apologize to Eva. And so, I did.

*Eva, my beautiful friend who I love, while I can't speak for all my people, I can speak for me. And I want to say that I am deeply sorry, for the pain my people caused your people. I'm sorry for all the dehumanizing language. I'm sorry for all the things I was brought up on — that Palestinians aren't real people and don't have a culture, and they don't belong here and they're not even here. I'm sorry for all that. I'm sorry for my participation in it. I'm sorry it took me so long to unpack it myself.*

*And I really hope and pray that there will come a day when your people and my people can see each other as human beings and we can just be. We can just be. Wherever it is that we need to be. Wherever it is that we want to be. Wherever we need to call home. That we can respect each other's history. That we respect each other's need for a home. That we respect each other's need for freedom, for justice, for security, for history, for culture, for whatever it is that human beings need. I pray that you and I will be just neighbors. And friends. Without having to carry all this baggage. Without having to live in fear of all this violence. This is my prayer. And I'm sending you, Eva, from my heart to your heart, human to human, just so much love. And gratitude for this conversation.*[194]

Something happened in that moment. A weight lifted off my shoulders, and I think off of Eva's as well. When we spoke later, she was light and bright. She told me that she didn't realize until that moment how much she wanted and needed an apology. It was, in fact, what was called for right then.

For a split second, I thought to myself, maybe something about this exchange speaks to something bigger that is needed between our two peoples.

And then, my reverie was broken. A participant in the webinar pinged me. She sent me a note saying she felt "uncomfortable" because I did all the apologizing and Eva did not. She was seeking some kind of reciprocity. A balance. A two-sided exchange. Otherwise, it was unfair.

---

[194] GADIP Gender and Development in Practice, "Webinar - Conflict in the Middle East: how can women contribute to the peace process?" October 14, 2024, YouTube video, 1:31:44, https://www.youtube.com/watch?v=PZZz4iJx4Hw&list=PLyw9 ntxS-kikAUsI-XvSeqSm7- i_pMCB2&index=2&ab_channel=GADIPGenderanddevelopment inpractice.

I explained that I did not need an apology from Eva. This was what was needed at that moment, nothing else. I also said that, anyway, I don't believe in reciprocal apologies. This is a lesson I learned from my thirty-three years of marriage. If person A has hurt person B and person B asks for an apology, and after person A apologizes they say, "Okay, now it's YOUR turn to apologize", that can have a devastating effect on the experience. Because in that moment, B's hurt becomes somehow their own fault. They end up having to apologize for being hurt. That is victim blaming. And it makes the entire apology disingenuous. If a person needs an apology, they should get an apology, unconditionally. So, no, I don't think that just because Eva asked me to apologize I need to ask her to apologize in return.

Furthermore, I don't hold Eva responsible for the pain of my people. She is not a terrorist, she doesn't have a violent bone in her body, and she has not hurt me. Jews and Israelis have been through some terrible things. But I don't feel that Eva needs to apologize to me for them. That never even occurred to me. Perhaps there will come a day when I feel differently, when I would be the one asking Eva to apologize to me. But this wasn't it.

Actually, I was quite happy that Eva accepted my earlier pushback of her statement about what Jews wanted in 1948. Eva responded openly and retracted something that was hurtful to me. That was enough for me.

I shared these thoughts with the participant who made that comment — a Christian peace activist currently working in Ukraine. We chatted for a while. But I don't think she was convinced.

Upon reflection, I think there is something more to be said about this apology thing. I don't think that the Israeli-Palestinian conflict should be seen within a framework of two equal sides, of a balance. While it's true that we are two peoples with roughly the same number of people inhabiting one land, the current situation is not one of balance. Because ultimately, I have rights. I am not afraid of being arrested, of me or my children being detained, or of having my house demolished. I travel freely; I'm not afraid of being strip searched at checkpoints or at airports, I go to the beach whenever I want, and in general I come and go as I please without fear of losing my personal status. That is privilege. That is power. That is what it means to be part of the hegemonic group. And this is what Palestinians mean when they call Israeli Jews colonizers. We are the ones with power here.

And so, when a Palestinian asks me, as an Israeli Jew, to acknowledge wrongdoing, it is not about balance and reciprocity. It is about unequal distribution of power. And about the pain that my people have caused her people. And we need to acknowledge this imbalance of power if we are ever going to change our realities.

My exchange with Eva around apologizing felt very powerful and stayed with me for days afterward. It confirmed some of the core ideas that guide me today. One is that the physical violence around us is enabled by verbal violence. If we work to change our language and discourse, ripple effects will undoubtedly follow.

I also learned the power of an apology, even in political contexts. Collective, political apologies for actions that hurt entire peoples have been used to ease conflict in many locations — Australia, Japan/South Korea, Canada, New Zealand, Armenia, and perhaps most notably, South Africa's Truth and Reconciliation Commission.[195] Certainly the

---

[195] Wenzel, Michael, Farid Anvari, Melissa de Vel-Palumbo, and Simon M. Bury. "Collective apology, hope, and forgiveness." *Journal of Experimental Social Psychology* 72 (2017): 75-87; David, Roman, and Pui Chuen Tam. "Political apologies and their acceptance: Experimental evidence from victims and perpetrators nations." *British Journal of Social Psychology* 63, no. 1 (2024): 273-294; Awale, Arya, Christian S. Chan, Katy YY Tam, and Minoru Karasawa. "Perceived warmth of offending group moderates the effect of intergroup apologies." *Group Processes & Intergroup Relations*

different circumstances of these apologies made some more effective at conflict resolution than others. But it strikes me that this is an approach desperately needed in the Israel-Palestine context. Not only has there been immense pain, but the tradition of refusing to apologize or even acknowledge wrongdoing contributes to the perpetuation of violence. This has been the main point of this book, and my experiences with Eva solidified this understanding.

When people ask me whether there are viable ways to bring about peace, I have many answers. Certainly, one answer is to direct them to Forum 1325, ALLMEP, A Land for All, the Geneva, Itach-Ma'aki, and other organizations doing the work of finding solutions.

But really, what I need to say first, is what Eva has taught me: *Peace begins within*. We first have to make peace inside our own hearts. We need to acknowledge our own role in perpetuating violence, and renounce it. We need to stop fighting with our words and our minds and our clever rhetoric. If we start there, all else can follow.

---

25, no. 5 (2022): 1372-1394; Blatz, Craig W., Karina Schumann, and Michael Ross. "Government apologies for historical injustices." *Political Psychology* 30, no. 2 (2009): 219-241; Bavelas, Janet. "An analysis of formal apologies by Canadian churches to First Nations." *Occasional Paper* 1 (2004): 317-338.; Sarah van Gelder, "Desmond Tutu and the Power of Apology", *Yes Magazine*, Jan 11, 2022, https://www.yesmagazine.org/social-justice/2022/01/11/desmond-tutu-power-of-apology; Chapman, A. R. (2007). Truth commissions and intergroup forgiveness: The case of the South African Truth and Reconciliation Commission. *Peace and Conflict*, *13*(1), 51-69.

# Revisiting My Jewish State

A lot has changed in me since I sat in Tomer's Zionism class in 1984. I went from being a good religious Zionist who left my life in Brooklyn behind to build a loyal, idealistic, dedicated family in Israel, to gradually questioning the language and ideas that girded me. After years of quiet questioning, my 2014 *Lilith* essay that publicly launched my shift in ideas and led to a decade of activism in various peace-seeking spaces, I barely resemble my former self. When I moved to Israel in 1993, I was a hat-and-long-skirt-wearing bright-eyed Jewish educator intent on convincing my fellow Jews to love Israel and dedicate their lives to Judaism. Today, I spend countless hours peeling back the layers of indoctrination, unraveling the lies that we are still being fed, and figuring out if there is a way to a humane future for the people of this land. I do this while still living in Israel, where my children and their spouses serve in the IDF, still marking Jewish holidays though no longer as an Orthodox Jew, and with no immediate plans to leave, as tempting as that idea sometimes seems.

I have spent much of this war listening to stories of pain — from all sides of this conflict: My friend whose peace-loving son was killed in the Gaza rim on October 7. Another friend who lost many family members in Gaza. The mother of a hostage who was eventually killed. A Palestinian citizen of Israel sitting in her safe room while rockets are flying overhead. A Jewish mother of seven living on the Lebanon border who doesn't have a safe room. Doctors volunteering in Gaza who have witnessed horrors. Parents of IDF soldiers who cannot sleep. Or who get the dreaded phone call. Or worse. Activists from countless different organizations and groups clamoring for an end to all this. So many protesters demanding a ceasefire, a return of the hostages, and new leadership. Images from the Nova festival and the October 7 attack sear my heart. The images from Gaza prevent me from ever really sleeping at night. The photos of soldiers whose lives are treated as cheap and expendable by the heartless Israeli government, always wondering who will be next, fill me with anger and fear, over and over again. And most recently, the swelling of antisemitic sentiment around the world into acts of everyday violence as the world begs Israel to stop this war.

Is it possible to hold on to hope throughout all this? Is it possible to truly believe in a shared humanity?

If we were to try to answer this question based solely on social media exchanges, the answer would be a resounding no. But I'm not ready to end things there, because I believe that we can fix the way we speak to one another, and because many solutions can emerge from there.

The true answer, I believe, I learned already in elementary school: I have to be human before I can be a Jew. We all do.

The current situation in Israel is based on one definition of a Jewish state. It is based on a need for a Jewish majority, no matter what. Some people take that idea even further and imagine a Jews-only space. This definition is not a viable one. Because in order to create that kind of reality, the Jewish state would have to continue to engage in unconscionable violence, dehumanization of the Other, and permanent apartheid. And that won't work. Firstly because on the practical level, with continued trauma-inducing violence for the foreseeable future, large numbers of Israeli Jews will either die or leave. But more importantly, with that kind of future, we will no longer be a Jewish state, or a human state. We will be a state of bloodshed and inhumanity.

I refuse to allow all this to become the definition of being Jewish. I refuse to accept the premise that the actions of this government as representation of Judaism. This is not my Judaism.

Hence, we need to redefine what it means to be a Jewish state. I would like to believe that being Jewish means being kind first. This is, after all, the teaching of Hillel the Elder: What you don't want to be done to you, do not do unto others. Some call this the "Golden Rule". It is, in theory, the core of being Jewish. And so, for this country to be a Jewish state, it needs to be guided by the unshakeable tenet that we are all human beings first. Everything else is interpretation.

Once we accept that principle, practical solutions open up to us. Whether the answer is a federation, a confederation, a binational state, or some other solution, it doesn't matter to me. I just want to live in a place where all human beings are treated as human beings. Because if the ethos of my society is one where people are safe, then it would be a place where I as a Jewish woman will be safe, too.

That is how I would define a Jewish state: one where all human beings are free to thrive. What a great Jewish state that would be to live in.

# Epilogue

By the time you read this, I will have probably lost a few friends and made some enemies. Or maybe I will have also made new friends. That would be a wonderful surprise. But I'm also bracing myself for the hard stuff.

In the decade or more since I started talking back to the culture that I come from, I have been called names — a self-hating Jew, antisemite, traitor, Hamas-lover, or perhaps more gently, an ignoramus. Some people have felt the need to "educate" me about my own life. Others have assumed I am a writer for Al-Jazeera. I get cursed, along with my children (*grrr...*). Some people have wished me dead or kidnapped, or fated to an eternity of *karet*, cut off from the Jewish people.

In the world I come from and mostly still inhabit, being "pro-Israel" is a given. I'm Jewish, Israeli, and American from Orthodox Jewish Brooklyn, New York. I have lived in Israel for most of the past 30-plus years. My family pays Israeli taxes, serves in the Israeli army, and worships according to Jewish tradition. In this world, political opinions have limited wiggle room. Sure, people get into arguments about which party to vote for, but it's all within the accepted parameters. That is: If you're Jewish, ergo you are a Zionist, you support Israel, and Palestinians are your enemy. That's just how it is. Now pass the challah, please.

Since the events of October 7, these lines in the sand have become even more pronounced.

I get it, to a certain degree. Jews of the world are, for the most part, frightened and battling a steep rise in antisemitism. Jews I speak to everywhere are terrified. These experiences are real. And for some people going through that, this book is at best irrelevant or at worst a slap in the face. One of my podcast interviewees – a self-described progressive American Jewish activist – told me straight out that she doesn't care whether the war in Gaza is justified. She has no interest in discussing it. She wants to talk about antisemitism, that's it.

Against this backdrop, this book will likely come across as tone-deaf in some spaces. After all, the expectation in Jewish communities is for us to "stand together" — whatever that means — and fight to protect the Jews using whatever tools we have. It's a longstanding strategy, and for many Jews today, it remains ummutable. Indeed, Netanyahu exploited the power of this message from the very start. He hasn't backed down from it because he understands that this is what Jews of the world for the most part want to hear right now. He has led The People of the Book, experts in texts and language, in how to narrate this war in ways that suit him. His talking points remain potent tools against The World. I have been well-trained in that craft, and I have in fact done exactly that for most of my life. In that cultural context, this book will make no sense to many people.

Still, despite all of that — with all the fears, the collective traumas, and the millenia of weaving threads about meanings of Jewishness — I believe this moment demands that we strive to look beyond fear with courage and honesty. That we find ways not to sacrifice our own humanity on the altar of elegant self-martyring narratives. Because these habits provide too convenient of an excuse to avoid looking at our own actions. In the name of fear, we often misread the events around us, including our own problematic role in perpetuating human suffering.

Also, this reasing is often just plain wrong. For example the violent clashes in Amsterdam between Israel and pro-Palestinian soccer fans that are being labeled in the Jewish world as a *"pogrom"* were actually instigated by violence by the *Israelis*. The Jewish Israelis began the cycle of violence by climbing onto porches where Palestinian flags were hanging and pulling them down.[196] The fear that Jews feel around the world is in some cases self-inflicted. As hard as that is to hear.

The knee-jerk response of calling all criticism of Israel antisemitism is not only wrong; it's also unsustainable. It will destroy not just the Palestinian people but our own souls. I am deeply worried about who we are becoming as a people.

And so I'm speaking out. To my own people. Most of whom may respond badly.

I know the cost of writing this book. *And still, she persisted.* I've chosen to write it because I believe it is imperative for me to share what I know. I need to speak out about the language war we are all stuck in the middle of — the spoken war that supports the deadly military war that continues to claim countless lives. The current violence is intolerable, and utterly crushing.

I have come to understand unequivocally that until we all face the truth about ourselves, there will never be peace. If we — and by "we" I mean Jews, Israelis, and supporters of Israel — don't start being honest and operating with integrity and humanity, the bloodshed will continue. I need to say these things out loud. To protect my family, my people, the residents of this land, and humanity – ours and everyone else's.

I am writing this book because I am horrified at what my people are doing, as if in my name, and I am equally alarmed by the verbal arguments that are used to justify those actions. I'm also ashamed of my own participation in all this for many years. Or maybe angry at myself for taking so long to unpack all the indoctrination. Either way, I'm done with all that.

---

[196] Loveday Morris, Meg Kelly, Imogen Piper, Souad Mekhennet and Koba Ryckewaert, "How antisemitism, Israeli nationalism and anger over Gaza clashed in Amsterdam," *Washington Post,* December 18, 2024, https://www.washingtonpost.com/investigations/2024/12/18/amsterdam-attacks-israeli-football-fans/.

One question I sometimes get asked is this: Do you still love Israel? Or, similarly, Are you still a Zionist?

There are, indeed, many things that I love and admire about Israel. Living in a place that has a history, connection, and purpose for your people and your ancestors offers a kind of everyday meaningfulness that I daresay many people in the Western world don't experience. I understand and fully appreciate the significance of having a safe haven for Jews, one where we have deep history. That need is not something I take for granted.

Also, there is a lot to love in everyday Israeli culture. People jump to help others in need. The Israeli stance of fearlessness and defiance has its moments of value. And of course, the food in Israel is the best kosher cuisine in the world. And other bits. Israelis tend to be travel adventurers. They are at ease about planning. They believe that everything is possible. The weightlessness of *"hakiol y'hye beseder"* or *"shanti"* — a hippy "it will all be okay" belief system — filters into everyday life in small and big moments. These things make me smile. Sometimes.

On a more difficult issue, I also understand why Israelis love the army. I was in that headspace for a long time. So many soldiers are driven by honor, valor, and commitment to the collective. They are often so courageous and giving that they are willing to lay down their lives to protect their families, their people, their heritage. Those are beautiful values in their own way. I am deeply proud of my kids and their service. My children are beautiful people and they serve in the army because they care about others. Truly. That may be hard for me to explain in mixed Jewish-Palestinian settings. It's hard to even say out loud. And I'm also horrified by a lot of what I see happening in the army. But I'm also proud of my amazing kids. I live with the internal contradiction on a daily basis.

I grapple with my love-hate relationship with Israel and Israeliness from the place of a broken heart. Each aspect of Israel that I say I love is also couched in pain and remorse.

The flipside of a willingness to fight for your own people, for example, is that you have to believe that some human beings are not your people. And we know where that leads. The same dynamics that cherish Jewish honor and valor are deeply embedded in dehumanizing the other. That reality is devastating to me.

There are other troubling flipsides to the Israeliness that so many Jews love. Take, for example, the idea of Israel as a safe haven for Jews. Today, that notion is questionable. Israel may in fact be the most *dangerous* place for Jews to live right now. Too many war fronts to count, rockets flying overhead, terror attacks, and mandatory army conscription all put Jewish Israeli lives at great risk every day. And those are just physical risks. There are also increasing financial risks as the endless war takes its eonomic toll, haredi political *machers* drain national resources, and Israeli life becomes economically untenable.[197]

Also, there are other ways in which it is unsafe for Israelis to live in Israel right now, some of which I have noted: the fact that you could get arrested or fired from your job for expressing any anti-Bibi opinions or wearing a "Fuck Ben-Gvir" T-shirt, the fact that peaceful protesters were being severely beaten by the police, the fact that Bibi supporters have attacked families of the hostages, etc. It is not just Palestinian citizens of Israel who do not necessarily feel safe in Israeli society right now, but also many left-wing Israelis who fear retribution for expressing opposition to the government. That is what life in Israel under this government and under this war

---

[197] JPost Staff, "Jerusalem's economic woes: Israel's deficit increased twice initial predictions," *Jerusalem Post,* January 1, 2025   https://www.jpost.com/business-and-innovation/all-news/article-835643;

has become like. The complete lack of interest in democratic norms has become a feature of this government. So there's that.

And there is the risk to our collective soul, an issue that is not yet on the Jewish communal agenda. Jewish sovereignty has proven to be a blessing and a curse – and today I would probably say that it is more of a curse. The current Israeli leadership seems uninterested in the morality of being in power, or demonstrating even the most basic commitment to governing with integrity. Corruption seems to be the norm. And in fact, it can be argued that the Israeli government is in fact the direct cause of at least most of these threats to Israelis' lives and Jewish lives. The only path that the Netanyahu government ever follows is violent onslaught, and that has only created more violence and more bloodshed on all fronts.

Moreover, regarding the Israeli cultures of kindness and mutual care, unfortunately it usually pertains only to members of the tribe. The rallying cry of war, for example, is "*Am Yisrael Chai*" — the Jewish people live. The exclusion of non-Jews from such sentiments reflects the harsh and painful reality that the Israeli culture is also often deeply racist. I shared some of my experiences in this realm, such as when I approached some organizations to help support Palestinian women of Jaffa and they declined. Even among some so-called solidarity organizations, the idea of taking care of Palestinian Israelis was beyond what they were willing to consider. Certainly there are other groups defying those norms, as I described. But there is an everyday racism in Israel that is very hard to stomach.

Some of that everyday racism in Israel seems almost mundane – but that is just a testament to how normative it is. For instance, I recently needed to hire someone to replace a door in my house, and the company that was most highly recommended came with the slogan, "Jewish workers only". Apparently that's a common advertising pitch. Similarly, when my building was looking to hire cleaners, one of the neighbors strongly suggested that we only hire Jews. (We voted him down, thankfully).

Israeli culture, then, is a confusing thing to love. I want to embrace the beautiful aspects of it, but they are often entangled with some of the ugliest parts. And safe haven? Not even sure about that anymore either.

And then there is the elephant in the room. That is, everything in Israel that's meant to demonstrate great success — buildings, infrastructures, institutions, the hi-tech industry, the non-profit sector — was all built on the backs of Palestinians. Massive, expensive cities sprawled on locations where Arab villages were destroyed, whose descendants became refugees. Everywhere I look in Israel there are signs of the erased history of others. Jews tend to vehemently reject the word "colonialism" to describe Israel's history. But if we're being honest...

I often wonder how long this feeling will last. Sometimes I think to myself, *everyone's home is built on someone else's pain*. Probably every residence in the world was once the location of a bloody struggle over ownership. Indigenous peoples around the world can testify to this. So can Jews, the wandering people. My husband's grandparents were violently removed from their homes in Hungary in 1943 and sent to the Auschwitz extermination camp where they lost 80-90% of their families – and in the blink of an eye, other Hungarians simply moved into their homes and that was the end of that. Perhaps this is the way of the world. *To the victor go the spoils*. People will power win. Everyone else moves on. Those who suffered learn to live with it and get on with their lives. Or something. Maybe we are all living on the buried ruins of someone else's pain. Maybe we all build our houses on someone else's blood.

But that is not an excuse. I do not want to actively and knowingly participate in that kind of violence. Traveling through this country after having heard so many stories of

Palestinians who were brutally removed from or pushed off their lands fills me with a very deep shame. And so many of those families and their descendants are still here. Israeli leaders have vehemently rejected all possible discussions of Palestinian refugees. And yet, how can we not discuss this? How can we, the Jewish people with our own history of that kind of trauma, not be highly aware of what Palestinians are saying about this? Am I and my people no different that the Hungarian gentiles of World War II? Do our leaders think that if we just wait it out long enough, people will forget and move on? That is just so wrong.

Sometimes I think the main problem with the Jewish state is this: The Jewish people have not systematically faced the transition from vulnerable marginalized community to hegemonic authority. We are now the majority, the ones with the power, the ones in charge. We have never done the hard work of asking ourselves what kinds of sovereign leaders we want to be. We keep responding to non-Jews as if they are all Nazis and we are the ones threatened with extermination. And we refuse to hear what Palestinians are saying to us. We refuse to hear their pain. We label all forms of resistance "existential threats" – even a little boy with a rock, even a teacher dancing on Tik Tok, even a guy with a curse word on his t-shirt. The resistance graduated from the slingshot to October 7th for the simple reason that we are not listening. We, the Jewish people, have collectively stopped engaging with those who we live alongsire, and we stopped feeling other people's pains. Instead we blame everyone but ourselves, craft simplistic 3000 year old narratives, and lean heavily on our own victimhood. But we failed to notice that the narrative isn't true anymore. We missed our own transition from oppressed to oppressor.

But here we are. We have arrived. We are now the ones causing the harm, dehumanizing the other, and oppressing the vulnerable. And it utterly breaks my heart.

With all that about my relationship with Israel — a complex mixture of love and hate, of ownership and disownership, of power and disempowerment, of rootedness and displacement, of self and other — I'm still here. My family is here. My children are raising their families here with partners who are also rooted here. I'm not going "back" to Brooklyn, or to Poland, or to Hungary. Even with my broken heart and horror about what we as a people are doing, I'm still here. And so, somehow, I have to make peace with all this. And I need to help build a future where my descendants can also exist here, along with everyone else who wants and deserves to be here.

And so here I am, as a contribution to that effort, putting this book into the world. Because as my friend Eva Dalak teaches me, peace begins within. From our peace within, we can work on creating peace out there in the world.

# Bibliography

A Land for All, "From Conflict to Reconciliation: A new vision for Palestinian-Israeli peace Draft for discussion," A Land for All, https://www.alandforall.org/wp-content/uploads/2021/02/booklet-english.pdf.

A Land for All, "Shared and Agreed Founding Principles," A Land for All, https://www.alandforall.org/english-program/?d=ltr.

ABC News, "Parents create 'Goodies Not Guns' to discourage violent Halloween costumes for kids," *ABC News*, October 22, 2017, https://abcnews.go.com/Lifestyle/parents-create-goodies-guns-discourage-violent-halloween-costumes/story?id=50634572.

Abdulrahim, Raja, et al., "Gaza in Ruins After a Year of War," *The New York Times*, October 7, 2024, https://www.nytimes.com/interactive/2024/10/07/world/middleeast/israel-gaza-destruction-hamas-war.html.

Abu-Ras, Wahiba, and Rozena A. Mohamed, "Child poverty and youth unemployment in Palestine." *Poverty & Public Policy* 10, no. 3 (2018): 354-370.

Abuamer, Majd, "Detection, Neutralization, and Destruction: The Limits of Israel's Strategy against Gaza's Tunnels." *Al-Muntaqa: New Perspectives on Arab Studies* 7, no. 1 (2024): 70-79. https://www.jstor.org/stable/48775005.

ACRI, "Two More Reforms to End Housing Discrimination," *The Association for Civil Rights in Israel*, October 13, 2021, https://www.english.acri.org.il/post/__364.

Aderet, Ofer, "Testimonies from the Censored Deir Yassin Massacre: 'They Piled Bodies and Burned Them'," *Haaretz*, July 16, 2017, https://www.haaretz.com/israel-news/2017-07-16/ty-article-magazine/testimonies-from-the-censored-massacre-at-deir-yassin/0000017f-e364-d38f-a57f-e77689930000.

Agam Goldstein, Almog, "I was a captive of Hamas. After I was freed, I was imprisoned by online trolls." *Washington Post*, August 21, 2024, https://www.washingtonpost.com/opinions/2024/08/21/hamas-israel-hostages-antisemitism/.

Aghaalkurdi, Mohammed, "Polio Threatens Gaza Today. Tomorrow, It Could Be Cholera." *The New York Times*, October 14, 2024, https://www.nytimes.com/2024/10/14/opinion/gaza-polio-infectious-disease.html.

Al Jazeera English, "Israel's Itamar Ben-Gvir calls police 'landlords' of Jerusalem," May 21, 2023, YouTube, https://youtube.com/shorts/CJFUAw8o40Y?si=icsYE3KJAUt-4zgK.

Allon, Gideon, "'No doubt' Netanyahu preventing hostage deal, charges ex-spokesman of Families Forum," *Times of Israel*, April 26, 2024, https://www.timesofisrael.com/no-doubt-netanyahu-preventing-hostage-deal-charges-ex-spokesman-of-families-forum/.

AP and Jeremy Sharon, "UN report says Palestinian detainees in Israel subjected to torture, mistreatment," *Times of Israel*, July 31, 2024, https://www.timesofisrael.com/un-report-says-palestinian-detainees-in-israel-subjected-to-torture-mistreatment/.

Asad, Adam and Yaron Kaplan, "Most Arab Israelis: October 7 Attack Does Not Reflect Islamic, Palestinian, or Arab Society Values," *Israel Democracy Institute*, December 26, 2023, https://en.idi.org.il/articles/52016 .

Asad, Adam, "What's it like being an Arab-Israeli after October 7", *Ynetnews*, November 15, 2023, https://www.ynetnews.com/article/rjkpezg4p.

Associated Press, "Israeli nationalists march through Palestinian area of Jerusalem, some chanting 'Death to Arabs'," June 5, 2024, YouTube, https://www.youtube.com/watch?v=g8O-6e9M864&ab_channel=AssociatedPress.

Avishai, Bernard, "Netanyahu's Government Takes a Turn Toward Theocracy," *The New Yorker*, January 7, 2023, https://www.newyorker.com/news/daily-comment/netanyahus-government-takes-a-turn-toward-theocracy.

Awale, Arya, Christian S. Chan, Katy YY Tam, and Minoru Karasawa, "Perceived warmth of offending group moderates the effect of intergroup apologies." *Group Processes & Intergroup Relations* 25, no. 5 (2022): 1372-1394.

Ayalon, Ami and Anthony David, *Friendly Fire: How Israel Became Its Own Worst Enemy and the Hope for Its Future* (Steerforth, 2020).

B'Tselem, "Israeli settlers threaten and attack Palestinian olive harvesters in the village of al-Mughayir, Ramallah District. Soldiers threaten and drive away the harvesters," *B'Tselem*, October 15, 2024, https://www.btselem.org/video/20241015_israeli_settlers_attack_palestinian_olive_harvesters_and_soldiers_threaten_and_drive_away_the_harvesters_in_the_village_of_al_mughayir_in_ramallah_district#full.

B'Tselem, Statistics on Palestinian minors in Israeli custody, *B'Tselem*, September 2, 2024 https://www.btselem.org/statistics/minors_in_custody.

Barkan, Ross, "How the Israeli-Palestinian Conflict Drove a Wedge Into the Democratic Party," *The New York Times*, February 7, 2024, https://www.nytimes.com/2024/02/07/magazine/israel-october-7-democrats.html.

Bavelas, Janet, "An analysis of formal apologies by Canadian churches to First Nations." *Occasional Paper* 1 (2004): 317-338.

Benhabib, Seyla, *Situating the Self: Gender, Community, and Postmodernism in Contemporary Ethics* (Routledge, 1992).

Benyair, Michael, "Former AG of Israel: With great sadness I conclude that my country is now an apartheid regime," *The Journal*, February 10, 2022, https://www.thejournal.ie/readme/israel-apartheid-5678541-Feb2022/.

Bertrand, Natasha and Katie Bo Lillis, "Exclusive: Nearly half of the Israeli munitions dropped on Gaza are imprecise 'dumb bombs,' US intelligence assessment finds," *CNN*, December 14, 2023, https://edition.cnn.com/2023/12/13/politics/intelligence-assessment-dumb-bombs-israel-gaza/index.html.

Bigg, Matthew Mpoke, "Gazans Are So Malnourished That They Could Face Famine, Report Warns," *The New York Times*, October 17, 2024, https://www.nytimes.com/2024/10/17/world/middleeast/gaza-malnourished-famine-warnings.html.

Bisset, Victoria, Júlia Ledur, and Leslie Shapiro, "Monitoring the status of hostages still in Gaza after Hamas's attack," *Washington Post*, November 26, 2024, https://www.washingtonpost.com/world/interactive/hamas-hostages-israel-war-gaza/

Blatz, Craig W., Karina Schumann, and Michael Ross, "Government apologies for historical injustices." *Political Psychology* 30, no. 2 (2009): 219—241.

Blum, Ruthie, "The myth of Gaza's 'innocent' majority," *JNS*, May 31, 2024, https://www.jns.org/the-myth-of-gazas-innocent-majority/.

Bob, Yonah Jeremy and Tovah Lazaroff, "Netanyahu actively sabotaging hostage deal, sources say," *Jerusalem Post*, July 16, 2024, https://www.jpost.com/israel-hamas-war/article-810551.

Brooks, Andrew, and Mark Griffiths, "Beyond Apartheid Israel." *Political Geography* 114 (2024): 103193; Raby, Sarah. "The humanitarian crisis of the Israeli occupation and settler colonialism in the West Bank and Gaza." (2023).

Carmel, Joel, "'Together We Will'…Speak the Truth. Only Then Can We 'Win.'"*Jewschool,* April 11, 2024, https://jewschool.com/together-we-will-speak-the-truth-only-then-can-we-win-174196.

Chacar, Henriette and Maayan Lubell, "Israeli finance minister suspends funds to Arab towns, East Jerusalem," *Reuters*, August 8, 2023, https://www.reuters.com/world/middle-east/israeli-finance-minister-suspends-funds-arab-towns-east-jerusalem-2023-08-08/.

Channel 4 News, "The hardline Israeli settlers planning their future homes in Gaza," October 22, 2024, YouTube video, 7:49, https://www.youtube.com/watch?v=riLA5r8D4ac.

Chapman, A. R. (2007). "Truth commissions and intergroup forgiveness: The case of the South African Truth and Reconciliation Commission." *Peace and Conflict, 13*(1), 51-69.

Damon, Arwa, "Opinion: How the suffering in Gaza is different from other conflicts," *CNN*, May 7, 2024, https://edition.cnn.com/2024/05/05/opinions/israel-gaza-psychological-trauma-damon/index.html.

"Database of Israeli Incitement to Genocide," *Law for Palestine,* January 15, 2024, https://law4palestine.org/wp-content/uploads/2024/02/Database-of-Israeli-Incitement-to-Genocide-including-after-ICJ-order-27th-February-2024-.pdf.

David, Roman, and Pui Chuen Tam. "Political apologies and their acceptance: Experimental evidence from victims and perpetrators nations." *British Journal of Social Psychology* 63, no. 1 (2024): 273-294.

Davidovich, Joshua, "By allowing towns to segregate, Israel may cross a different kind of red line," *Times of Israel*, July 13, 2018, https://www.timesofisrael.com/by-allowing-towns-to-segregate-israel-may-cross-a-different-kind-of-red-line/.

Davies, Wyre, "'I had to bulldoze my house' – Palestinians face spike in Israeli demolition orders in East Jerusalem," *BBC*,

October 17, 2024,
https://www.bbc.com/news/articles/c0lwpg9xrxdo.

Easton, Scott D., Najwa Sado Safadi, and Robert G. Hasson III. ""We Deal With Symptoms Rather Than Causes": Antipoverty Policy Making in Occupied Palestinian Territories." *Journal of Loss and Trauma* 22, no. 8 (2017): 631-645.

Ebrahim, Nadeen and Mike Schwartz, "'He got out of Gaza, but Gaza did not get out of him': Israeli soldiers returning from war struggle with trauma and suicide," *CNN*, October 21, 2024, https://edition.cnn.com/2024/10/21/middleeast/gaza-war-israeli-soldiers-ptsd-suicide-intl/index.html.

Elitsoy, Z. Aslı. "A 'Jewish State' or a 'State for All Its Citizens'?: Palestinian Demands for Redefining the Boundaries of the Israeli National Identity and the Jewish Response." *İsrailiyat* 7 (2021): 4-17.

Eljamal, Mekarem (2020). "Alienations and Articulations: Tracing Israeli Land Policies Through History," Agora Journal of Urban Planning and Design, 106-119.

Erlanger, Steven and Natan Odenheimer, "They Refused to Serve. Now They're Supporting Israel's War Effort," *The New York Times,* Oct. 29, 2023, https://www.nytimes.com/2023/10/29/world/europe/israel-reservists-hamas-war.html.

Fabian, Emanuel, "IDF: Deaths of 29 of 170 soldiers in Gaza op were so-called friendly fire, accidents," *Times of Israel*, January 1, 2024 https://www.timesofisrael.com/idf-deaths-of-29-of-170-soldiers-in-gaza-op-were-so-called-friendly-fire-accidents/.

Falah, Ghazi-Walid. "The (im) possibility of achieving a peaceful solution to the Israeli-Palestinian conflict." *Human Geography* 14, no. 3 (2021): 333-345.

Federal Forum, "Building a Shared Future for Israel-Palestine," *Challenge*, https://challenge.org.il/federal-forum/.

Filipovic, Jill, "The Problem With 'Feminist' Men," *The New York Times*, May 8, 2018, https://www.nytimes.com/2018/05/08/opinion/schneiderman-abuse-feminist-men.html.

Fink, Rachel, "Israeli TV Exposé Uncovers Alleged Deep Corruption of Key Netanyahu Minister," *Haaretz*, May 27, 2024, https://www.haaretz.com/israel-news/2024-05-27/ty-article/.premium/israeli-tv-expose-uncovers-alleged-deep-corruption-of-key-netanyahu-minister/0000018f-bab5-d0b7-abdf-feb7c40f0000.

Fisher, Clara, et al., "UN Security Council Resolution 1325 in Peacekeeping: Challenges and Opportunities," The Elliott

School of International Affairs, The George Washington University and Women in International Security (WIIS), August 2016, https://wiisglobal.org/wp-content/uploads/UN-Security-Council-Resolution-1325-in-Peacekeeping-Challenges-and-Opportunities.pdf.

Forum 1325 for Political Agreement, "An Introduction to Diplomatic Solutions (Hebrew)," January 2, 2024, YouTube video, https://www.youtube.com/watch?v=w9uISKe9c94&ab_channel=Forum1325forPoliticalAgreement.

Forum 1325 for Political Agreement, "The Federal Proposal: Between one nation and two nations, the combining solution" (Hebrew), February 12, 2024, YouTube video, 1:20:06, https://www.youtube.com/watch?v=xQuCDza9ysg&ab_channel=Forum1325forPoliticalAgreement.

Frenkel, Sheera, "Israel Secretly Targets U.S. Lawmakers With Influence Campaign on Gaza War," *The New York Times*, June 5, 2024, https://www.nytimes.com/2024/06/05/technology/israel-campaign-gaza-social-media.html.

Friedson, Felice and Giorgia Valente, "Most Palestinians support West Bank groups but don't back Hamas, researcher says," *Jerusalem Post*, August 23, 2024, https://www.jpost.com/israel-hamas-war/article-815996.

GADIP Gender and development in practice, "Webinar - Conflict in the Middle East: how can women contribute to the peace process?" October 14, 2024, YouTube video, 1:31:44, https://www.youtube.com/watch?v=PZZz4iJx4Hw&list=PLyw9ntxS-kikAUsI-XvSeqSm7-i_pMCB2&index=2&ab_channel=GADIPGenderanddevelopmentinpractice

Gantus, Layla, "The Many Civil and Human Rights Challenges Facing Israel's Palestinian Citizens," *Carnegie Foundation*, February 28, 2024, https://carnegieendowment.org/posts/2024/02/the-many-civil-and-human-rights-challenges-facing-israels-palestinian-citizens?lang=en "Geneva Initiative: The Accord," *Geneva Accord*, https://geneva-accord.org/the-accord/.

Gitzin, Mickey, "Buying into 'Together We Win' Means We All Lose," *NIF*, Jul 30, 2024, https://nifcan.org/buying-into-together-we-win-means-we-all-lose/.

Glausiusz, Josie, "The Israel—Hamas conflict one year on: researcher resilience in the face of war," *Nature*, October 7,

2024, https://www.nature.com/articles/d41586-024-03263-y.

Glausiusz, Josie, "Would the world be more peaceful if there were more women leaders?" *Aeon*, October 27, 2017, https://aeon.co/ideas/would-the-world-be-more-peaceful-if-there-were-more-women-leaders.

Glazer, Hilo and Itay Mashiach, "'Systematic Witch Hunt:' What Persecution of Arab-Israelis Looks Like Amid Gaza War," *Haaretz*, Nov 2, 2023, https://www.haaretz.com/israel-news/2023-11-02/ty-article-magazine/.highlight/systematic-witch-hunt-what-persecution-of-israeli-arabs-looks-like-amid-gaza-war/0000018b-90db-db7e-af9b-fbdb254e0000.

Goldenberg, Tia, "A former Mossad chief says Israel is enforcing an apartheid system in the West Bank," *AP News*, September 6, 2023, https://apnews.com/article/israel-apartheid-palestinians-occupation-c8137c9e7f33c2cba7b0b5ac7fa8d115.

Goldenberg, Tia, "Harsh Israeli rhetoric against Palestinians becomes central to South Africa's genocide case," *AP News*, January 18, 2024, https://apnews.com/article/israel-palestinians-south-africa-genocide-hate-speech-97a9e4a84a3a6bebeddfb80f8a030724.

Goldenberg, Tia, "Israelis are protesting for democracy but Palestinians say occupation ignored," *PBS*, August 3, 2023, https://www.pbs.org/newshour/world/israelis-are-protesting-for-democracy-but-palestinians-say-occupation-ignored.

Gonen, Yoana, "May Golan: Minister for Rolling Back the Status of Women," *Haaretz*, April 9, 2023, https://www.haaretz.com/opinion/2023-04-09/ty-article-opinion/.premium/may-golan-minister-for-rolling-back-the-status-of-women/00000187-6233-dde0-afb7-7e3320a50000.

Gorenberg, Gershom, "Israel's Fragile Democratic Future," *The New York Times*, February 7, 2024, https://www.nytimes.com/2024/02/07/opinion/israel-democracy-netanyahu-war.html.

Goldstein-Almog, Agam. "I was a captive of Hamas. After I was freed, I was imprisoned by online trolls." *Washington Post*, August 21, 2024, https://www.washingtonpost.com/opinions/2024/08/21/hamas-israel-hostages-antisemitism/.

Goodman, Ilana, "NBC4: Largest poster in the world features 173 Israeli hostages," *Israel National News*, December 20, 2023, https://www.israelnationalnews.com/news/382256.

Graham-Harrison, Emma and Quique Kierszenbaum, "'It is a time of witch hunts in Israel': teacher held in solitary confinement for posting concern about Gaza deaths," *The Guardian*, January 13, 2024, https://www.theguardian.com/world/2024/jan/13/it-is-a-time-of-witch-hunts-in-israel-teacher-held-in-solitary-confinement-for-posting-concern-about-gaza-deaths.

Greve, Joan E, Chris McGreal, and Will Craft, "Five things we learned from our reporting on the US's pro-Israel lobby," *The Guardian*, August 16, 2024, https://www.theguardian.com/us-news/article/2024/aug/16/congress-election-pro-israel-lobby-aipac.

Gross, Judah Ari ,"Does the IDF need donations of equipment? It's complicated. The military is unequivocal that there are no major shortages, so why are units still asking for gear?"*EJewish Philanthropy*, October 12, 2023, https://ejewishphilanthropy.com/does-the-idf-need-donations-of-equipment-its-complicated/.

Groves, Stephen, "DeSantis says US shouldn't take in Palestinian refugees from Gaza because they're 'all antisemitic'," *AP News*, October 15, 2023, https://apnews.com/article/desantis-israel-hamas-gaza-palestinian-refugees-water-73a468f8d030e083844d16e82684c406.

Haaretz Staff, 'Astonishing': Atwood Responds to 'The Handmaid's Tale' Becoming Israeli Protest Symbol, *Haaretz*, Mar 18, 2023, https://www.haaretz.com/israel-news/2023-03-18/ty-article/.premium/astonishing-atwood-responds-to-the-handmaids-tale-becoming-israeli-protest-symbol/00000186-f5ae-dd8e-a7d7-f7ef02e90000.

Halper, Jeff, "Decolonizing Israel, Liberating Palestine." *London: Pluto. doi* 10 (2021).

Hasson, Nir, "New Jerusalem 'Apartheid Road' Opens, Separating Palestinians and Jewish Settlers", *Ha'aretz*, Jan 10, 2019, https://www.haaretz.com/israel-news/2019-01-10/ty-article-magazine/.premium/new-apartheid-road-opens-separating-palestinians-and-west-bank-settlers/0000017f-e8cc-df2c-a1ff-fedda5460000

Heller, Mathilda, "Gwyneth Paltrow, Gal Gadot, other celebrities express outrage, grief at murdered hostages," *Jerusalem Post*, September 2, 2024,https://www.jpost.com/israel-hamas-war/article-817348.

Hendrix, Steve, "Israel's massive democracy movement is ready for war", *Washington Post,* October 24, 2023, https://www.washingtonpost.com/world/2023/10/24/israel-democracy-protesters-war-aid/.

Henkin, Dr. Yagil, "A new security doctrine is needed, even if the price is perpetual war," *Israel Hayom*, October 24, 2024, https://www.israelhayom.com/2024/10/24/a-new-security-doctrine-is-needed-even-if-the-price-is-perpetual-war/.

Holzman-Gazit, Y. (2016). Land expropriation in Israel: law, culture and society. Routledge.

Horovitz, Michael, "Panelist on right-wing TV calls to free Rabin assassin, to audience applause; is booted," *Times of Israel*, July 31, 2023, https://www.timesofisrael.com/tv-panelist-sacked-after-calling-to-free-assassin-yigal-amir-to-audience-applause/.

Hubbard, Ben, et al., "Getting around the West Bank is never easy, but it's a lot harder if you are Palestinian. That's no accident." *The New York Times*, October 13, 2024, https://www.nytimes.com/interactive/2024/10/13/world/middleeast/west-bank-roads.html.

Ibsais, Ahmad, "I've never felt more disillusioned as a Palestinian," *The Guardian*, May 17, 2024, https://www.theguardian.com/commentisfree/article/2024/may/17/palestinians-gaza-news-coverage.

IMEU Institute, "The 7 Most Racist Israeli Laws," *IMEU Institute for Middle East Understanding*, March 6, 2023, https://imeu.org/article/the-7-most-racist-israeli-laws.

Ingram, David, "Israeli government sparks outcry with X videos saying 'there are no innocent civilians' in Gaza," *NBC News*, June 14, 2024, https://www.nbcnews.com/tech/social-media/israel-posts-video-saying-are-no-innocent-civilians-gaza-rcna157111.

*Israelism*, https://www.israelismfilm.com/.

Jamal, Amal, "Jewish sovereignty and the inclusive exclusion of Palestinians: Shifting the conceptual understanding of politics in Israel/Palestine." *Frontiers in Political Science* 4 (2022): 995371.

Johnson, Walter, "Guns in the Family," *Boston Review*, March 23, 2018, https://www.bostonreview.net/articles/walter-johnson-guns-family/.

Joronen, Mikko, and Mark Griffiths, "Ungovernability and ungovernable life in Palestine." *Political Geography* 98 (2022): 102734.

JPost Staff, "Former IDF chief of staff blames Netanyahu of sacrificing remaining hostages," *Jerusalem Post*, September 22,

2024, https://www.jpost.com/breaking-news/article-821255

Kadman, Noga, Erased from Space and Consciousness: Israel and the Depopulated Palestinian Villages of 1948 (Indiana University Press, 2015).

Karam, Dana, "The West Bank Apartheid/Separation Wall: Space, Punishment and the Disruption of Social Continuity." *Geopolitics* 22, no. 4 (2017): 887-910.

Karni, Dana, "Israeli minister says it may be 'moral' to starve 2 million Gazans, but 'no one in the world would let us'," *CNN*, August 6, 2024, https://edition.cnn.com/2024/08/06/middleeast/israeli-minister-smotrich-starve-gazans-intl/index.html?utm_source=substack&utm_medium=emai.

Keinon, Herb, "Israeli solidarity stays strong one month after Hamas-Israel war," *Jerusalem Post*, November 11, 2023, https://www.jpost.com/arab-israeli-conflict/gaza-news/article-772568.

Kelly, Mary Louise, Erika Ryan, Linah Mohammad, and Courtney Dorning, "For this Israeli general, the horror of Oct. 7 meant a return to the battlefield," *NPR*, November 7, 2023, https://www.npr.org/2023/11/07/1211329918/for-this-israeli-general-the-horror-of-oct-7-meant-a-return-to-the-battlefield.

Kershner, Isabel, "Back From War, Reserve Soldiers Set Their Sights on Israel's Politics as Usual," *The New York Times*, Feb. 28, 2024, https://www.nytimes.com/2024/02/28/world/middleeast/israel-reserve-soldiers-gaza.html.

Khalaf, Mohammad Shukri, "The position of Arab Israelis on the events of October 7, 2023," *Zeitgeschichte Online*, October 6, 2024, https://zeitgeschichte-online.de/themen/position-arab-israelis-events-october-7-2023.

Khatib, Rasha, Martin McKee, and Salim Yusuf. "Counting the dead in Gaza: difficult but essential." *The Lancet* 404, no. 10449 (2024): 237-238, https://www.thelancet.com/journals/lancet/article/PIIS0140-6736(24)01169-3/fulltext.

Kilander, Gustaf, "Lauren Boebert poses her children with guns in Christmas photo," *The Independent*, December 8, 2021, https://www.independent.co.uk/news/world/americas/us-politics/lauren-boebert-guns-children-christmas-b1972033.html.

Kingsley, Patrick and Isabel Kershner, "Revenge Attacks After Killing of Israeli Settlers Leave West Bank in Turmoil," *The New York Times*, February 27, 2023, https://www.nytimes.com/2023/02/27/world/middleeast/israel-palestinians-west-bank.html

Kingsley, Patrick and Isabel Kershner, "The Israeli Government's Plan to Overhaul the Judiciary: What to Know", *The New York Times*, March 29, 2023, https://www.nytimes.com/article/israel-judiciary-crisis-explainer.html.

Kingsley, Patrick, "Mass Protests Over Government's Court Plans Sweep Israel", *The New York Times*, March 9, 2023, https://www.nytimes.com/2023/03/09/world/middleeast/israel-judicial-protests-netanyahu.html?s.

Konrad, Edo, "The 'pact of silence' between Israelis and their media," *+972 Magazine*, October 16, 2024, https://www.972mag.com/israeli-media-pact-of-silence-gaza/.

Kraner-Tucci, Ruby, "Art attack: Creative campaigns to ensure hostages are not forgotten," *The Jewish Independent*, January 29, 2024, https://thejewishindependent.com.au/public-art-takes-hostage-crisis-to-the-streets-in-many-forms.

Krever, Mick et al., "Netanyahu derailed a potential Gaza hostage deal in July, Israeli newspaper reports," *CNN*, September 4, 2024, https://edition.cnn.com/2024/09/04/middleeast/netanyahu-derailed-hostage-deal-in-july-intl/index.html.

Kubovich, Yaniv, "'No Civilians. Everyone's a Terrorist': IDFSoldiers Expose Arbitrary Killings and Rampant Lawlessness in Gaza's Netzarim Corridor," *Haaretz*, Dec 18, 2024, https://www.haaretz.com/israel-news/2024-12-18/ty-article-magazine/.premium/idf-soldiers-expose-arbitrary-killings-and-rampant-lawlessness-in-gazas-netzarim-corridor/00000193-da7f-de86-a9f3-fefff2e50000.

Landler, Mark, "'Erase Gaza': War Unleashes Incendiary Rhetoric in Israel," *The New York Times*, November 15, 2023, https://www.nytimes.com/2023/11/15/world/middleeast/israel-gaza-war-rhetoric.html.

Lazaroff, Tovah, "'There are no innocents in Gaza,' says Israeli defense minister," *The Jerusalem Post*, April 8, 2018, https://www.jpost.com/arab-israeli-conflict/there-are-no-innocents-in-gaza-says-israeli-defense-minister-549173.

Levine-Schnur, Ronit, Constitutional Property Rights in Israel and the West Bank (July 10, 2021). *Oxford Handbook on the Israeli*

*Constitution* (Aharon Barak, Barak Medina and Yaniv Roznai, eds., Oxford University Press).

Levy, Natalie, "Arabs in segregated vs. mixed Jewish—Arab in Israel: their identities and attitudes towards Jews." *Ethnic and Racial Studies* 46, no. 12 (2023): 2720-2746.

Lieberman, Jonathan, "Being an Israeli right now means making the ultimate sacrifice — opinion," *Jerusalem Post*, January 6, 2024, https://www.jpost.com/opinion/article-780828.

Lipka, Michael, "Israeli Jews, Arabs have different perspectives on discrimination in their society," *Pew Research Center*, May 25, 2016, https://www.pewresearch.org/short-reads/2016/05/25/most-israeli-jews-do-not-see-a-lot-of-discrimination-in-their-society/.

Livni, Ephrat "Conditions in Gaza Worsen Amid Israeli Strikes," *The New York Times*, October 9, 2024, https://www.nytimes.com/2024/10/09/world/middleeast/gaza-israel-military-strike.html .

Livni, Ephrat, "Surge in Violence by West Bank Settlers Draws Ire of Israel's Allies," *The New York Times*, July 16, 2024, https://www.nytimes.com/2024/07/16/world/middleeast/settler-violence-west-bank.html.

Lonsdorf, Kat, "The war is in Gaza, but Palestinians in the West Bank are targeted with violence too," *NPR*, October 12, 2024, https://www.npr.org/2024/10/12/g-s1-27704/west-bank-palestinians-violence-israel-settlers.

Lubell, Maayan, "Israel adopts divisive Jewish nation-state law," *Reuters*, July 19, 2018, https://www.reuters.com/article/world/israel-adopts-divisive-jewish-nation-state-law-idUSKBN1K9022/.

Lubell, Maayan, "Tel Aviv police chief quits, citing government meddling against protesters," *Reuters*, July 6, 2023, https://www.reuters.com/world/middle-east/tel-aviv-police-chief-quits-citing-government-meddling-against-protesters-2023-07-05/.

Lustick, Ian S. "Annexation in right-wing Israeli discourse—The case of Ribonut." *Frontiers in Political Science* 4 (2022): 963682.

Maanit, Chen, "Israeli Police Recommend Closing Case Against Yeshiva Head Who Said All Gazans Should Be Killed," *Haaretz*, June 18, 2024, https://www.haaretz.com/israel-news/2024-06-18/ty-article/.premium/police-recommend-closing-case-against-yeshiva-head-who-said-all-gazans-should-be-killed/00000190-27d9-d95e-a3ff-effdb62c0000.

Magid, Jacob, "Abbas denouncing Hamas, but criticism kept private due to IDF 'aggression' — top aide," *Times of Israel*,

December 7, 2023, https://www.timesofisrael.com/abbas-denouncing-hamas-but-criticism-kept-private-due-to-idf-aggression-top-aide/.

Magid, Jacob, "Netanyahu issues list of 4 'nonnegotiable' demands as hostage talks slated to restart," *Times of Israel*, July 7, 2024, https://www.timesofisrael.com/netanyahu-issues-list-of-non-negotiable-demands-as-hostage-talks-slated-to-restart/.

Magid, Jacob, "US slams 'irresponsible' calls by Smotrich and Ben Gvir for emigration of Gazans," *Times of Israel*, January 3, 2024, https://www.timesofisrael.com/us-slams-irresponsible-calls-by-smotrich-and-ben-gvir-for-emigration-of-gazans/.

Mallapaty, Smriti, "Gaza: Why is it so hard to establish the death toll?," *Nature*, September 24, 2024, https://www.nature.com/articles/d41586-024-02508-0.

Margalit, Ruth, "Itamar Ben-Gvir, Israel's Minister of Chaos," *The New Yorker*, February 20, 2023, https://www.newyorker.com/magazine/2023/02/27/itamar-ben-gvir-israels-minister-of-chaos?utm_source=substack&utm_medium=email;

Margulies, Joanie "Increased tensions, identity struggles: How Givat Haviva helped Arab Israelis cope post Oct. 7," *Jerusalem Post*, October 24, 2024, https://www.jpost.com/israel-news/article-825666

McCluskey, Mitchell and Richard Allen Greene, "Israel military says 2 civilians killed for every Hamas militant is a 'tremendously positive' ratio given combat challenges," *CNN*, December 6, 2023, https://edition.cnn.com/2023/12/05/middleeast/israel-hamas-military-civilian-ratio-killed-intl-hnk/index.html.

McGreal, Chris, "Amnesty says Israel is an apartheid state. Many Israeli politicians agree," *The Guardian*, February 5, 2022, https://www.theguardian.com/commentisfree/2022/feb/05/amnesty-israel-apartheid-israeli-politicians-agree.

McKernan, Bethan, "A precious resource: how Israel uses water to control the West Bank," *BBC*, May 17, 2023, https://www.theguardian.com/world/2023/may/17/how-israel-uses-water-to-control-west-bank-palestine.

Meidan, Tal, "Women Are Leading Israel's Biggest-ever Protest Movement," *Haaretz*, Mar 22, 2023, https://www.haaretz.com/opinion/2023-03-22/ty-article-opinion/.premium/women-are-leading-israels-biggest-ever-protest-movement/00000187-09f8-d1cf-a7af-fdf8d66f0000 .

Middle East Eye, "Clip resurfaces of Israeli MK encouraging her son to say he wants to 'kill Arabs'", August 9, 2023, YouTube video, 1:00, https://www.youtube.com/watch?v=emWISZ_k4BM&ab_channel=MiddleEastEye.

Middle East Monitor, "Debunked: Israel has 'no partner for peace'", *MEMO*, November 22, 2023, https://www.middleeastmonitor.com/20231122-debunked-israel-has-no-partner-for-peace/.

Milstein, Adam, "Exposing the vile antisemitism of the 'Pro-Palestinian' activists," *Jerusalem Post*, June 23, 2024, https://www.jpost.com/opinion/article-807374.

Montana Right Now, "Are gun-related Halloween costumes falling out of favor?" *Montana Right Now*, October 6, 2017, https://www.montanarightnow.com/news/are-gun-related-halloween-costumes-falling-out-of-favor/article_bc275b81-b6b0-5d06-8380-59a499440268.html.

Morris, Loveday, Meg Kelly, Imogen Piper, Souad Mekhennet and Koba Ryckewaert, "How antisemitism, Israeli nationalism and anger over Gaza clashed in Amsterdam," *Washington Post*, December 18, 2024, https://www.washingtonpost.com/investigations/2024/12/18/amsterdam-attacks-israeli-football-fans/ .

Ner-David, Haviva, "Jews and Arabs hoped to fill a truck with aid for Gaza civilians. We ended up filling 300," *JTA*, August 26, 2024, https://www.jta.org/2024/08/26/ideas/jews-and-arabs-hoped-to-fill-a-truck-with-aid-for-gaza-civilians-we-ended-up-filling-300.

Nimni, Ephraim. "The twilight of the two-state solution in Israel-Palestine: Shared sovereignty and nonterritorial autonomy as the new dawn." *Nationalities Papers* 48, no. 2 (2020): 339-356.

Nuriel, Carole, "Arab Israeli mobilization and solidarity in response to the Hamas massacre," *Times of Israel Blogs*, Nov 21, 2023, https://blogs.timesofisrael.com/arab-israeli-mobilization-and-solidarity-in-response-to-the-hamas-massacre/

Odenheimer, Natan, Bilal Shbair, and Patrick Kingsley, "How Israel's Army Uses Palestinians as Human Shields in Gaza," *The New York Times*, October 14, 2024, https://www.nytimes.com/2024/10/14/world/middleeast/israel-gaza-military-human-shields.html.

Oppenheimer, Rabbi Yehuda L, "Who Is the Baal HaBayit?" *Jewish Press*, November 16, 2022, https://www.jewishpress.com/judaism/torah/who-is-the-baal-habayit/2022/11/16/.

Orbach-Yozgof, Nikola. "Blended cities in Israel." *Israel Affairs* 27, no. 5 (2021): 984-1004; "Israel's mixed cities: Jews still wealthier, but economic gaps may be closing — report," *Jerusalem Post*, May 23, 2023, https://www.jpost.com/israel-news/article-743914.

Paterson, Chris, "Too many journalists and aid workers are being killed in Gaza despite rules that should keep them safe," *The Conversation*, April 30, 2024, https://theconversation.com/too-many-journalists-and-aid-workers-are-being-killed-in-gaza-despite-rules-that-should-keep-them-safe-227201.

PBS News, "Military experts discuss Israel's use of unguided bombs and harm to civilians in Gaza," December 15, 2023, video, 7:23, https://www.pbs.org/newshour/show/military-experts-discuss-israels-use-of-unguided-bombs-and-harm-to-civilians-in-gaza.

Peterson, Bruce, "The scary power of cognitive dissonance," *Star Tribune*, October 21, 2024, https://www.startribune.com/the-scary-power-of-cognitive-dissonance/601165383.

Picheta, Rob. "More than 40,000 Palestinians have been killed in 10 months of war in Gaza, health ministry says," *CNN*, August 16, 2024, https://edition.cnn.com/2024/08/15/middleeast/gaza-death-toll-40000-israel-war-intl/index.html.

Prince-Gibson, Eetta, "Israel's protest movement caught between anger and solidarity," *The Jewish Independent*, March 9, 2024, https://thejewishindependent.com.au/israels-protest-movement-caught-between-anger-and-solidarity.

Rahmanan, Anna, "The Artists Behind the 'Kidnapped' Posters Plastered Around the World," *Observer*, October 23, 2023, https://observer.com/2023/10/the-artists-behind-the-missing-posters-plastered-around-the-world/.

Reich, Eleanor H., "Israel's far-right kingmaker joins memorial for racist rabbi," *AP News*, November 10, 2022, https://apnews.com/article/middle-east-religion-jerusalem-israel-d1500820cd52562638506cc59843b789.

Reiff, Ben, "'No democracy with apartheid': Inside the radical bloc at Israel's anti-gov't protests," *+972 Magazine*, January 25, 2023, https://www.972mag.com/radical-bloc-israel-protests-tel-aviv/.

Reuters, "Israeli women form human chains to protest planned judicial overhaul," March 8, 2023, *Ynetnews,* https://www.ynetnews.com/article/hy1smwl1n .

Riba, Naama, "Why Are These Israeli Protesters Dressed Up Like 'The Handmaid's Tale?'", *Haaretz,* March 1, 2023, https://www.haaretz.com/israel-news/2023-03-01/ty-article/.premium/why-are-these-israeli-protesters-dressed-up-like-the-handmaids-tale/00000186-9d65-df48-ab96-bd65cc790000.

Robinson, Kali, "What to Know About the Arab Citizens of Israel," *Councill of Foreign Relations*, October 26, 2023, https://www.cfr.org/backgrounder/what-know-about-arab-citizens-israel.

Rose, Emily, "Israeli troops killed hostages, mistaking their cries for help as ambush -military," *Reuters*, December 28, 2023, https://www.reuters.com/world/middle-east/israeli-troops-killed-hostages-mistaking-their-cries-help-ambush-military-2023-12-28/.

Rozanes, Nathalie, "The Gaza war is an environmental catastrophe," *+972 Magazine*, September 5, 2024, https://www.972mag.com/gaza-war-environmental-catastrophe/.

Rubin, Shira, "Politicians called them 'traitors.' Now they're manning Israel's home front," *Washington Post*, October 15, 2023, https://www.washingtonpost.com/world/2023/10/14/israel-brothers-in-arms-gaza-border/ .

Schejter, Iddo and Gavriel Fiske, "Police use considerable force near PM's home to disperse protesters urging hostage deal," *Times of Israel*, September 3, 2024, https://www.timesofisrael.com/police-use-considerable-force-near-pms-home-to-disperse-protesters-urging-hostage-deal/.

Schwartz, Roy, "Israelis Need to Update Their Mantra 'Together We Will Win'", *Haaretz*, Jan 25, 2024, https://www.haaretz.com/opinion/2024-01-25/ty-article-opinion/.premium/can-israelis-win-together-against-dangers-lurking-at-home/0000018d-3ca3-d35c-a39f-befbb1d50000.Sella, Adam, "Large Antigovernment Protest Returns to Tel Aviv, as Criticism of Netanyahu Mounts." *The New York Times*, Feb. 17, 2024, https://www.nytimes.com/2024/02/17/world/middleeast/tel-aviv-protest-netanyahu-israel.html.

Sella, Adam, "The Fight Within the Fight: Where Does the Occupation Fit in the Judicial Overhaul Protests?" *Haaretz*, July

6, 2023, https://www.haaretz.com/israel-news/2023-07-06/ty-article/.premium/the-fight-within-the-fight-where-does-the-occupation-fit-in-judicial-overhaul-protests/00000189-2abb-dcb5-a5df-6fff82320000.

Shalom, Zaki. "The Controversy Surrounding Prime Minister Netanyahu's Position Regarding the Two-State Solution—Background and Implications." In *Polarization and Consensus-Building in Israel*, pp. 240-260. Routledge, 2023.

Sharon, Jeremy and Michael Bachner, "Ben Gvir widely panned for warning of renewed Jewish-Arab intercommunal riots," *Times of Israel*, October 11, 2023, https://www.timesofisrael.com/ben-gvir-widely-panned-for-warning-of-renewed-jewish-arab-intercommunal-riots/.

Sharon, Jeremy, "Ben Gvir calls to 'encourage emigration,' resettle Gaza at ultra-nationalist rally," *Times of Israel*, May 14, 2024, https://www.timesofisrael.com/ben-gvir-calls-to-encourage-emigration-resettle-gaza-at-ultra-nationalist-rally/.

Sharon, Jeremy, "'It is doable': 10 Likud MKs to attend conference calling for 'resettling Gaza'," *Times of Israel*, October 16, 2024, https://www.timesofisrael.com/it-is-doable-10-likud-mks-to-attend-conference-calling-for-resettling-gaza/.

Sheizaf, Noam, "This is a war of choice. Netanyahu's choice," *+972 Magazine*, July 16, 2014, https://www.972mag.com/this-is-a-war-of-choice-netanyahus-choice/.

Sherwood, Harriet, "Court upholds law banning Palestinian spouses from living in Israel," *The Guardian,* January 12, 2012.

Shiff, Einav, "We have to talk about the disturbing things from Shoval ben Natan's funeral," [Hebrew] *Ynet*, October 28, 2024, https://www.ynet.co.il/news/article/yokra14128906#autoplay .

Sixty Minutes, "60 Minutes travels to Israel to report on historic protests," September 18, 2023, YouTube video, 5:13, https://www.youtube.com/watch?v=kt3aVD8HLXc&ab_channel=60Minutes.

Skelley, Geoffrey "Pro-Israel groups spent big to oust two Squad members in primaries. But they didn't splash cash to oppose all high-profile progressives," *ABC News*, September 17, 2024, https://abcnews.go.com/538/pro-israel-groups-spent-big-oust-squad-members/story?id=113675889.

Sokol, Sam, and Charlie Summers, "Far-right violence, chants of 'Death to Arabs,' at Jerusalem Day Flag March in Old City," *Times of Israel*, June 6, 2024, https://www.timesofisrael.com/jerusalem-day-flag-march-marred-by-far-right-violence-under-shadow-of-war/.

Sokol, Sam, "Far-right minister: Hostage deal throws war goals in trash to save only 22-33 hostages," *Times of Israel*, May 1, 2024, https://www.timesofisrael.com/far-right-minister-claims-hostage-deal-throws-war-goals-in-trash-to-save-hostages/.

Syed, Armani, "What Palestinian Children Face in Israeli Prisons," *Time*, December 15, 2023, https://time.com/6548068/palestinian-children-israeli-prison-arrested/.

Stephens, Bret, "Hamas Bears the Blame for Every Death in This War," *The New York Times*, October 15, 2023, https://www.nytimes.com/2023/10/15/opinion/columnists/hamas-war-israel-gaza.html.

Summers, Charlie, "At Tel Aviv confab, Israel's embattled peace camp seeks to revive itself post-Oct. 7," *Times of Israel,* July 2, 2024, https://www.timesofisrael.com/at-tel-aviv-confab-israels-embattled-peace-camp-seeks-to-revive-itself-post-oct-7/.

Sztokman, Elana and Eva Dalak, "Women Ending War S1 E5: The everyday work of peace building, w/Dr. Fakhira Halloun and Yael Treidel," August 5, 2024, YouTube video, 46:21, https://www.youtube.com/watch?v=3W-HNBU_sQI&list=PLyw9ntxS-kikAUsI-XvSeqSm7-i_pMCB2&index=15&ab_channel=ElanaSztokman.

Sztokman, Elana and Eva Dalak, "Women Ending War S1 E9: A Plethora of partners: Nivine Sandouka of ALLMEP & Naomi Sternberg of Geneva Institute," September 3, 2024, YouTube video, 56:12, https://www.youtube.com/watch?v=76bZ0h6Fui8&list=PLyw9ntxS-kikAUsI-XvSeqSm7-i_pMCB2&index=24&t=7s&ab_channel=ElanaSztokman.

Sztokman, Elana, "3 myths about the war in Gaza," *The Roar*, Substack, September 12, 2024, https://elanasztokman.substack.com/p/3-myths-about-the-war-in-gaza.

Sztokman, Elana, "Amy Coney Barrett and the Women Who Uphold the Patriarchy," *Lilith*, October 27, 2020, https://lilith.org/2020/10/amy-coney-barrett-and-the-women-who-uphold-the-patriarchy/.

Sztokman, Elana, "Bennett responds like an abuser, with gaslighting not compassion," *The Jewish Independent*, May 17, 2022, https://thejewishindependent.com.au/bennett-responds-like-an-abuser-with-gaslighting-not-compassion-2

Sztokman, Elana, *Conversations with My Body: Essays on My Life as a Jewish Woman* (Lioness Books, 2022)

Sztokman, Elana, "Israeli mothers like me are fed up with having our children used as cannon fodder," *JTA*, May 29, 2024, https://www.jta.org/2024/05/29/ideas/israeli-mothers-like-me-are-fed-up-with-having-our-children-used-as-cannon-fodder .

Sztokman, Elana, "My Political Evolution," *Lilith*, August 12, 2014, https://lilith.org/2014/08/my-political-evolution/. https://www.theguardian.com/world/2012/jan/12/israel-palestinian-spouses-ban.

Sztokman, Elana, "Rockets, Bombs and Babies: Wartime in the Maternity Ward," *Lilith*, June 9, 2021, https://lilith.org/2021/06/rockets-bombs-and-babies-wartime-in-the-maternity-ward/.

Sztokman, Elana "Tackling Trump in the Israeli media," *A Jewish Feminist*, November 9, 2019, http://jewfem.com/index.php?option=com_easyblog&view=entry&id=668&Itemid=497.

Sztokman, Elana, "The problem is not antisemitism; It's Bibi," *The Roar*, Substack, September 27, 2024, https://elanasztokman.substack.com/p/the-problem-is-not-antisemitism-its.

Sztokman, Elana, "The problem with women," *The Roar*, December 28, 2022, https://elanasztokman.substack.com/p/the-problem-with-women?utm_medium=reader2.

Sztokman, Elana, *The War on Women in Israel: A Story of Religious Radicalism and the Women Fighting for Freedom* (Sourcebooks, 2014).

Sztokman, Elana, *When Rabbis Abuse: Power, Gender, and Status in the Dynamics of Sexual Abuse in Jewish Culture* (Lioness Books, 2022).

Sztokman, Elana, "Why It's Hard To Be a Zionist and a Feminist," *Forward*, November 17, 2009 https://forward.com/life/119097/why-its-hard-to-be-a-zionist-and-a-feminist/

Tait, Robert, "Palestinian baby killed in arson attack 'by Israeli settlers'," *The Telegraph*, July 31, 2015, https://www.telegraph.co.uk/news/worldnews/middleeast/israel/11774900/Palestinian-baby-dies-in-fire-started-by-Israeli-settlers.html.

Tanis, Fatma, "Friendly fire and accidents have killed a lot of Israeli soldiers in Gaza. Here's why." *NPR* January 26, 2024

https://www.npr.org/2024/01/26/1226977365/israel-idf-
gaza-middle-east-deaths.

Tavris, Carol and Elliot Aronson, *Mistakes Were Made (but Not by
Me): Why We Justify Foolish Beliefs, Bad Decisions, and Hurtful Acts*
(Mariner Books, 2015).

TOI Staff, "Anti-overhaul protesters rally for women's rights
outside religious courts", *Times of Israel*, July 18, 2023,
https://www.timesofisrael.com/anti-overhaul-protesters-rally-
for-womens-rights-outside-religious-courts/.

TOI Staff, "IDF spokesman says Hamas can't be destroyed,
drawing retort from PM: 'That's war's goal'," *Times of Israel*,
June 20, 2024, https://www.timesofisrael.com/idf-
spokesman-says-hamas-cant-be-eliminated-will-remain-in-
gaza-if-no-alternative/.

TOI Staff, "Members of Israel's negotiating team accuse
Netanyahu of intentionally sabotaging hostage deal talks —
report," *Times of Israel*, August 20, 2024,
https://www.timesofisrael.com/liveblog_entry/members-
of-israels-negotiating-team-accuse-netanyahu-of-
intentionally-sabotaging-hostage-deal-talks-report/.

TOI Staff, "On '60 Minutes,' anti-overhaul protest leaders decry
threat 'from inside' Israel," *Times of Israel*, September 18, 2023,
https://www.timesofisrael.com/anti-overhaul-protest-
leaders-decry-threat-from-inside-israel-on-60-minutes-
segment/.

Tondo, Lorenzo, "Israeli government accused of trying to
sabotage Gaza ceasefire proposal," *The Guardian*, July 7,
2024,
https://www.theguardian.com/world/article/2024/jul/07
/israeli-government-accused-of-trying-to-sabotage-gaza-
ceasefire-proposal.

Tondo, Lorenzo, "'We will not go away': Israeli demolitions leave
Bedouin homeless," *The Guardian*, June 6, 2024,
https://www.theguardian.com/world/article/2024/jun/06
/israeli-demolitions-bedouins-homeless-negev.

Tova in Israel, "Guns and Purim", Tova in Israel, March 21, 2016,
http://tovainisrael.com/blog-posts/guns-and-purim/.

UN Women, "A Global Study of UN Security Council Resolution
1325," *UN Women*, https://wps.unwomen.org/resources/.

UN Women, "Fact Sheet The Global Study of UN Security
Council Resolution 1325: Key Messages, Findings, and
Recommendations," UN Women,
https://wps.unwomen.org/resources/fact-sheets/Fact-
Sheet-and-Key-messages-Global-Study-EN.pdf.

United States Institute of Peace, *What is UNSCR 1325?* https://www.usip.org/gender_peacebuilding/about_UNSCR_1325 .

van Gelder, Sarah, "Desmond Tutu and the Power of Apology", *Yes Magazine*, Jan 11, 2022, https://www.yesmagazine.org/social-justice/2022/01/11/desmond-tutu-power-of-apology .

Warzel, Charlie "I'm Running Out of Ways to Explain How Bad This Is," *The Atlantic*, October 10, 2024, https://www.theatlantic.com/technology/archive/2024/10/hurricane-milton-conspiracies-misinformation/680221/.

Waxman, Dov, "Jewish response to Hamas war criticism comes from deep sense of trauma, active grief and fear," *The Conversation*, October 30, 2023, https://theconversation.com/jewish-response-to-hamas-war-criticism-comes-from-deep-sense-of-trauma-active-grief-and-fear-216340.

Wenzel, Michael, Farid Anvari, Melissa de Vel-Palumbo, and Simon M. Bury. "Collective apology, hope, and forgiveness." *Journal of Experimental Social Psychology* 72 (2017): 75-87.

White House. "Background Press Call on Efforts to Secure the Release of Hostages in Gaza," *The White House*, September 4, 2024, https://www.whitehouse.gov/briefing-room/press-briefings/2024/09/04/background-press-call-on-efforts-to-secure-the-release-of-hostages-in-gaza/.

Wintour, Patrick, "UN chief 'shocked' by 'misrepresentation' of comments in row with Israel," *The Guardian*, October 26, 2023, https://www.theguardian.com/world/2023/oct/25/israel-says-it-will-ban-un-staff-after-secretary-generals-comments.

Wintour, Patrick, "US demands proof that Israel does not have starvation policy in northern Gaza," *The Guardian*, October 16, 2024, https://www.theguardian.com/world/2024/oct/16/urgent-un-security-council-meeting-called-amid-pressure-on-israel-to-allow-aid-into-gaza .

Wollaston, Sam, "Kids and Guns review — a terrifying look at the heart of American culture," *The Guardian*, July 31, 2014, https://www.theguardian.com/tv-and-radio/2014/jul/31/kids-and-guns-tv-review-francine-shaw.

Youssef, Nancy A. and Jared Malsin, "Israel Struggles to Destroy Hamas's Gaza Tunnel Network," *Wall Street Journal*, January 28, 2024, https://www.wsj.com/world/middle-east/israel-struggles-to-destroy-hamass-gaza-tunnel-network-fb641122

Ze Ba'avir, Calculated Risk - The Policy that Led to October 7th (Not Accidental)," YouTube video, October 2, 2024, https://www.youtube.com/watch?v=0r4Y0DEeGCw&ab_channel=%D7%96%D7%94_%D7%91%D7%90%D7%95%D7%95%D7%99%D7%A8.

Zhou, Li, "The argument that Israel practices apartheid, explained," *Vox*, October 20, 2023, https://www.vox.com/23924319/israel-palestine-apartheid-meaning-history-debate.

Zureik, E., Lyon, D., & Abu-Laban, Y. (2010). Surveillance and control in Israel/Palestine. *Population Territory and Power. London: Routledge*

# Acknowledgments

This book exists thanks to the powerful women who have sustained me during this long and terrible war. My deepest gratitude goes to:

Jessica Kaz, for holding space, even during the darkest times, and encouraging me to keep writing all those years ago.

Dr. Roberta Levy Schwartz, for 35 years of friendship generosity, and showing up — to really, really showing up.

Eva Dalak, for sisterhood and love across oceans and divides, for opening her heart to me in order to activate peace.

Dr. Fakhira Halloun, for partnership, friendship, and heartfelt, safe exchange of ideas, even when it's complicated.

Sally Gottesman, for believing in me with generosity and vision, and for ensuring that my words get out into the world.

Dora Bender, Dr. Warda Sada, and all the women of Forum 1325, for keeping hope alive.

Anat Asia, for guided healing in many realms, along with her NVC partner and my teacher, Nadia Mahmoud Gaol, for so many invaluable life lessons, and especially for exposing me to the dictum, "Connect before you correct."

Khadijeh Dassuky, for many real talks about the real lives of women in this country.

Sarah Ain Linder, for support and collegiality over the years because the personal really is political.

Sally Berkovic, for encouraging me to write this book, and for also being a great writing *chevruta* over the years.

Reva Mann, my wonderful writing partner, meticulous reader and editor, and friend.

Dr. Rabbi Reverend Haviva Ner-David, for a 30+ year friendship, for being a quintessential safe space.

Susan Goodman Jackson, for the healing, listening, and for redefining family.

Laura Herschlag, for providing refuge, great food, love, and a great view, rockets and all.

Ruthie Lang, for teaching me the value of checking in, and an occasional great escape to the beach.

Dr. Sharon Weiss Greenberg, for real feminist friendship.

Sigal Kirsch, my longtime partner in facilitating women's dialogue, for teaching me so much, with patience and love.

Loolwa Khazzoom, for the fierce, fiery sisterhood.

Maayan Sharon, editor par excellence – thorough reader, sharp thinker, and newfound friend.

To my podcast guests, for entrusting me with your stories and knowledge, and for the collaboration.

To my coven of healers: Re'eli, Suri, Inbal, Zita, and Noa, for saving my life over and over again.

To my beta readers, followers, subscribers, and friends, thank you for all the likes, shares, chats, and meaningful exchanges. These moments nourish and sustain me.

And especially to my beautiful, loving, magical family. My spouse, Jacob, and our children and their miraculously growing families. With boundless gratitude and awe.

A special shout out to the people and organizations doing the real work of building a shared society based on humanity, non-violence, and mutual understanding: A Land for All, ACRI, All its Citizens, Alliance for Middle East Peace (ALLMEP), Breaking the Silence, B'Tselem, Combatants for Peace, Encounter, Givat Haviva Center for Jewish-Arab Education in Israel, Hand in Hand, Ir Amim, Itach-Ma'aki, Kids4Peace, Kulna Yaffa, Machsom Watch, Mothers Against Violence in Israel, Neve Shalom Wahat al-Salam School for Peace, Nonviolent Communication, Parents Against Child Detention, The Parents Circle-Families Forum, Road to Recovery, Standing Together, Tag Meir, Tech2Peace, Tomorrow's Women, and many others doing this holy work.

Where there's life, there's hope.

# Index

260 | ELANA SZTOKMAN

# About the Author

Dr. Elana Sztokman (she/her) is an award-winning author, anthropologist, educator, and Jewish feminist Israeli-American peace activator. This is her seventh book.

Follow her Substack newsletter, *The Roar*, and follow her podcast Women Ending War, with Muslim Palestinian peace activators and citizens of Israel Eva Dalak and Dr. Fakhira Halloun.

Author page: www.elanasztokman.net
Substack: https://elanasztokman.substack.com/
YouTube: https://www.youtube.com/@elanahope
Facebook:
https://www.facebook.com/WomenEndingWar
Bluesky: @elanahope.bsky.social